Explore t

NELLES

CYPRUS

Authors:
*Samantha Stenzel, Nita Clothier, Andreas Demetropoulos,
Lana der Parthogh, Mary F. Finch, Kerin Hope, Ken MacKenzie,
K. McElroy, Ted Petrides, Corinne Vallois*

*An Up-to-date travel guide with 148 color photos
and 13 maps*

**Third revised edition
1999**

Dear Reader: Being up-to-date is the main goal of the Nelles series. Our correspondents help keep us abreast of the latest developments in the travel scene, while our cartographers see to it that maps are also kept completely current. However, as the travel world is constantly changing, we cannot guarantee that all the information contained in our books is always valid. Should you come across a discrepancy, please contact us at: Nelles Verlag, Schleissheimer Str. 371 b, 80935 Munich, Germany, tel. (089) 3571940, fax. (089) 35719430, e-mail: Nelles.Verlag@t-online.de

Note: Distances and measurements, including temperatures, used in this guide are metric. For conversion information, please see the *Guidelines* section of this book.

LEGEND

★★	Main Attraction *(on map)*	
★★	*(in text)*	
★	Worth Seeing *(on map)*	
★	*(in text)*	
❽	Orientation Number in Text and on Map	
▪	Public or Significant Building	
■	Hotel	
▪	Shopping Center / Market	
✝	Church	
C	Mosque	

Larnaca *(Town)*
Church *(Sight)* — Places Highlighted in Yellow Appear in Text

✈ ✈ International Airport / National Airport

Khionistra (1612) — Mountain (altitude in meters)

\ 13 / — Distance in Kilometers

☀ — Beach

◎◎◎ Luxury Hotel Category
◎◎ Moderate Hotel Category
◎ Budget Hotel Category
(for price information see "Accomodation" in Guidelines section)

Line of Demarcation	
Expressway	
Principal Highway	
Main Road	
Provincial Road	
Secondary Road	
Road closed to Traffic	
1 2 Route Number	
Ferry	
⸸ Lighthouse	
∴ Ancient Site	

CYPRUS
© Nelles Verlag GmbH, 80935 Munich
  All rights reserved

Third Revised Edition 1999
ISBN 3-88618-156-1
Printed in Slovenia

Publisher:	Günter Nelles	**Cartography:**	Nelles Verlag GmbH
Managing Editor:	Berthold Schwarz	**Color**	
Project Editor:	Samantha Stenzel	**Separation:**	Priegnitz, Munich
English Edition Editor:	Chase Stewart	**Printed by:**	Gorenjski Tisk

TABLE OF CONTENTS

GUIDELINES

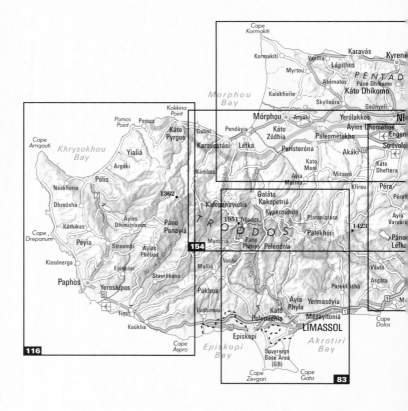

M E D I T E R R A N E A N

S E A

CYPRUS

0   10   20 km

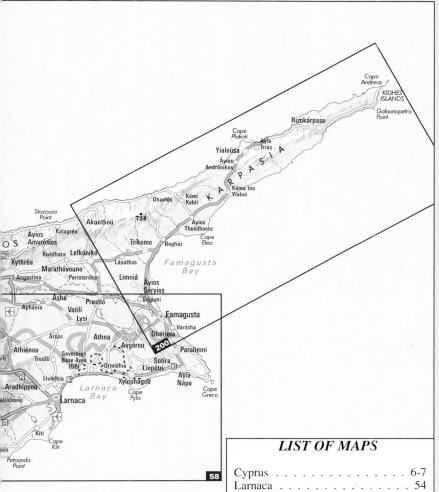

ΠΕΤΡΟΣ   Ο ΚΗΦΑΣ   Ο ΑΓΙΟΣ ΜΑΤΘΑΙΟΣ   Ο ΑΓΙΟΣ

APHRODITE'S ISLAND

The charms of "Aphrodite's Island," as Cyprus is known, are manifold and manifest. The weather is sunny and dry for a good part of the year and the sea is enticing, blue and crystal clear. Cyprus has picturesque mountain villages, remote monasteries, crusaders' castles, exquisite Roman mosaics and imposing temples. The tiny Byzantine churches tucked away in the folds of foothills contain unforgettable masterpieces by artists often long forgotten.

Cyprus is the third-largest Mediterranean island after Sicily and Sardinia. Those seeking isolation can find it even during peak season, if they are willing to wander off the beaten track. In recent years, the government has launched a number of programs to encourage the preservation of traditional communities, especially in the interior. Cyprus has a homey charm, innate in the character of the friendly locals who have never lost their enthusiasm for welcoming visitors.

Cyprus is also known as the "Island of Love," largely due to the legacy of Aphrodite, the Goddess of Love. It is steeped in romantic settings, and its fine cuisine and wine lend themselves to the pursuit of hedonistic pleasures. Even more telling is a love of life, which lies deep within the soul of the Cypriot, embracing good company and camaraderie.

Although Cyprus is quite prosperous, and the island's inhabitants enjoy a relatively high standard of living, one is tempted to say that the simple pleasures of family life and authentic hospitality are more important than material gain. Em-

Preceding pages: The hills of the Akamas Peninsula in the autumn light. A Cypriot priest sits with his wife. Richly decorated iconostasis in Kato Lefkara. Left: Aphrodite, the Goddess of Love, who walked ashore on Cyprus from the sea.

phasis in this guide is on steering you to places where you will have the opportunity to meet and talk to Cypriots, with the firm belief that person-to-person contact is a meaningful part of a visit to another country.

A concerted effort has been made to develop tourism in a thoughtful manner, although some participants have succumbed to the flashier aspects. Many potential visitors view Cyprus only as a sea, sun and fun spot. They may be pleasantly surprised when they discover the vast store of historical treasures and natural wonders that await them. In recent years, the Cyprus Tourism Organization (CTO), tour operators, and the press have encouraged visits by people interested in exploring unspoiled areas. Wherever possible, stress in this guide has been placed on the appreciation and preservation of the natural environment. The formation of national parks on the Akamas Peninsula in the Paphos District, Athalassa in the Nicosia District, and Cape Greco in the Famagusta District will go a long way towards establishing firmer controls over a precious heritage.

The proximity to and occupation by a variety of cultures has left a definite imprint on the Cypriot lifestyle. A proper British cream tea in a mountain village can be followed by a Mediterranean-style siesta. Spending the evening in Nicosia, it is possible to have a dinner of Cypriot specialties with Middle Eastern origins, such as *talatouri* and *houmous*, while listening to the call of the *muezzin* (announcer of hours of prayer) from a mosque in northern Cyprus. The Turkish sector is just across the "Green Line" separating the last divided capital in Europe.

Yes, bitter lemons are found among the blossoms on Cyprus. The pain of the division in 1974 and its continued schism is a prevalent aspect of island life. It will not hinder your appreciation of all the joys Cyprus has to offer, but it is a sad reality that cannot be ignored.

Ancient Roots of Cyprus

Cyprus is at the crossroads of a number of civilizations and, because of this position, has absorbed the influence of many other cultures. It has had a tumultuous past in many ways, struggling under the yoke of a succession of conquerors, only becoming an independent state in 1960. As difficult as this existence has been, the outside influences have created a fascinating diversity in its archeological and artistic development, all of which have contributed to the formation of its own unique identity.

Tackling the many millennia of Cypriot history may appear to be a formidable and perhaps unnecessary task for the average visitor, yet even casual reading on the subject will greatly enrich one's appreciation of the island. The Cyprus Tourist Organization has printed a booklet, *Cyprus: 9,000 Years of History and*

Above: The Neolithic settlement of Tenta at Kalavasos in the "Copper Belt."

Civilization, a brief capsule history of the entire island followed by descriptions of the sights of each district.

For readers who want a thorough immersion into the island's history, *Footprints in Cyprus*, edited by Sir David Hunt, is an excellent reference book. Experts on each period of the island's history give an analysis of it in 12 articles, illustrated with color panels and black-and-white sketches. The chronology followed throughout the book is a modification of one used in *An Archeological Guide to the Ancient Kourion Area and the Akrotiri Peninsula,* edited by Helena Wylde Swiny.

Epipaleolithic Period (8500-7000 B.C.)

It is difficult to pinpoint an exact date or origin for the first civilization on Cyprus. Evidence indicates that well before 6000 B.C. a series of related communities were already established on Cyprus, which disappeared as mysteriously as they had begun. It seems strange that settled communal life existed on the adjacent Anatolian and Syrian coasts before 7000 B.C., yet this fertile island appears to have been uninhabited.

We cannot say, however, that there is no evidence of habitation before 7000 B.C., since radiocarbon dating traces tools found in a cave on the Akrotiri Peninsula back to 8500 B.C. Most likely, these implements did not belong to permanent Epipaleolithic residents, but were left by passing hunters, who might also have been responsible for eradicating the pygmy hippopotami once prolific on the island.

Neolithic Period
(7000-3500 B.C.)

In the Neolithic Period about 15 communities altogether were formed along the north coast or in the short river valleys of the Troodos Mountains in the south. The largest was Khirokitia in the Larnaca District, with an estimated 2,000 inhabitants. Although the distances between these communities were great, they have many characteristics in common. The buildings were huddled together on the tops and slopes of hills, much as those of contemporary mountain villages. The beehive hut was popular, but a collapsed flat roof of one building at Khirokitia indicates that not all of the dwellings were standardized. The circular buildings were made of stone and mud brick. Many researchers believe these early inhabitants practiced ancestor worship. This may explain why the dead were buried beneath the floor, with a space for offerings. One generation was piled on top of another, and several layers of floor were a common result.

The interiors at Khirokitia typical of this period have hearths used for heating and cooking. The smoke which gathered in the upper level was used for curing venison from fallow deer. Evidence of

early stock breeding and hunting have been found, but no nearby fields for crops. Early communities were familiar with clay, but stubbornly continued to produce stone bowls. For this reason, archeologists label that period the Aceramic Neolithic.

The Ceramic Neolithic begins with the settlement of Sotira at Teppes near the village of Kandou in the Limassol District, dating back to the second half of the fifth millennium B.C. The so-called Neolithic Revolution had taken place, and human beings had domesticated such animals as the sheep, pig and dog. Grains such as wheat and barley were cultivated and supplemented by gathering nuts and berries, wild olives and grapes.

Two notable innovations occurred that distinguished Sotira from Khirokitia. The dead of the settlement were also buried in simple pits, but in a separate cemetery under the floors of the dwellings. The bodies were still forced into a contracted position and weighted down with a stone, indicating a superstitious fear of the dead. The other change is the first appearance of pottery, hence the name Ceramic Neolithic. Surprisingly, the pottery was not a crude form as one would expect, but was so-called combed ware, hand made from reddish clay with a distinctive wavy decoration made by a comb-like instrument. Beads of blue-green picrite from Troodos were used for pendants in Sotira and were found in other settlements in the north, indicating that exchange took place between communities. No evidence exists for external trade.

Although no great advances over the Khirokitia civilization appear to have occurred in the Sotira groups, their numbers increased, but not greatly in comparison to mainland groups. This is perhaps indicative of the vulnerability of many island communities, which were more susceptible to countless diseases, earthquakes and invasions. A general population shift occurred around 4000 B.C., and

small fluctuating communities were common into the Bronze Age. Urbanization came late here in comparison to other civilizations.

Chalcolithic Period
(3500-2500/2300 B.C.)

Pottery has been extremely useful in aiding the dating of sites and indicating patterns of trade and communication. The red-on-white ware, using a thick white slip (clay solution) on often coarse clay, then decorated with rich ornamental patterns in red paint, is most characteristic of southern Cyprus Chalcolithic communities. Examples of it from Erimi and Souskiou are on display in the Cyprus Museum in Nicosia and at the Pierides Foundation Museum in Larnaca. Other types of pottery are in the Cyprus Museum or in the various district museums.

Above: Early Bronze Age clay model of a temple with three-headed horned god. Right: Boat-shaped bowl (Middle Bronze Age).

Changes occurred in the transition from the Neolithic to the Chalcolithic Period. The word Chalcolithic is a combination of the Greek words for copper (*chalkós*) and stone (*líthos*). It was during this period that metalwork appeared for the first time. The earliest copper objects, such as chisels, hooks and jewelry, gave hints of the island's later exploitation of these resources. Some of these have tiny amounts of tin added and obsidian also appears, both indicating contact with Anatolia, perhaps through maritime trade. Few sites of the long period from 4000-2500 B.C. have been excavated. The evidence of cult buildings, introduction of the stamp seal, and imports suggest the development of more sophisticated societies with social hierarchies and administration of goods and properties. The wealth of burial objects in the shaft graves at Souskiou near Palea Paphos is striking.

It is difficult to reconstruct ensuing events with any certainty since little information exists from Kyrenia or the west Nicosia District, key areas in the transition to the Bronze Age. Events in the west were dramatic, with all Late Chalcolithic settlements but Kissonerga abandoned while Lemba was destroyed by fire. Kissonerga survived the transition into the Bronze Age, but was later abandoned. By this time chamber tombs, the hallmark of the arrival of the Bronze Age, had been constructed and urn burials occurred.

Bronze Age:
Early and Middle Cypriot
(2300-1900 B.C. and 1900-1625 B.C.)

The transition to a full bronze-using culture came surprisingly late. Most of the evidence of this period comes from family chamber tombs, most notably from Vasilia to the west of Kyrenia and from Vounos, located to the southeast of Kyrenia. The cemetery at Vasilia was distinguished by a sumptuous display of

"nouveau riche" artifacts stashed in the impressive plaster-lined complexes of up to 16 meters in length. Large stone vessels were found along with a form of pottery known as Philia, early red polished ceramic ware, distinguished by a variety of sometimes elaborate shapes.

Some of the clay models of open-air scenes are charming vignettes of daily life, a revealing form of naive art. One version from Vounos on display in the Cyprus Museum features seated and standing figures, including dancers and a mother with child, observing an area with penned bulls. This scene indicates that the circular mode of dwelling had persisted. The bulls, combined with bulls' heads used for terminals in other models, suggest a cult had developed in Early Bronze Age religion, perhaps connected with fertility. The large cemetery at Vounous is characterized by its elaborate burial sites complete with slaughtered cattle, cult vessels, pottery, replicas of daggers and sheaths, and decorated long copper pins.

A concentration of sites occurs along the "copper belt" of the northeastern foothills of the Troodos, from the Bay of Morphou in the north to Kalavasos in the south. The interest in the exploitation of copper may indicate some of this was done for export, rather than for strictly local needs. Alambra, south of Nicosia, is notable for its implements with traces of copper and the radical innovation of aligned rectangular buildings and streets.

Imported Asian and Minoan pottery, Egyptian stonework and Cycladic pottery found in cemeteries give solid proof that by 2000 B.C. Cyprus was involved in trade with adjoining lands of the Eastern Mediterranean. The first forts, built during this era, indicate unrest. They were built along the edges of the central plain and on the Karpasia Peninsula, most notably at Nitovikla. These structures are not close enough to the sea to be designed as protection from sea invaders, so they must have been a response to internal conflicts. It is notable that Nitovikla was violently destroyed.

19

By 1650 B.C., large-scale export of pottery to the Levant and Egypt had begun, and joined the flourishing export of copper to Mesopotamia. At the same time, this trading generated the first urban development.

Bronze Age: Late Cypriot (1625-1050 B.C.)

Cyprus finally emerged from its isolation in the Late Bronze Age. An increase in trade encouraged growth of major urban areas, both in the inland agricultural communities and the major harbors. Morphou on the north coast flourished, as did the ports of Enkomi, Hala Sultan Tekke and Maroni in the south.

Free communication existed throughout the island, and copper ore was brought to industrial centers and harbors. Artistic expression thrived, especially in

Above: Female figure with double-hoop earrings (Late Bronze Age). Right: Delicately crafted gold necklace (seventh century B.C.).

pottery. The extremely hard base ring ware, including a small poppy-head-shaped jug thought to have held opium in a liquid form, and white slip ware are uniquely Cypriot. These forms dominated the local industry for over three centuries and became very popular in the Near East and Aegean.

Palea Paphos was an especially prosperous region, and a vase of serpentine found here shows the earliest *cartouche* of an Egyptian Pharaoh (oval ring enclosing the king's name) ever found in Cyprus. This is an indication that the western part of the island also had relations with both Egypt and the Levant. Trade with the Aegean was a new development that had profound effects upon Cypriot culture. Mycenean merchants came to Cyprus seeking copper, for which they traded advanced wheel-made pottery with figured scenes, which influenced the development of Cypriot pottery. Other indigenous art forms, such as jewelry, seal engraving and faience, now incorporated strong Aegean elements.

Kalavasos flourished during the 14th and 13th centuries B.C., but was abandoned before the 12th century B.C. Chamber Tomb No. 11, crammed with an extraordinary amount of gold, ivory and glass objects, tells the story of Cypriot wealth developed through the exchange of Mycenean goods and those of other countries. Enkomi and Hala Sultan Tekke showed signs of similar wealth.

Until this time Cyprus had no form of writing, essential for a trading culture, but it now borrowed a Minoan script, Linear A of Crete, to develop the Cypro-Minoan syllabic. Although long documents in the form of baked clay tablets have been found only at Enkomi, there is evidence of script throughout the island. The text on these tablets, using the 80 characters of the Cypro-Minoan syllabic script, has never been deciphered. It is certainly not lists or inventories, as was the case in Minoan palaces, but most likely poetry.

Despite the peaceful nature of developments, cities were fortified, perhaps with an inkling of what lay ahead. Kition built a mud brick city wall, and in Enkomi a fortress was constructed. Workshops for smelting copper have also been found in these settlements. Generally, the standard of living seems to have been very high. The existence of clay and limestone bathtubs, lavatories and advanced drainage systems proves this.

After 1250 B.C., the peaceful period of the Bronze Age in the Eastern Mediterranean ended. Enkomi and Kition were destroyed by unknown invaders. The main Mycenean centers in the Peloponnese were destroyed and deserted. By the time Enkomi was rebuilt, it included a fair proportion of Mycenean immigrants who had come to Cyprus to reestablish themselves. Enkomi's new architecture was quite advanced with an orderly grid plan, and important buildings were constructed of enormous rectangular blocks like those of the Near East. Excavation of the city wall brought rudimentary cyclopic masonry to light, and in Kition archeologists found square bastions that were set at intervals before the city wall.

The Mycenean merchants were replaced by the "Peoples of the Sea." These fortune hunters sailed eastward and were perhaps joined by others from Anatolia. They turned to piracy and raided the coastal towns of Cyprus, with devastating effect. Further waves of immigration to Paleokastro-Maa and Pyla by Achaeans, a Homeric name for Mycenean Greeks, were resisted. Nevertheless, by the beginning of the 11th century, the process of colonization was completed and the Mycenean element was dominant.

This is one of the most formative and far-reaching periods in Cypriot history. The Mycenean aristocracy was at the forefront of politics and culture, but continued to absorb influences from the indigenous culture and from the Syro-Palestinian coast through continued

trade. One very significant event occurred during this period: Greek was introduced on the island and from this time on, Cyprus was a predominantly Greek-speaking country.

A renewal of contacts with the Aegean took place during the early 11th century. Some of the people who had settled on Cyprus after the Dorian invasions were probably Cretans, since the Minoan influence is evident in excellent ceramics and jewelry. A new wheel-made pottery called proto-white painted ware is an unmistakable blend of imported Greek and Cypriot motifs and techniques.

The Cretan influence was also evident in religious rituals, with the introduction of the Minoan fertility goddess with arms raised in benediction found in the sanctuaries of Kition, Enkomi and elsewhere. In funerary architecture, the tomb now had a rectangular chamber with a long narrow *dromos* (passage), similar to those on Crete and Rhodes and quite different from the typical Cypriot tomb in which the chamber opens out of a small vertical shaft. Examples of these were found at Kourion, Salamis, and in the Paphian cemetery of Palea Paphos.

Cypro-Geometric Period
(1050-750 B.C.)

The substitution of iron tools and weapons for bronze gave this period the name of Iron Age, now usually classified as the Geometric Period. More important was the consolidation of the capital cities of the ancient Greek kingdoms as entire Mycenean communities fled from mainland Greece. The Aegean Greeks had descended into a Dark Age of illiteracy and poverty, while the Cypriot Greeks still exhibited reasonable prosperity in their new environment. The earliest syllabic Greek inscription was found on a bronze *obelos* (pointed pillar) in a rich tomb of Palea Paphos. It is in the genitive case, as it would later be formed in the Cypriot and Arcadian dialects. The earlier script was adapted to the Greek syllabary known as Cypro-Classical, so we have evidence that the art of writing never vanished in Cyprus as it did in Greece.

Very little is known about any urban site in this period due to the lack of excavations. What is known has been gleaned from the tombs. It seems that some of the Greek kingdoms absorbed the native communities. Thus, the sites of Episkopi near Kourion and Idalion were completely deserted by the end of the 11th century B.C. The Cypriot cities founded by Greeks, including Salamis, Soli, Marion-Arsinoë, Palea Paphos and Kourion, formed the basic structure of modern Cyprus.

One community never taken over by the Greeks was Amathus on the south coast. Amathus was first settled in the 11th century and was independent and prosperous, trading with equal ease with

Right: An Archaic goblet decorated with a sphinx, the symbol of wisdom.

both Greeks and Levantines. It became one of the leading states of the Geometric Period, and was as powerful as the Greek kingdoms.

The period between 950 and 850 B.C. was uneventful and stagnant for the most part. Then, in the ninth century, Kition was settled by Phoenicians (inhabitants of the kingdom located on what is now the Syrian and Lebanese coast) as part of their determined western expansion which led them as far as Sardinia, Sicily and even Spain. It was given the name of "New Town," indicating that it was considered a Phoenician colony. This was confirmed by the rulership of a governor who reported to the King of Tyre, the principal Phoenician city. The colonists at Kition dedicated the splendid temple they built on the ruins of a Late Bronze Age sanctuary to the Phoenician goddess of fertility Astarte, whose identity was easily assimilated into the Cypriot cult of Aphrodite.

At first the Phoenicians settled in at Kition and took a deceptively non-aggressive stance. Their initial impact was on the artistic development. They introduced the shallow metal bowl with figured scenes inside, and the red slip ware and black-on-red ware. Regional ceramic styles became clarified during the Cypro-Geometric Period, with eastern potters being more inventive in the use of motifs such as rosettes, lotus flowers and figured themes, while the more conservative westerners favored small circles.

The eighth century B.C. was one of expansion and increased prosperity. Greece was recovering from its Dark Age and trade was resumed. The mainland Greek traders quickly learned the Phoenician alphabet, but the Cypriot Greeks continued to resist it. They clung to their more complicated syllabic forms, even though the Phoenician alphabet was in use at Kition. Although the mainland Greeks adopted the *polis* system, a network of small city-states, this system never took hold in

Cyprus. The Cypriots were exposed only to an absolute monarchy leaning towards despotism. The 10 or so kingdoms remained completely independent of one another and were often prone to serious conflicts.

One unifying factor was the recitation of Homer's epics of the *Iliad* and *Odyssey* at public festivals, encouraging a common cultural pride shared by mainland and Cypriot Greeks. The Cypriot Greeks had their own epic poet, Stassinos, who claimed to be Homer's son-in-law and who wrote his now lost poem *Cypria* as a prelude to the *Iliad*.

The revival of Mycenean burial customs by the inhabitants of Salamis added Homeric accents to their unique funerary blend of native, Eastern and Greek rituals. The extraordinary wealth of the Salaminian royalty at the end of the Geometric Period is evident from their nine huge tombs and the richness of the grave goods, including ivory-inlaid furniture and ornate bronze cauldrons. Nothing was spared to provide comfort for the de-parted in the next world. The rituals included slaughtering the deceased's chariot horses and burying them with the owner together with their richly decorated harnesses.

Evidence of other adapted Homeric burial details was quenching the pyre with wine and cremation. A homey touch was provided by including iron skewers and tongs in the tombs so that in the next world the royalty could have a cookout over charcoal for new friends, thus maintaining their reputation for hospitality.

Cypro-Archaic Period (750-475 B.C.)

The Cypro-Archaic Period was one of fluctuating rules and influences. At its beginning, Assyria began to be aggressive towards its neighbors, although at first the Cypriot kingdoms were spared and kept their autonomy. Cyprus eventually submitted to Sargon II of Syria in 709 B.C., who erected a stele at Kition to commemorate the event. At this time he boasted seven Cypriot kingdoms paying him

23

homage; in later records we read of 10 kingdoms, and by the fifth century there were 11.

Assyrian domination ended in 663 B.C., and Cyprus then enjoyed almost a hundred years of autonomy. During this period the Cypriot culture flourished and produced many of the finest Archaic art forms. A brief period of Egyptian rule (about 560-540 B.C.) fostered Cypriot trade with Egypt and a Cypro-Egyptian school of sculpture. Shortly afterwards, Cypriots shifted allegiance to the Great King of Persia, having to pay tribute and put their forces at his command, but they retained some form of independence.

The Cypriot kingdoms, with the exception of Amathus, joined in the Ionian Revolt in 499 B.C. to rid themselves of Persian oppression. Persia retaliated by laying siege to all the Cypriot cities. One

Above: These sandstone heads demonstrate Assyrian influence. Right: A bas relief of Sargon II. Far right: Bronze statue of Roman Emperor Septimus Severus.

by one all the cities succumbed, including Soli, which had valiantly held out for five months. Religion always played an important role in Cypriot life. During the Cypro-Archaic Period, inhabitants became familiar with a number of foreign deities, including the Phoenician and Egyptian gods. Rituals surrounding the worship of gods included sacred banquets and ritual dances accompanied by musicians playing lyres, pan-pipes and tambourines. It was customary to offer a gift appropriate for the deity, such as a dove for Aphrodite. Animals were sacrificed, incense was burned and the priests wore animal masks.

Worshippers dedicated limestone or terra cotta figures representing themselves or the deity and left them grouped around the altar of the sanctuary or buried them in the tombs. The main sanctuaries had their own workshops, and a huge number of objects were produced. Over 2,000 figures were found at the sanctuary of Ayia Irini, many of which are on display at the Cyprus Museum in Nicosia.

Colossal statues of limestone and terra cotta reflect both Egyptian and Eastern Greek influences. Artists overcame the limitations of soft limestone by using paint and engraving to add details. These statues often provide a fascinating reflection of clothing, hair and jewelry styles of the time. Some common facial characteristics are an oval shape, protruding eyes, long plaited hair and the mysterious "archaic" smile.

The first century of the Cypro-Archaic Period was the zenith of Cypriot civilization. Although Cyprus had three foreign rulers in quick succession, it also had a century of independence which allowed it to finally fully explore its own culture and art forms. Works of art created at this time had a definite Cypriot flavor, incorporating outside influences without mindlessly imitating them.

Classical Period (475-325 B.C.)

The Classical Period began when Cyprus was in a state of turmoil after its final defeat by the Persians in 498 B.C. During this era, Cyprus was caught between two warring factions, Greece and Persia. Persia kept a tight rein on Cyprus after the ill-fated Ionian Revolt of 499 B.C. The Cypriot kings paid tribute to the Great King of Persia and had to contribute ships in time of war, as they did in 480 B.C. for Persia's naval war against Athens.

A despotic form of government for the city-states reached its peak. The King had absolute power and was supported by princes and princesses who formed a supreme court. The King also took on the function of high priest in Paphos, inheriting the role of Kinyras, thought to be the founder of Aphrodite's Sanctuary. Only in Idalion was the system somewhat more democratic.

Toward the beginning of the fourth century B.C., the Cypriots made their most significant bid for unity and independence. King Evagoras I emerged as a Cypriot national hero at a time when the weary populace desperately needed someone to believe in. A clever and at-

25

tractive young man, he seized the throne of Salamis away from the Phoenician ruler Abdemon in 411 B.C. He was the dominant figure in the politics of Cyprus for the next 40 years, forging the destiny of Salamis as the most influential city of Cyprus. Evagoras introduced the Greek alphabet to Cyprus, and the Athenians honored him with a decree in 410 B.C.

He elicited the help of Artaxerxes II of Persia, who later turned against him, in Athens' war against Sparta. He fought alone for 10 years against the Persians, hoping to extend the rule of Salamis over the whole island. Evagoras essentially saw his dreams come true by 391 B.C. By 380 B.C., after the defeat by the Persians, he maintained the throne of Salamis but lost control of the other cities. Around 374 B.C. he was murdered by a eunuch.

Because of all the turmoil between the Cypriot city-kingdoms and conflicts between the Greek cities and Persians, forti-

Above: Alexander the Great during the Battle of Issos in 333 B.C.

fied communities were of prime importance to their kings. The structures at Idalion, Palea Paphos and Ayia Irini all had siege walls constructed.

The conflicts between Greece and Persia for control of Cyprus had repercussions in art as well. Attic pottery from Greece continued to dominate, and classical Greek influences are evident in sculpture, too. Greek sculptors were breaking away from the rigidity of the Archaic style and strove to create a perfect human form with both expressiveness and movement.

The pro-Greek stance of Evagoras I and his followers led to the adoption of Greek forms to the exclusion of native art, which, unfortunately, in some cases had become stagnant and repetitive. On the other hand, though there was little peacetime for Cypriots to practice their art forms, some fine works reflecting the Cypriot character were produced.

The Cypriot kings supported Alexander the Great when he assumed control in 333 B.C. and backed him in the naval battle against Tyre. Although this seemed like an advantageous move, when Cyprus became part of the Hellenistic world it also lost part of its identity.

Hellenistic Period (325-58 B.C.)

The city-states had maintained some freedom under the Persians, but lost this under Alexander, who was determined to spread Greek culture. After Alexander died in 323 B.C., his generals turned Cyprus into a battleground while struggling to inherit his kingdom. They destroyed the city-kingdoms of Kition, Lapithos, Marion and Kyrenia. In 294 B.C., Cyprus was conquered by Ptolemy I, Alexander's general, who had taken control of Egypt. Former kings who were hostile were sent off to Egypt. King Nikokreon of Salamis, overall ruler, was the only opposition left to total Ptolemaic domination. He was given a sentence of death, but he chose to kill himself and his wife followed suit. The Cypriot royal line came to an abrupt end. In one fell swoop, the city-kingdoms were eliminated, and Cyprus was absorbed into the Hellenistic state of Egypt.

The Ptolemies acquired Cyprus mainly for the supply of copper, grain and timber, and as a ship-building center. By the early second century, the capital had been transferred from Salamis to Paphos, an ideal location for ship building close to Egypt.

The government was reorganized as a military command under the control of a *strategos* – or governor general – who was under the authority of the King of Egypt. Although the city-kingdoms had been abolished, during the 300 years that the Ptolemies ruled some freedoms were preserved. The Ptolemies were of Greek origin and their culture was Hellenistic. The mother goddess Astarte was still worshipped, although Aphrodite was recognized as the most important deity. Greek cults flourished.

Many of the buildings of this period were supplanted by later Roman ones or were destroyed by earthquakes. Gymnasia are recorded as well as theaters, including the one at Kourion, which survives today. The Kourion Theater was built in the second century B.C. on the basis of a Greek plan, in which the central section of the fan-shaped auditorium together with the entire orchestra and a large part of the stage building were cut into the hillside. The theater was used for performances in both the Greek and Roman periods and was an integral part of the city's amusement.

The initial form of Greek drama probably originated in the songs and dances performed for the fertility rites at the country festival of Dionysus, who became the patron god of the theater. The festivals took place in a central clearing near a temple, perhaps on a threshing floor, which might have been the original model for the theater.

Greek drama was subdued, related to nature and usually highly moral, while in comparison Roman drama was more emotional and exaggerated. The only Cypriot playwright on record was Sopatros, who lived in Paphos in the third century B.C. Only 25 lines of a burlesque comedy survive, in which he ridiculed the famous philosopher Zeno of Kition.

Ordinary citizens were buried in irregular simple chamber tombs cut into the rock. The noble Ptolemaic aristocrats were laid to rest in style in elaborately cut-out chambers set in Doric courtyards in Paphos. This was an imitation of similar ones in Alexandria in Egypt, which were so sumptuous that they were mistakenly called "Tombs of the Kings."

In the Hellenistic Period, Cyprus lost some of its independence under the Ptolemies, and its culture became more cosmopolitan. But some art forms, such as sculpture, retained their native quality. Zenon of Kition, who died about 264 B.C., was the founder of the Stoic School

of Philosophy in Athens. However his work was outside Cyprus. The intellectual life on the island itself at this time was mostly mediocre.

Roman Period (58 B.C.-A.D. 330)

Strabo describes how the last Ptolemaic King of Cyprus, an uncle of Cleopatra, was deposed by the Romans in 58 B.C. and preferred death to becoming a high priest. Eleven years later, Cyprus was given back to Cleopatra by Caesar, officially confirmed by Mark Antony in 36 B.C. However, in 22 B.C., the island became a separate Roman Senatorial Province ruled by a proconsul.

Greek remained the official language, as was true in the rest of the Eastern Empire. Rome seemed to have little interest in Romanizing Cyprus. The Cypriots, in contrast, were initially enthusiastic about showing their loyalty to the Emperor. It

Above left: Cleopatra. Above right: Julius Caesar. Right: Constantine the Great.

seems they received meager reward for this from the Roman side. In A.D. 212, when Caracalla offered Roman citizenship to all males living in the empire, few took him up on it.

The Roman Period, which spurred a productive agricultural economy, was one of the most prosperous throughout Cypriot history. Strabo mentions the island had good wine and olive oil and was self-sufficient in grain. The arts flourished, yet few Cypriots gained international fame. Most of the ruins you will see around Cyprus date from Roman times. Information from this period has largely been gleaned from inscriptions, because few events so significantly disturbed the *Pax Romana* that they were reported to the outside world. One of the few violent episodes was the Jewish Insurrection of A.D. 116, which resulted in a bloodbath among the non-Jewish population of Salamis, pointing out the need for adequate military forces on the island.

Otherwise, the most frequent cause for bloodshed during this period was the popular form of Roman entertainment, the gladiatorial games at ancient Kourion (indicated by the mosaic in the House of Gladiators), Salamis and Paphos. The island was divided among 12 or 13 cities. Nea Paphos, which had been founded at the end of the fourth century B.C., was the seat of the Roman proconsul. At this time it reached its golden age. Palea Paphos (Kouklia), site of the world-renowned Temple of Aphrodite, became the sanctuary of the new capital. Pilgrims arriving from the harbor crossed through the Holy Gardens. Proconsul Sergius Paulus distinguished himself by converting to Christianity in A.D. 45, after a visit from St. Paul accompanied by St. Barnabas, a citizen of Salamis.

Although Cyprus proudly touts its reputation as the first country to be ruled by a Christian governor, Christianity seemed to make little headway on the island before the fourth century A.D. Obvious signs of decline in the third century A.D. can be attributed to Cyprus' loss of favor within the Roman world, resulting in its subordination to Antioch.

Early Byzantine Period
(A.D. 330-649)

In A.D. 330, the Byzantine Period was ushered in with Constantine the Great having founded a new capital for the East Roman or Byzantine Empire on the site of ancient Byzantium. He dubbed it "New Rome," although it was commonly known as Constantinople. But for many people it was and still is simply "The City."

The name Istanbul, used today, probably derives from the Greek expression *eis tin polin*, "to the city." The administration of the eastern provinces, including Cyprus, was here.

The first two centuries of this period were peaceful and prosperous. Religious history was in the forefront after Constantine officially recognized Christianity in 313. In the late fourth century A.D., Emperor Theodosius ordered all pagan temples to be closed, which sounded the knell for the rituals at the Temple of Aphrodite in Paphos. However, vestiges of the worship of the Goddess of Love continued for some time and can even be found today.

Traditionally, St. Barnabas of Salamis, the 12th apostle who replaced Judas, was the founder of the Church of Cyprus. St. Barnabas was with St. Paul in A.D. 45 during the aforementioned visit in which he converted the Roman Proconsul Sergius Paulus to Christianity.

Besides St. Barnabas, three Cypriot saints who lived during the Byzantine Era are revered on the island. The first is St. Spyridon, a pious and colorful figure who was tortured during the terrible persecution of the Christians (A.D. 303-305) in the time of Emperor Diocletian. But he survived to become Bishop of Tremithus in the Larnaca District. His remains were transported to Corfu, and he is now the beloved patron saint there.

The second saint is the Palestinian hermit Hilarion, who settled near Paphos. The third saint was Epiphanios, also of Palestine, who was elected bishop of the prestigious Constantia-Salamis Church in 401.

Of more immediate consequence to the local populace was St. Helena's visit to Cyprus about 327 A.D. The mother of Emperor Constantine was returning from Jerusalem and carried with her fragments of the "True Cross," as well as the Cross of the Penitent Thief. According to popular legend, a 36-year-long drought and famine ended immediately when she arrived. She founded the monastery at Stavrovouni after being prompted to do so in a dream, and a gold-encased fragment of the cross now hangs in its church.

The recognition of Christianity generally seemed to make life easier for the inhabitants. Harsher Roman laws were repealed, and the death penalty was rarely

imposed. Concubinage was abolished and gladiator matches were replaced by chariot races. The lot of laborers, who were confined to the land on which they were born, was not improved in this sense. But stricter control over the officials governing them, who had been pocketing tax funds, gave them fairer treatment.

The Church of Cyprus, originally controlled from Antioch, won its independence in 478 after Cypriot Archbishop Anthemios had discovered St. Barnabas' remains and brought them to Constantinople. He also presented St. Barnabas' handwritten copy of the Gospel to Emperor Zeno, who was so overwhelmed by this gift that he confirmed the autocephaly of the Cypriot Church and extended great privileges to its archbishop, including the rights to carry a scepter instead of a staff and to sign documents in the imperial purple ink.

During the fifth and sixth centuries, the urban areas enjoyed a high standard of living as a result of renewed trade, but

Above: The Byzantine Church of St. Barnabas and Hilarion (early 10th century).

Cyprus didn't regain the levels of prosperity of late Roman times. Two monks brought silk worms to Cyprus from the Far East and, within a short time, the fine silks of Cyprus were world-renowned and commanded high prices.

Arab Invasions (A.D. 647-965)

The first of the Arab raids that would continue intermittently for the next three centuries took place about 647. Salamis-Constantia was sacked and never recovered. The harbor towns of Paphos, Kourion and Lambousa were depleted as the inhabitants began to move to safer territory inland and settled on higher ground, such as Ktima near Nea Paphos. Cyprus was once again caught between two warring factions, in this case the Byzantines and the Arabs.

During the next turbulent 300 years the island changed hands 11 times, and taxes were extremely high since at times both the Moslem Caliph and Byzantine Emperor collected them. During this period, thousands of Christians were killed or taken as slaves.

Late Byzantine Period (A.D. 965-1191)

Cyprus was reconquered in A.D. 965 by Emperor Nikephoros II Phokas and was once again a Byzantine province. This ushered in a second golden age in the economic as well as cultural fields.

The Byzantine Period as a whole was an extremely prolific era and much of Byzantine art reflected the prosperity but, unfortunately, only a tiny percentage of the total output survives today. Mosaic work, mural painting, icon painting, ivory sculpture and metal work were the main forms, reaching their peak during the mid-Byzantine Period.

The splendid relief work on silver plates found at Lapithos, now called Lambousa, shows a remarkable craftsmanship. Other art forms reflect transitions of this period. Only a few of the remarkable wall mosaics of the period survived the iconoclastic period. These include the *Virgin and Child*, originally in the Kanakaria Church on the Karpasia Peninsula, which was recently crudely dismantled by smugglers who tried to sell it in the United States. A court decision has returned it to the Cypriot Church.

The mosaic is in the hieratic orientalized style, while the similar *Virgin and Child* of the Panayia Angeloktisti in Kiti shows the movement and human forms characterizing the classical style that dominated Byzantine art in the centuries after the collapse of iconoclasm.

These two styles, the hieratic and the classical, were also evident in church paintings which comprise one of the most outstanding and unique contributions Cyprus has made to the world.

The surviving Byzantine churches are small and simple stone structures, little treasure troves of incredible beauty. Few secular buildings remain from this period other than the St. Hilarion Castle in Kyrenia District.

Richard the Lionhearted (1191-1192)

When the Byzantine Empire waned in the late 12th century, Cyprus fell into the hands of the Crusaders. After a brief interlude of independence (1184-91) under the tyrant Isaac Comnenos, Richard the Lionhearted of England overran the island. After plundering a sufficient amount to repay his expenses, he decided the island was more bother than it was worth and sold it to the Knights Templar, who proved to be decadent and cruel rulers. The Cypriots planned a bloody insurrection and the Templars hastily retreated after slaughtering so many people in Nicosia that blood ran in the streets. In 1192, Richard then presented Cyprus to Guy de Lusignan, former King of Jerusalem, and the Lusignan dynasty began.

Lusignan Dynasty (1192-1489)

The rule of the Franks in Cyprus, the *Frankokratia* as the Greeks called it, was largely based on the feudal system. The dynasty was most successful in avoiding internal dissension, notably civil war. But, once again, Cyprus suffered because of the conflict between foreign interests, in this case the Genoese and Venetians, who both coveted the island.

The Lusignans were absolute rulers whose dynasty was notoriously laden with intrigues. Women played a dominant role. Conflicting accounts exist on the status of the common people. Some travelers described the luxury of the rulers and then commented on the oppression of the peasantry. Others describe them as good-natured slothful people whose main solace was in the hearty local wine. Whichever version was true, the main

Above: Richard the Lionhearted, reluctant ruler of Cyprus in 1191. Right: Caterina Cornaro, Queen of Cyprus (1473-89).

burden for the populace was being subjected to an alien rule, for the Lusignans made no effort to bridge the cultural and social gap. Under Amaury de Lusignan (1194-1205) Roman Catholicism became the official religion. The Orthodox bishoprics were dissolved and the native clergy was persecuted and imprisoned. Some were even burned at the stake.

One of the more positive aspects of the Lusignans' heritage are the medieval architectural monuments, including the fairy-tale castles of St. Hilarion, Buffavento and Kantara, the square keep of Kolossi, which housed the Knights of St. John, and part of the Manor House at Kouklia. These are the first completely exotic architectural elements in Cyprus. The stately Western European Gothic style structures include the cathedrals of St. Sophia in Nicosia, St. Nicholas at Famagusta and the Abbey of Bellapais. The Lusignans built most of Famagusta's churches, which once numbered 365. By a quirk of fate, all of these monuments lie in northern Cyprus.

The highly ambitious and quixotic ruler Pierre I (1359-69) captured Alexandria, but had to retreat when his knights abandoned him. He was also thwarted in his plan to conquer Jerusalem and was assassinated upon his return to Cyprus. The Lusignan dynasty went into rapid decline. In 1372, riots between the Genoese and Venetians at the coronation of Pierre II, the 12-year-old son of Pierre I, led to the seizure of Famagusta by the Genoese. In 1426, the Mamelukes of Cairo invaded, forcing the Lusignans to take an oath of allegiance and to pay an annual tribute to the Sultan. Queen Helena Paleologa, a Byzantine princess, tried to help the Cypriots, and her illegitimate stepson Jacques II ousted the Genoese from Famagusta with the aid of the Venetians. They cleverly matched him up with Venetian beauty Caterina Cornaro. This set the stage for Venice's acquisition of Cyprus, fulfilling a long-desired goal.

Venetian Period (1489-1571)

The Venetians acquired Cyprus at a time when their role as a Mediterranean superpower was starting to appear rather shaky. After Constantinople fell to the Turks in 1453, the trading nations of Christian Western Europe moved defensively. No longer welcome as privileged merchants in Ottoman-controlled cities, the Venetians tried to protect their business interests as best they could. Cyprus was strategic as a stopover on the lucrative sailing routes to the Levant.

Venice already ruled Crete (less than a week's sailing time from Cyprus in good weather), as well as ports and islands scattered around the coast of Greece, which provided a network of safe harbors for the state-owned galleys that carried sugar, valuable spices and textiles. Merchant ships brought pilgrims from all over Europe to the Holy Land and returned with cargoes of wine, timber, grain and cheese from Cyprus or Crete.

A skillful mix of diplomacy and intrigue eventually secured Cyprus for the Venetians. The key to the conspiracy was a woman, Caterina Cornaro, who came from a prominent family of Venetian aristocrats. She married King Jacques II, the last of the Lusignan rulers. He was an energetic playboy who enjoyed hunting and took little interest in the island's welfare. She appears as an almond-eyed beauty in a portrait by Titian. But apparently she lacked the lively independence of earlier Cypriot queens.

When Jacques died in 1473 under suspicious circumstances (Venetian skill in eliminating enemies through poison is sometimes cited), his infant son Jacques, born posthumously, was proclaimed king. He died a year later. Caterina became Queen of Cyprus and a focus for political scheming on the island. She had already been officially adopted as a "daughter of the Venetian Republic," a ruse ensuring that if she died without an

heir, Cyprus would automatically become part of the Venetian Empire.

However, the Spanish were also keen to take over the island. A large number of Catalans had already settled there. In 1473, shortly after Jacques died, the Catalan party murdered Caterina's uncle and closest adviser. They even came close to toppling her, but a Venetian fleet came to the rescue.

Six years later, another Spanish-inspired plot, directed by an aristocratic Venetian rebel, was hatched. Once again Venetian forces intervened to save Caterina from assassination.

Continuing unrest on Cyprus eventually persuaded the Venetian Council of State that only direct rule could ensure its loyalty. Even Caterina was suspected of secretly sympathizing with the Spanish faction. Her brother Giorgo was given the task of persuading her to abdicate in favor of the *Serenissima*, the "Most Serene Republic."

Caterina was reluctant to give up the trappings of monarchy, but agreed when

she was allowed to keep the title of Queen and granted a handsome pension with a stately home at Asolo, close to Venice. In 1489, she formally ceded the kingdom to the Doge of Venice at a ceremony in St. Nicholas' Cathedral in Famagusta before setting sail for home.

For the Cypriots, Venetian rule proved even harsher than the feudal system of the Lusignans. Administrators were sent out from Venice every two years – three *Rettori* and a *Capitano* who took charge of the military. But Cyprus was an unpopular posting compared to islands like Crete or Corfu. In their reports home, the bureaucrats complained about poor water quality and severe droughts, the burning summer heat, plagues of locusts and frequent outbreaks of disease.

The Lusignan nobles were allowed to keep their estates, but lost their political power when the old *Haute Court* (High

Above: The domed fountain in Ayia Napa Monastery. Right: Famagusta Gate, part of the city wall of Nicosia.

Court) was abolished. They thoroughly resented being governed by Italian republicans. Ordinary Cypriots found themselves taxed more heavily and required to work two days a week for the State without being paid.

As new routes to the East were opened up and the Turks tightened their grip on the eastern Mediterranean during the early 16th century, Venetian power declined. The island's administration grew more corrupt and inefficient. For thousands of Cypriots, emigration was the answer. The island's population declined markedly during the later years of Venetian rule: people forgot their fears of the Ottomans and settled in southeastern Turkey.

One reason for the Venetians' bad reputation as administrators was the home government's reluctance to allocate enough funds to its colonies, even when the Turkish threat started to loom large. Cyprus was always strapped for cash to pay troops stationed there and to improve its fortifications. Yet, the island contributed substantial revenues, especially from the administration's monopoly on salt, which was collected from the lake beds of Larnaca District and regularly exported to Venice.

Both *Commandaria* wine and sugar from Cyprus were also much in demand. Locally-grown cane was crushed and processed at sugar mills on big estates like Kolossi outside Limassol. It was a highly profitable business, as sugar was becoming an important luxury in northern Europe. Fine crystalline sugar was shipped to Venice in the form of large cones, pressed from a mold. Another luxury product sent to Venice and very much in demand was the *beccafico*, a small fig-eating bird which was snared and then pickled in brine.

The Venetians had little interest in completing elegant public works in a colony intended to be a military outpost. Apart from the fortifications, there are few striking architectural or artistic remnants from their days in power.

One rare example is the Monastery of Ayia Napa, completed just before the Turkish invasion. In the cloistered courtyard is a carved marble fountain covered by a dome supported on pillars.

In the north of the island, Venetian work can be seen on the finely decorated iconostasis at the Monastery of Ayios Mamas in Morphou. In Famagusta, part of a Venetian loggia, including coats of arms sculpted in marble, survives next to the cathedral. Nearby, part of the impressive façade of the Venetian *Palazzo del Provveditore* still stands.

By far the most striking monuments from the days of Venetian rule are the circular walls of Nicosia, with their 11 heart-shaped bastions (each named after a prominent Venetian family) and the imposing fortifications of Famagusta. Venetian military planners, it seems, were not interested in maintaining the medieval castles in the Kyrenia Mountains in the northern part of Cyprus.

Turkish Invasion (A.D. 1570)

After the Turks captured Egypt in 1517, it was clear that Cyprus was under threat. But it was not until 1567 that Nicosia was fortified by Francesco Barbaro. The Lusignan palace and a Dominican monastery were demolished to make way for the Paphos Gate, one of three tunnel entrances to the walled city. The best preserved of them is the Famagusta Gate, now restored as a cultural center. Its thick wooden doors are probably original.

At Kyrenia, the Venetians rebuilt the medieval castle overlooking the harbor. At Famagusta, the administrative center had walls, standing 15 meters high in some places and 8 meters thick, rebuilt on Lusignan foundations and strengthened by 15 bastions. The Sea Gate, its iron portcullis still visible, was built in 1496. The Citadel, known as Othello's Tower, dates from 1492.

Shakespeare's *Othello, the Moor of Venice* may have been an officer nick-

named *Il Moro* for his dark-complexion, who served at Famagusta in the 1540s and who was banished for an unrecorded crime.

When the long-expected Turkish invasion finally came, the Venetian defenses eventually yielded to heavy bombardment and superior numbers. In March 1570, the Ottoman Sultan Selim II (son of Suleyman the Magnificent) ordered Venice to hand over Cyprus.

The Venetians refused; instead, they organized a relief force with the help of the Papacy and King Philip II of Spain. But it turned back in September and never reached Cyprus.

In the meantime, an Ottoman army landed on the south coast, led by Lala Mustapha Pasha. The Venetians thought Famagusta would be attacked first. In fact, Mustapha marched on Nicosia.

Above: Engraving of the southwest gate of Famagusta, target of the siege by the Turks in 1570. Right: Cyprus country folk in holiday dress during the Ottoman Period.

The city was defended by an inept commander, Nicolo Dandolo. The siege began on July 25 and lasted only six weeks. Mustapha's troops stormed into the city on September 9 and massacred 20,000 residents. Dandolo's head was sent to Famagusta, the Turks' next target. In the meantime, Kyrenia surrendered without a cannon being fired.

The Venetian commander at Famagusta was Marcantonio Bragadino, a more determined character who was assisted by a professional soldier, Astorre Baglioni. The ten-month siege of Famagusta was an epic of heroic defense. 8,000 Venetian and Greek troops were heavily outnumbered by an Ottoman force that rose to 200,000 as the siege wore on.

Despite ferocious bombardment from the 145 Ottoman guns, it was not until June 1571 that a breach was made in the walls. Even then, it was valiantly held by the starving defenders, who by that time were reduced to eating stray cats. By August 1, only 400 troops were fit to fight

and gunpowder supplies had almost run out. Bragadino offered to surrender. A cease-fire was negotiated, and it seemed at first that Mustapha intended to recognize the Christians' brave defense by granting them safe passage home.

But the truce was quickly broken. Most of the defenders were massacred on the spot. Bragadino suffered a horrific fate. Mustapha himself sliced off his ears and nose; two weeks later he was flayed alive. His skin was stuffed with straw and brought triumphantly to Constantinople, where it was publicly displayed.

Ten years later, a Venetian stole his remains and took them back to Venice, where they are now kept in an urn in the Church of Santi Giovanni e Paolo.

Famagusta was renamed Magosa by the Turks, and the Cathedral of St. Nicholas became the Lala Mustapha Pasha Mosque, in honor of the man who made Cyprus a Turkish possession. Two years later, the Venetians formally renounced all claims on the island and turned westward in the hope of protecting Crete.

"He who would become and remain a great power in the East must hold Cyprus in his hand," is an oft-quoted statement epitomizing the island's checkered history over many centuries. No sooner had Cyprus thrown off the yoke of one foreign power than another emerged to take its place.

After the conquest of Egypt, the Ottomans needed Cyprus for the control of the eastern Mediterranean. Another theory, more bizarre but not totally without historical evidence, is that the Sultan, known as "Selim the Sot," had long coveted the island because of the fame of its wines.

It is incontestable that by this time Venetian rule had atrophied, and conquest by the expansionist Ottomans, whatever the Sultan's personal motives, had become virtually inevitable.

The ten-month siege and subsequent fall of Famagusta is widely regarded as marking the start of the Turkish Era of occupation, although it was not until March 1573 that a formal treaty was concluded between Venice and the *Porte*.

Above: The aqueduct of Larnaca, built in 1746, has a total of 75 arches.

Ottoman Era (1571-1878)

Turkish rule was despotic, inefficient and corrupt, with occasional spasms of cruelty, but it had some redeeming features, especially in the earlier stages. The Ottoman administrators conferred upon their Cypriot subjects a number of elementary rights and favors denied to them by previous conquerors. First, the Turks abolished serfdom, which brought about a gradual transformation in the status of the ordinary peasants. On payment of a modest sum, the peasant acquired possession of his soil, with right of succession going to his dependants.

More important, the Turkish authorities reestablished the supremacy of the autocephalous Greek Orthodox Church, which had languished or been humiliated during centuries of Latin ecclesiastical domination under the Lusignans and Venetians. With the benefit of hindsight, this concession to the Greeks stands out as one of the most important developments of the Ottoman Era, and one that is richly paradoxical. Greek Orthodox properties seized by the Turkish troops during their initial wave of occupation were even handed back to their rightful owners.

The procedure adopted by the Turks was to work through the Church, according it civil functions which gradually acquired greater importance than its religious functions. In Cyprus, the Greek Archbishop came to be treated as the temporal, not merely the spiritual leader of his community. He was allowed the formal title of *Ethnarch*, and in practice was often the most important figure after the Turkish governor.

In the early 19th century, a traveler convened this picture of the secular activities of the Archbishop: "The Governor and the Archbishop deal more largely in grain than all of the other people of the island put together; they frequently seize upon the whole yearly produce, at their own valuation, and either export it or re-tail it at an advanced price." The Archbishop played a key role in assessing tax contributions in all sorts of ways and served as both representative of his community and interlocutor.

To some extent, his responsibilities dovetailed with those of an important functionary of the Ottoman Empire bearing the awesome title of the Dragoman (or the interpreter) of the Palace. This post had been invented by the Ottomans because they were not motivated to learn the languages of the various peoples they conquered. They therefore needed an intermediary in every territory to serve primarily as an interpreter. As the office became institutionalized, the Dragoman acquired immense power. For example, he was exempt from paying taxes and had access to the Sultan in Constantinople as a key Ottoman official.

Despite the tolerant attitude of the Turkish authorities toward the Cypriot Church, the first two centuries of Ottoman rule were an era of stagnation and hardship for Greeks and Turks alike. Historian Sir George Hill writes about "plague, locusts, drought, famine and earthquakes, especially in the 17th century." The benighted Cypriot villagers might have added a man-made tribulation tax. Some of the revenue went to the Porte, some went into the Governor's coffers, virtually none was used for the betterment of the island. The slow decay of the architectural monuments left by the Lusignans and Venetians was met with utter indifference.

An interesting social phenomenon from the Turkish Period is the group known as *linobambakoi*, literally translated as "flax-cottons." They were Greek or Latin Christians who ostensibly adopted the Moslem faith, mainly to avoid paying higher taxes. They gained a reputation for being wily, chameleon-like people, many of whom lived in the area of Tillyria near Pomos on the northwest coast.

Construction during the Turkish Period consisted of mosques, Moslem monasteries, called *tekke*, caravansaries (inns for caravan travelers), libraries, forts and tombs, called *türbe* in Turkish. Many aqueducts and fountains were built that still exist today.

Beneath the surface, there were inevitable rumblings of unrest, not confined to the Greek community. In 1799, a mutiny occurred in the Turkish army, the origins of which are still obscure. Five years later, serious rioting erupted in Nicosia, sparked by rumors of food shortages on top of more general economic grievances. The protestors were mainly Turks, significantly the prime targets.

During the 19th century, Cyprus was sucked into the vortex of European power politics slowly but inexorably, and its fate was increasingly determined by events and historical forces outside the island. The most catalytic of these was the Greek War of Independence which started with an anti-Turkish revolt on March 25, 1821. It continued for nearly a decade until the mainland Greeks, with backing from Britain, France and Russia, emerged triumphant in the new-born nation-state. Inevitably, their achievement had a profound psychological effect on the Cypriots. It did not spark off an immediate agitation for *Enosis* (the union of Cyprus with Greece), but the idea began to germinate in Greek Cypriot minds.

The immediate response of the Turkish authorities to the news of the 1821 uprising was alarm bordering on panic. The governor at that time was the infamous Küchük Mehmet ("Little Mehmet"), described by the French consul as a "harsh, vulgar and fanatical man."

Fearing that a similar revolt might soon be staged on the island, he persuaded the Sultan to send in thousands of extra troops whose arrival led only to bloody clashes and atrocities. Although by this time the Greek population had been systematically disarmed, Küchük Mehmet

drew up a list of 486 people, including the leaders of the Church, whom he regarded as potentially subversive. They were inveigled into attending a ceremony close to his palace, where they were arrested and then executed in a massacre that went on for several days.

The first to meet their end were Archbishop Kyprianos and his three Metropolitans. Altogether 470 out of the 486 were murdered in barbarous fashion. Archbishop Kyprianos was hanged from a mulberry tree as a "public spectacle." He acquitted himself with dignity up to the end, and his memory is still revered by devout Greek Cypriots.

During the mid 19th century, Cyprus enjoyed a period of relative docility, even though the idea of *Enosis* was gradually gaining momentum beneath the surface. The Turkish authorities, both in the Porte and on the island, gradually recognized

Above: Benjamin Disraeli, British Prime Minister (1874-80). Right: Lord Kitchener (1850-1916), Earl of Khartoum.

that stability was in their interest. In 1839, Sultan Mahmud II drew up his program of reforms known as the *Tanzimat,* which was promulgated by his son and successor after his death. The *Tanzimat Charter* guaranteed the security and property of all Ottoman subjects, regardless of religion or race.

In Cyprus, the administration of the island was reorganized along more rational lines. More important, the whole system of taxation regularized and the pernicious practice of "farming" the public revenues was to be abolished. But implementation of these reforms was another matter. In George Hill's succinct phrase, the *Tanzimat Charter* was "a great advance – on paper."

By this time, it was too late for the Sultanate to revitalize its sluggish imperial administration or even to retain its hold of the island. Cyprus' future was to be determined by the sweep of events in Europe, where the great powers were now locked in bitter regional rivalries in the new era of imperialist expansionism.

British Period (1878-1960)

Britain's interest in Cyprus was essentially strategic throughout the 82 years of its control of the island, which was ironically the same time span as that of the Venetians. The British Era, however, encompassed momentous changes in world affairs, including two world wars, which naturally affected Cyprus, just as they did everywhere else.

The genesis of the British involvement is traceable to an idea in the mind of one man: Benjamin Disraeli, who was Prime Minister from 1874 to 1880. He had nursed an almost sentimental interest in Cyprus ever since he visited it as a young man in 1831. In a letter at that time, he described the island as "the rosy realm of Venus, the romantic Kingdom of the Crusades." Sentimentality, however, was overlaid by astute opportunism in the way

Disraeli engineered Britain's acquisition of Cyprus.

In 1877, war broke out between Russia and Turkey, and soon the armies of the Czar were almost literally at the walls of Constantinople. Forced to sue for peace, Sultan Abdul Hamid II accepted the terms of the Treaty of San Stefano (signed on March 3, 1878), dismembering much of his European empire and creating a new and greater Bulgaria with access to the Black Sea and the Aegean. The other great powers were dismayed by this implicit extension of Russian influence. Their pressure obliged the Czar to agree to an international conference, the famous Berlin Congress, to settle relevant frontier issues.

Before the congress convened, Disraeli upstaged all his rivals with what seemed at the time a diplomatic masterstroke. He entered into secret negotiations with the Sultan to secure British control of Cyprus, which in his grand design would serve as a bulwark against any further Russian expansionism. Cyprus was also a staging area on the route to India, the so-called "Jewel in the Crown" of Britain's developing empire. An agreement known as the Convention of Defensive Alliance was signed between Britain and Turkey on June 4, 1878, a few days before the Congress of Berlin started. For Disraeli, it was a triumph, albeit a rather flashy one.

In the Cyprus Convention, the Sultan accepted that the island should be occupied and administered by Britain as *une place d'armes* (in other words, a base), but remain under his suzerainty. Thus, in international law, Cyprus continued to be a Turkish possession, but to all intents and purposes this marked the end of the Turkish Era.

In the early years of the British Period, a number of foreigners passed through and either left their mark on or gave their impressions of the island. The island's first trigonometrical survey of the land was done by Lord Kitchener beginning in

1881. Rupert Gunnis mentions a fig tree near the Church of St. Reginos that had excellent fruit which was never eaten because it caused the people who ate it to break out in boils. Lord Kitchener wanted to cut it down because it interfered with his observations of the landscape. However, for some strange reason, the villagers objected. They built him a special platform so that he could see over it and the tree was spared.

The wandering French poet Arthur Rimbaud was not divinely inspired by Cypriot landscapes during his visits. Instead, he seemed to be unusually industrious. In 1878, while working on a marble quarry at Voroklini, he contracted typhoid. Rimbaud then went back to France to recuperate. He returned in 1880, and under his direction, a summer house for the high commissioner was built in Troodos. A plaque there commemorates the event.

Written impressions of this era of Cypriot history include the charming *A Lady's Appreciation of Cyprus* written by

Mrs. Lewis, and *In An Enchanted Isle*, vivid descriptions by W. H. Mallock.

At first the Cypriot Greeks welcomed the British, rather as they had initially welcomed the Turks 300 years previously. Prone to wishful thinking, they imagined that British rule might lead to *Enosis* or union with mainland Greece.

The Greeks lost no time in making their feelings known. No sooner had the First British High Commissioner, Sir Garnet Wolseley, set foot on the island than he was met by pro-Enosis groups calling for Cyprus' eventual integration with Greece. Yet, the first three decades of British rule – up to the end of World War I – proved to be a relatively uneventful period in which British officials sought to inculcate in the Cypriots the values of justice, orderly administration and honorable commercial behavior. The early colonial administrators were often classical scholars and gentlemen of means who recognized that Cyprus, with its complex history, was a *sui generis* case within the British Empire.

Sir Harry Luke mentions in *Cyprus, A Portrait and An Appreciation* the many notable advances made during British rule. Most of the roads in 1878 were described by Luke as "nothing more than indifferent mule and camel tracks." A complete system of roads and proper bridges was implemented. A concerted effort, especially in Larnaca, succeeded in eradicating endemic diseases such as malaria. The unfortunate side effect of the 1879 operation to fill in a mosquito-breeding marsh near the ancient temple of Kition resulted in the 13th-century B.C. acropolis being unknowingly razed.

The formation of a Forestry Service that set out to reforest the mountainous regions is one of the most noticeable and admirable achievements of British rule. In 1878, no post offices existed on the is-

land, yet by 1917-18, there were 65. Co-operatives were encouraged during these years and the successive rise in quality and standardization of product were especially noticeable in wines. This was aided by the availability of agricultural credit, eliminating the need to turn to "loan sharks." Sir Harry Luke levels his most serious criticism at the early administrations that "had allowed priceless remains of medieval Cyprus to go to rack and ruin." Other legacies of the British Period are less tangible. One will hear English spoken very often. The legal system, administration and law enforcement have been inspired by British models. The largest number of Cypriot emigrants went to England, not Greece.

As the tempo of world affairs quickened and Britain's role expanded, Cyprus came to be regarded in London as less important than Disraeli had made it out to be. Britain's overriding interest remained strategic, and the acquisition of a good harbor at Alexandria in Egypt made the British Treasury reluctant to spend money on developing the shallower ports of Cyprus. As Sir Harry Luke, a most distinguished colonial administrator, had put it, "Officials tended … to regard duty in Cyprus more as a stage in their careers or as climatic relief from torrid West Africa than as an end in itself."

Although the corrupt anomalies surrounding taxation disappeared, one particularly vexatious issue bedeviled relations between Britain and the islanders: the question of tribute. In the negotiations over the 1878 Convention, Britain agreed to give Turkey the average difference between the island's revenue and its expenditure during the last five years of Ottoman rule.

Although Turkey had spent next to nothing on the island, the difference was worked out to 93,000 British pounds per year, a burden which fell upon the Cypriots to pay. It was not until 1927 that tribute was abolished.

Right: The faithful honor their patron saint at Ayios Lazaros Church, Larnaca.

Enosis

During World War I, the idea of *Enosis,* or union with mainland Greece, received a sudden boost in the most unexpected manner. In 1915, Britain offered to cede Cyprus to Greece if the Greek government entered the war immediately on Britain's side. The offer was open for only one week. It was rejected, supposedly because of King Konstantinos' slight pro-German leanings, though his country eventually helped the Allied cause. A later generation of Greeks argued that by this gesture, Britain had virtually acknowledged the validity of *Enosis*, at least in principle.

The Cyprus Convention remained in force until World War I, when Turkey took the disastrous step of joining the Central Powers against Britain and its allies. In November 1914, Britain annexed the island, and in 1925, Cyprus formally became a British Crown Colony.

Throughout the interwar years (1918-39), relative calm prevailed on the island, except for a sudden paroxysm of political violence in 1931. A frenzied mob of *Enosis* backers attacked the Government House and burned it to the ground. Rioting spread throughout the island; six demonstrators were killed and 30 people injured. The British Administration took punitive measures and deported the Greek Cypriot ringleaders in the revolt, including two bishops. The Legislative Council, comprised of Greeks and Turks, and the Constitution were suspended. Cyprus was ruled by decree. The 1931 revolt was a foretaste of bigger trouble a quarter of a century later.

During World War II, although Cyprus escaped extensive onslaught from the Axis powers, a Cyprus Regiment was formed. Over 11,000 recruits served in Egypt, the Sudan, Libya and Palestine, and also took part in the 1940 Dunkirk Evacuation and the 1944 Italian Campaign. Meanwhile, momentous developments outside the island greatly influenced the future course of events. Greece's gallant resistance to both the

Above: A poster of Makarios III, the first president of the Republic of Cyprus, hung on a cedar tree.

Italians and the Nazis endeared the Greek nation to the British public. The Cypriot nationalists tried to exploit this favorable mood, but their efforts were negated by the mainland Greeks who started fighting against each other. During the 1940s, Cyprus presented a confused picture of overlapping conflicts: the Greeks wanted the British out, the Turks were determined to resist the Greeks, and the Greek Right and Left were locked in ideological differences.

During the early 1950s, the pace of politics in Cyprus quickened markedly, due largely to the emergence of a new and powerful figure, Michael Mouskos, later Archbishop Makarios III, first president of the Republic of Cyprus after 1960. Born in 1913, Makarios spent most of World War II in Greece, where he came in touch with political circles. When he returned to Cyprus and became Archbishop of the Church of Cyprus, he also revived the term of Ethnarch, signaling his intention of playing a dominant political and ecclesiastical role. Makarios masterminded a plebiscite on the subject of *Enosis*, with the result that 96 percent of Greek Cypriots were in favor of it.

Almost simultaneously in Athens, another personality had emerged to sway the course of Cyprus' history; Georgios Grivas, a colonel in the Greek army. Grivas was born on Cyprus in 1898, but moved to Athens at the age of 17, acquiring Greek citizenship.

He soon became more Hellenic than the mainland Greeks themselves. Fired by the *Megali Idea*, the irredentist dream of linking the Greeks of the eastern Mediterranean with their original motherland, Grivas felt he had a Messianic mission to bring about *Enosis*.

In the early 1950s, Grivas paid secret visits to the island to discuss his ideas with the Archbishop. The two men agreed on the basic principle, the desirability of *Enosis*, but due to personality differences, the relationship between them was strained from the outset. In the end, they became bitter enemies.

Both Makarios and Alexandros Papagos, Premier of Greece, endorsed Grivas' plan for military action in Cyprus. None of the parties, Grivas, Makarios or Papagos gave serious consideration to the reaction of the Turks, a miscalculation of gargantuan proportions since by this time the Turks were determined to prevent Greek conquest of the island.

In 1955, Grivas, under the *nom de guerre* of "The Leader Dighenis," a name he chose after a legendary Byzantine warrior of the 12th century, launched the campaign of EOKA, an acronym from the Greek words meaning "National Organization of Cypriot Fighters."

It lasted for nearly four bitter and bloody years. For the British, rightly or wrongly, the EOKA and all it represented was personified in one young man: Nikolaos Georgiades, otherwise known as Nikos Sampson. With his hit squad, he was responsible for the assassination of over 20 people in the streets of Nicosia. He was eventually captured and given the death sentence by the court, but this was commuted. He went on to play a nefarious role in Cyprus' troubles of the 1960s and 70s.

In March 1956, the British deported Makarios to the Seychelles where he was held under house arrest for a year. He was then allowed to move to Athens. Britain's decision to deport Makarios had been prompted not merely by the continuing violence for which they held him culpable, but by the breakdown of negotiations for a settlement in early 1956. In early February 1959, the leaders of Greece and Turkey met in Zurich, Switzerland. After five days of intensive negotiations, they broke the news to the world: a Cyprus solution had been found. The island would become an independent republic.

The Zurich Agreement, as it became known, provided for a presidential system in an independent state with a Greek president and Turkish vice-president. Under them was to be a Council of Ministers, composed of seven Greeks and three Turks. The House of Representatives was to have the same ratio, as were all civil service posts.

Britain, Greece and Turkey undertook to guarantee the settlement in a separate treaty, which proscribed both *Enosis* and Partition. It was also agreed that small contingents of Greek and Turkish troops should be stationed on the island, and that Britain should maintain two military bases as sovereign British territory.

On August 16, 1960, centuries of foreign occupation ended when the British flag came down and the Republic of Cyprus emerged as an independent state.

Independent Republic

The newly-born Republic started with many advantages, not least the native talents of its people and a plethora of good will from the international community. Soon, however, old rivalries and antagonisms, both ethnic and ideological, began to reappear. In addition, the Zurich Agreement, with its unwieldy machinery of government, proved to be much too complicated to be workable, even if maximum good will existed between the two sides. By 1963, it was visibly grinding to a halt.

A few days before Christmas 1963, fighting broke out again. The British government, invoking its right as a guarantor power, rushed troops into Nicosia to act as a peace-keeping force. Their arrival was warmly received at first, even by Makarios. But things eventually went sour. At this time, British officers drew a cease-fire line across Nicosia with a green pen. It became known as the "Green Line" and was extended across the island in 1974. It is 180 kilometers long and stretches from Kokkina in the northwest to Famagusta in the east.

In March 1964, the UN Security Council recommended that a United Nations Peace-keeping Force (UNFICYP), composed of soldiers from various countries, be assigned for three months to Cyprus. The agreement was renewed, and 30 years later, the forces are still stationed on Cyprus. A mediator was appointed "for the purpose of promoting a peaceful solution and an agreed settlement to the problem confronting Cyprus." Various mediators arrived, but no solution was found.

In March 1965, a report was transmitted by UN mediator Galo Plaza to the Security Council in which he made specific recommendations for a solution. These were that Cyprus should remain an independent state, the island should be demilitarized, there should be no partition or physical separation of the two communities, and a settlement should be reached in talks between the Greek and Turkish Cypriots. The Turks and Turkish Cypriots

Above: The traces left by the war on a school building in Famagusta.

rejected this agreement as unacceptable, saying that any settlement must include the prohibition of union with Greece along with the geographical separation of the two communities under a federal system of government. The partition suggested is the one that occurred in July 1974, when a coup against Makarios was engineered by the Greek junta and carried out by rebel units of the Cyprus National Guard led by Greek officers.

Everyone agrees that the anti-Makarios coup was a disastrous fiasco. The Presidential Palace was almost destroyed in the fighting that ensued. Makarios barely escaped and made his way to London. In his place, the Athens junta installed the notorious Nikos Sampson as president, and war fever mounted in Ankara. Sampson and his supporters were so engulfed in a civil war with the pro-Makarios forces and the leftists that the presidency lasted only eight days.

On July 20, 1974, Turkish troops landed on the Cyprus north coast around Kyrenia in what was said to be a preemptive move to prevent the Greek attack on the Turkish Cypriots. Turkey's president Bulent Ecevit invoked his country's right to intervene under the 1960 Treaty of Guarantee. Ecevit had flown to London to seek British cooperation. The British government declined, however, and advised restraint.

Turkey's military operation forced the resignation of Sampson and also brought about the downfall of the Athens junta. But in purely military terms, it was not a spectacular success. The Turkish forces failed to capture some of their main objectives, and even sank one of their own warships by mistake. Greek Cypriot resistance was tougher than might have been expected.

A second conference was held in Geneva to work out a political settlement. Respected statesman Konstantinos Karamanlis had become Prime Minister of Greece, while Glafkos Klerides, widely regarded as the most moderate of Cypriot politicians, had replaced Sampson as acting president of Cyprus. Ecevit proposed that Turkish Cypriots be given six autonomous districts or cantons where they could live in security. This arrangement would have given the Turks control of about 30 percent of the island, but it would have prevented a clear-cut partition. The Greek representatives hesitated and requested an adjournment of 36 hours. Ecevit rejected their request and immediately ordered a second military operation. From August 14 to 16, the Turkish army overran about 37 percent of the island. Partition was now a reality, and about 200,000 Greek Cypriots were displaced from their homes. Of them, only about 40,000 could later return to their houses.

The Turkish army still maintains a military presence on the island, and it is estimated they have about 40,000 soldiers in the north. In addition, tens of thousands of farmers from Anatolya have been settled in the northern sector since 1974, on land belonging to displaced Greek Cypriots. Since that time, many Turkish Cypriots have emigrated to Great Britain and other European countries, as agriculture in the Turkish-occupied northern part of Cyprus is now firmly in the hands of the mainland Turks.

In November 1983, Rauf Denktash, the prevailing leader in the north, proclaimed the Turkish zone to be an independent, sovereign state. The Turkish government now finances more than 50 percent of the domestic economy of the "Turkish Republic of North Cyprus." It has not been recognized, however, by any country other than Turkey. The rest of the Islamic world continues to maintain economic and political ties to the legitimate government of the Republic of Cyprus.

Attempts to resolve the problems of Cyprus have been undertaken time and again since 1974. The United Nations, under the leadership of Secretary General Boutros Boutros-Ghali, was long at the forefront of these attempts. In 1998, the United States, represented by special envoy Richard Holbrooke, undertook intense negotiations with both parts of Cyprus, Greece and Turkey. All suggestions for the resolution of the situation in the country have so far proved ineffectual due to the delaying tactics of Rauf Denktash, and the precondition he has set that North Cyprus be recognized as an independent state.

New problems arose in 1998: Turkey threatened that, in the event official EU entry negotiations with Cyprus were undertaken, Turkey would annex North Cyprus de jure and declare it a Turkish province. Furthermore, after the Republic of Cyprus order air defense missiles from Russia, Turkey declared it would carry out immediate air attacks on the missile sites if any attempt was made to station them on the island.

The European Union and the United States did not adopt a specific stance in regard to either of these affairs.

THE GATEWAY TO CYPRUS

**LARNACA
SOUTHWEST OF LARNACA
WEST OF LARNACA
NORTHEAST OF LARNACA
FAMAGUSTA DISTRICT
NATURE WALKS**

LARNACA

Once a quiet seaside village, **Larnaca** ❶ (Greek: *Lárnaka*) is today a major tourist center and a booming city bustling with activity. After the partition of the island in 1974 and the closure of the Nicosia International Airport, the Larnaca Airport was expanded to become the major international entry point on the island. The population has more than tripled in the last 20 years and continues to expand into outlying areas. The marina right on the main waterfront is well equipped. Its more than 400 berths attract many summer sailors, as well as year-round boaters who winter here in its well-protected harbor.

Much of modern-day Larnaca has literally been built over the site of ancient *Kition*, a city dating from the 13th century B.C., when it was inhabited by Myceneans who traded here. Larnaca succeeded Kition, some say it took its name from the ancient tombs and urns, in Greek the *larnax*, on which it was built. Sacked by invaders and crippled by an earth-

Preceding pages: The dramatic rocky cliffs of Protaras. At peace with a simple life, "Papas" Varnavas of the Stavros tis Minthas Monastery. Left: The pleasant palm-lined promenade of Phinikoudes, Larnaca.

quake, Kition disappeared as a city during the Dark Ages that encompassed the entire eastern Mediterranean, only to reemerge into history centuries later as a Phoenician town with strong links to the city of Tyre, in what is now Lebanon. It remained an important city up to the seventh century A.D., when it was destroyed in Arab raids.

Zeno the Stoic, who founded the ancient school of Stoic philosophy in Athens, is the city's most famous native son. When he died in Athens, the Athenians awarded him a golden wreath and a state tomb in their city. Lazarus, who according to the Bible was raised from the dead by Jesus, is said to have lived his second life here, after being expelled from the Holy Land by the Jews. According to tradition, Lazarus lived another 30 years before dying again, and was consecrated as the first Bishop of Kition. Larnaca still remembers the holy man and each year, on the penultimate Saturday before Easter, a procession with his icon starts from the Church of Ayios Lazaros early in the evening and passes through the main streets of the city, accompanied by bands, and then returns to the church.

From 1683 on, Larnaca was the seat of foreign consulates. Both during the Ottoman occupation of the island and the early days of British colonial rule, it was

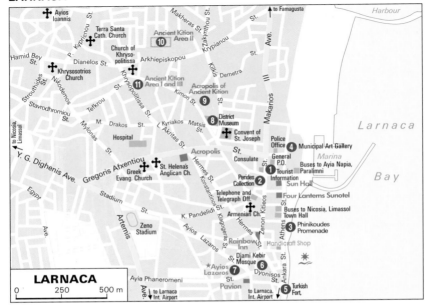

LARNACA

0   250   500 m

an important center of trade as well. These activities lent Larnaca a "continental" flavor, and it has been estimated that in 1816 about 1,000 Europeans lived here, a remarkable number for the time.

The diplomatic realm always provided a colorful accent to the community, even in its earliest days. Other colorful members of the diplomatic corps included General Luigi Palma di Cesnola, appointed American consul in 1865. At the same time, he was also the Russian consul. He was an archeology buff of dubious reputation who immediately set about excavating extensively at ancient sites all over the island, generally undisturbed by indifferent Turkish authorities. A dazzling collection of silver and gold supposedly from Kourion was discovered by Cesnola and sold to the Metropolitan Museum in New York. Only at Ormidhia outside Larnaca was any formal action taken against him in the courts, and he had to return his finds.

In the 1940s, the importance of Larnaca was overshadowed by the port cities of Famagusta and Limassol and, as one traveler noted, the city had fallen asleep. But the modern-day invasion of the island by the Turkish army proved to be a turning point, stopping the city's decline. Refugees from the 1974 invasion swelled its population, which is now estimated at around 60,000. Its port was enlarged, but more importantly for the city, an old unused airport runway to its south was hastily repaired and a new terminal set up to meet the urgent need of reestablishing air links after the closure of Nicosia International Airport during the invasion. The Nicosia Airport, today in the no man's land between the island's divided communities, is now used only by the UN peace-keeping force which mans a buffer zone along the island's Green Line.

Fifty days after Easter, Larnaca bursts into activity as it celebrates *Kataklysmos*, a festival unique to the island. Some say the ceremony, in which people flock to the sea and sprinkle each other with water, is in memory of Noah's salvation

Larnaca

from the Flood. Others say it is a thinly disguised pagan festival, perhaps to celebrate Aphrodite's birth or the resurrection of her lover Adonis.

Whatever its roots, *Kataklysmos* is an event which provides for five days of spirited festivities. At this time an annual fair takes place along the shore promenade, and the city organizes numerous concerts around town.

The Pierides Collection

The city's centrally-located **Tourist Office** ❶ on Demokratias Square is close to the post office and banks. A short distance to the south, at 4 Zenon Kitieos Street, lies the **Pierides Foundation** ❷, the most important privately-owned collection of Cypriot antiquities. Objects dating from the Neolithic Period up to Medieval times are exhibited in the museum's four rooms.

The Pierides Collection was mostly gathered by scholar and archeologist Demetrios Pierides (1811-1895) and his family, and is kept in their handsome white house with veranda. The fastidiously maintained museum provides an important record of Cyprus' cultural heritage, preserving important artifacts and objects which would otherwise have found their way to Europe and America. Over 2,500 pieces include excellent samples of the pottery of different periods.

Anthropomorphic pitchers, including one showing antlered deer, are displayed near steatite idols from Erimi and Souskiou. Attic black glazed ware imported from Greece is dated to 500 B.C. Idols of the goddess Astarte, Phoenician precursor of Aphrodite, are interesting, as is a solemn seventh-century B.C. terra cotta goddess with its arms raised to give a blessing.

Chalcolithic humor and zest for life are evident in the very important recent discovery from Souskiou, a 36-centimeter-high terra cotta vase of a male seated on a stool with his mouth agape and elbows resting on his knees. Water or wine poured into his mouth would spout from his prominent penis.

Model chariots and mounted warriors, a fine collection of ancient glass, a tomb inscription from Kition, and a collection of early maps of Cyprus are just some of the exhibits that have been painstakingly collected over the years. Note the brass-studded leather trunk in the hall, which once belonged to noted historian Rupert Gunnis. A collection of rare embroidery and costumes is in the stairwell, along with antique furniture. Before the exit is a room with carved and painted woodwork, and adjacent to it is the library displaying family portraits.

Phinikoudes and the Turkish Fortress

The most popular place for a stroll is the more than 70-year-old palm tree lined promenade between the Marina and the Turkish Fort known as **Phinikoudes** ❸, with its many restaurants and outdoor cafés. At its northern end, housed in two of five former warehouse buildings from the late 19th century, is the **Municipal Art Gallery** ❹ on Europe Square. Here temporary exhibitions of works by 20th-century Cypriot artists are mostly shown. Right next door, the **Museum of Paleontology** presents exhibits of fossils from around the world.

Moving south along Athens Street to the bottom of the road, you will come to the old **Turkish Fortress** ❺. Built in 1625 to defend the town, it later served as a prison and observation post for the port. It was also used as a prison by the British during the early part of their rule before they turned it into the police headquarters. Today the fort is a **Museum**, housing some exhibits from Kition and the *tekke* sites (dervish monasteries), along with photographs of local finds. Steps ascend to a wall which commands good sea views.

Church of Ayios Lazaros

Behind the fort is a square lined with shops, and the renovated **Djami Kebir Mosque** ❻. Slightly to the northwest lies the distinctive **★Church of Ayios Lazaros** ❼, one of Larnaca's oldest monuments, which has an intriguing history. It was built around the year A.D. 900 by the Byzantine Emperor Leo VI, above what was supposed to be the empty grave of Lazarus.

Lazarus probably traveled more after his (second) death than he had done during his lifetime. His body was said to have been transported from Kition – first to Constantinople, and then to its final resting place in Marseilles. According to a legend, the saint never smiled after his resurrection.

The tomb, probably discovered in the year 890, bears the Greek inscription: "Lazarus, the friend of Christ."

Above: Splendid interior of the Church of Ayios Lazaros in Larnaca.

Although little of the ninth-century building now remains, it was rebuilt in the 17th century on the original design and was later embellished with an impressive bell tower, one of the very few permitted by the Turks before 1857. Inside the church, the iconostasis, or wooden screen with icons, in front of the chancel has some of the island's most notable 18th-century carvings.

Of particular interest is a 17th-century icon of the *Raising of Lazarus*, in which a man can be seen holding his nose, according to the words of Lazarus' sister Martha quoted in the New Testament: "Lord, by this time he stinketh; for he has now lain for four days in this grave" (John 11:34). It is set in a carved frame and hangs on a pillar, seen as one enters the church by the south door. Beneath the altar floor is the marble sarcophagus which is believed to be Lazarus' tomb.

Occasional poetic touches provide a contrast to the church's overall pious dignity, such as the carved hand on the front of the pulpit which supports a dove and the serpent opposite which balances a lamp on its head.

Immediately behind the northwest corner of the church is a small **English Cemetery** where the tombstones bear the names of German, Italian, French and American missionaries, of British consuls and their families, and of merchants and seamen, with some stones bearing coats of arms.

Continuing south, away from the palm trees of the sea front, the road skirts a building and then continues along the coast towards the airport. A series of restaurants lines the road, some of them built right at the edge of the water.

A little fishing harbor is the departure point for diving expeditions to the *Zenobia*, a 12,000 ton ship that sank in 1980 a few miles offshore in clear Mediterranean waters, and which now attracts divers from clubs all over Europe.

The road continues to another series of restaurants along **Mackenzie Beach**, just before the airport. During the peak season and on weekends, when the beach directly below Larnaca's promenade is especially full, it is advisable to head out to Mackenzie or one of the beaches beyond the airport near Kiti.

District Museum

Also within walking distance of the town center and the Tourist Office, is the modern **District Museum ❽**, reached by turning left onto Gregoris Afxentiou Street and then right onto Kimon Street just past the Convent of St. Joseph. Open daily, the modern District Museum exhibits an interesting collection of antiquities found in the District of Larnaca, dating from the Neolithic to the Roman Periods. The well-lit displays feature finds from Kition, including a ceramic collection with graceful alabaster vases, tools, coins and lamps. Also notable are Mycenean kraters (mixing jugs) and an ivory figure of the ungainly Egyptian dwarf-god Bes. Wall cases hold many significant pieces which illustrate the area's history, including faience scarabs, limestone and cylindrical seals, and bone implements and engraved stone blocks from Khirokitia.

The Ancient City of Kition

To the northwest of the District Museum, further along Kimon Street, on the right-hand side of the road lie the amorphous ruins of the **Acropolis ❾** of the ancient city of Kition, a region today known as *Bamboula*. The passage of the centuries had already taken its toll, when, in 1879, the British army totally leveled what was left standing, using the debris to fill in marshlands in an attempt to eliminate malaria-bearing mosquitoes.

Further north, following Arkhiepiskopou Kyprianou Street to Leontios Makheras Street and then taking the third left, you will come to the entrance to the most important site of ancient Kition, known as **Kition Area II ❿**. Prior to large-scale investigations, it was thought Kition was a Phoenician colony dating back only to the ninth century B.C. New evidence proves it had a Mycenaean predecessor.

On the premises are the remains of five temples, including a Phoenician **Temple of Astarte**, built on the ruins of an earlier Bronze Age temple. Part of the northern city walls can also be seen, with the lower sections built of huge stones resembling Mycenaean cyclopean walls. Little remains of the subsequent Hellenistic Period and nothing at all of the Roman.

The remains of the five temples are found in Area II. Finds from the temples and adjacent areas have provided cogent clues as to the history of these civilizations and their life styles. Quantities of copper slag and evidence of copper-smelting workshops have been found dating back to the beginning of the 13th century B.C.

A large cache of ivory objects found in a room of the Holy of Holies includes a plaque with the Egyptian god Bes and a pipe, perhaps this was used to smoke opium, all bearing inscriptions in the undeciphered Cypro-Minoan script of the Late Bronze Age. The city was re-inhabited and rebuilt on a larger scale in about 1200 B.C. Based on evidence of the type of pottery they used, known as Mycenaean IIIc, these new inhabitants were refugees from the main centers of the Peloponnese.

Area I and **Area III** ⑪ of Kition are less important sites and are also much smaller. They lie to the south and southwest of Area II near the Church of Khrysopolitissa.

SOUTHWEST OF LARNACA

When heading south out of Larnaca towards the airport, Larnaca's **Salt Lake** stretches out on the right. It is the first natural landmark most travelers will notice upon arrival. In the winter months the lake fills with sea water and becomes a temporary habitat for flamingos, egrets and swans. Ornithologists and photographers prowl the area at this time, and anyone with an appreciation of beauty will be awed by the unforgettable sight of the graceful waterfowl.

A right turn after the lake brings you to the ****Hala Sultan Tekke** ②, one of the most important Moslem shrines. It attracts many pilgrims, especially on the religious holidays of *Shekir Bayram* and *Kurban Bayram*. Passing Turkish vessels used to lower their flag and fire a salute as a sign of respect.

Also known as the Tekke of Umm Haram, the shrine stands in a peaceful setting amid palm trees and gardens housing the tomb of Umm Haram, an aunt of the Prophet Mohammed. As the wife of the governor of Palestine she was part of the Sultan's entourage during the expedition to Cyprus in 647 under Caliph Oman.

She allegedly died here after falling from her mule.

Surrounded by the buildings of a former dervish monastery (Turkish: *tekke*), the octagonal mosque with a minaret was built in 1816 over the site of Umm Haram's grave. Three stones supposedly from Mount Sinai mark the tomb; one of these is said to have been miraculously suspended in the air for many centuries, but now lies on the ground. Outside the mosque there is a fountain for performing ablutions. Shoes must be removed before entering the mosque!

Fenced-in excavations to the west of the tekke have unearthed a **Bronze Age town**. Finds include Mycenaean pottery, ivory objects, and a delicate lotus-shaped

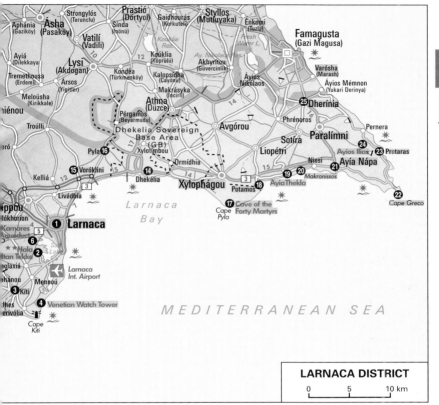

LARNACA DISTRICT

0   5   10 km

faience scepter head. In 1978, a cache of gold treasures was discovered. In 1979, a tomb yielded an impressive bronze trident, weapons and jewelry. Some of these finds are on display at the Turkish Fort in Larnaca.

A great place to stay in the area is the **Pasithea Hotel**. All the hotel's suites have a good view of the sea and are only a stone's throw from a fine quiet beach off the main road. Furthermore, this makes an ideal base for bird watchers who want to observe the migratory birds, such as flamingos, which flock to the nearby Salt Lake.

About 11 kilometers southwest of Larnaca is the village of **Kiti ❸**, famous for its **Church of Panayia Angeloktisti**,

the latter word meaning "built by angels." The church lies just north of the village center and contains an outstanding mosaic that dates from about the fifth century.

This masterpiece decorates the conch of the apse and depicts the *Virgin Mary Flanked by the Archangels Gabriel and Michael*, the latter being partly damaged from the neck down. The Virgin Mary stands on a footstool and holds the Christ Child in her left arm.

To the south of Kiti lies the tiny village of **Perivolia** and, to its southeast, **Cape Kiti**, with its small **lighthouse** that was erected in 1864. North of the lighthouse is a **Venetian Watch Tower ❹**, a solitary medieval monument in the surrounding

landscape. The tower itself is closed, but the Venetian coat of arms, the Lion of St. Mark, is still visible.

Adjacent to the District of Limassol is the picturesque village of **Zyyi** ❺, which had a long history as a carob-exporting port. Today the only reminders of this industry are a wooden pier and several stone warehouses. Fishing is now a main activity in this area. Fish restaurants on the beach are popular with tourists and residents alike, who come from Nicosia, Limassol and Larnaca to enjoy a good meal by the sea. It is near Zyyi that Saint Helena of the Cross is said to have come ashore about A.D. 325.

WEST OF LARNACA

One of the main attractions in the western part of Larnaca District is the monas-

Above: Hala Sultan Tekke, one of the most important Islamic shrines, on the Salt Lake of Larnaca. Right: Iconostasis in the Church of Panayia Angeloktisti, Kiti.

tery on Stavrovouni, the "Mountain of the Cross." It can be reached from the main Nicosia-Limassol highway. To get there from Larnaca, take the southwest turn out of town towards Limassol. First the road passes the **Aqueduct of Larnaca** ❻, called *Kamares*, the Greek word for "arches." Built in 1746 by Bekir Pasha, a wealthy Turkish governor of Cyprus, it supplied fresh water to the city of Larnaca from a series of wells. For nearly two centuries water was carried along channels in the aqueduct, which has 75 arches, before the system was replaced.

If you prefer not to take the highway, follow the road through the villages of Kalokhorio, Ayia Anna and Mosphiloti. In between **Ayia Anna** and **Mosphiloti**, a left turn leads to **Pyrga** ❼, a charming little village with many olive and carob trees. To the left when entering the village is **Ayia Marina**, a little domed 15th-century chapel in which fragments of paintings of Ayia Marina and other saints survive. Nearby is a mosque built in 1830.

One of the outstanding examples of Lusignan architecture is the little stone chapel of **Ayia Katherina**, known as the *Chapelle Royale*. It was built in 1421, probably by Lusignan King Janus. The monarch is pictured with his second wife, Charlotte de Bourbon, both of them wearing crowns, in the outstanding fresco *The Crucifixion* on the west end of the chapel. Other frescoes in the chapel, such as *The Last Supper* and *The Raising of Lazarus*, have French inscriptions beneath them. The historian Rupert Gunnis reports that this chapel used to be wrapped in cotton fabric by local women, a peculiar custom said to protect the village from illness.

Kornos ❽, just a few kilometers beyond, is notable for its simple but sturdy unglazed red pottery, mostly large *pithoi* (storage jars) made from the rust-colored soil of the area. These pithoi, which are about the size of a man, were set into the floor during the construction of a house, as they would have been too big to pass through the door later. Wander around the town for awhile, and take the time to stop

into one of the pottery studios to watch the locals producing their craft. Walks in the lowlands of the **Kornos Forest** in the direction of Lefkara are especially rewarding in early spring when wildflowers are in bloom.

Stavrovouni Monastery

Just outside Mosphiloti, turn onto the old Nicosia-Limassol road slightly before the highway towards **Kophinou**. The road soon forks left for the ascent to the Stavrovouni Monastery. The road has been improved in recent years, but care should still be taken after passing the military installation and the **Ayia Varvara Monastery ❾**, when it begins its torturously winding ascent to the dramatic site of Stavrouvouni. Walkers might want to hike the 6.5 kilometers uphill from the little Ayia Varvara Monastery to Stavrovouni.

Those who do not have a car will have to hire a taxi or hitchhike to get to Ayia Varvara since there are no buses. The trail

begins on a track opposite the sign pointing right to Spitoudhia.

Ayia Varvara is a dependency of Stavrovouni Monastery. Until recently, the fields and gardens of the hilltop monastery were cultivated. A noteworthy botanical feature of the monastery's gardens is that lotuses are cultivated here. The buildings date from the 18th century.

The monks here sell olive oil and honey, and one of them, a painter, offers his works of art for sale in his studio opposite the entrance to the monastery. The quality of these works, produced primarily for tourists, perhaps leaves something to be desired.

If you are driving, it is advised to proceed slowly, as the military often stages maneuvers hereabouts. It is also possible that you will be pulled over by them.

The **Stavrovouni Monastery** ⑩, considered the oldest in Cyprus, commands

Above: The hilltop location of Stavrovouni Monastery provides for a spectacular panoramic view.

spectacular views of the Troodos Mountains, the southeast of the island and the sea from its perch on a rocky peak. While women are not allowed inside the facility, the view from here is so terrific that this in itself is reason enough for making the trip. The peak, well over 600 meters in height, was known in ancient times as Olympos, and was adorned by a temple to the goddess Aphrodite. According to tradition, it was claimed in the name of Christianity by Empress Helena, the mother of Constantine the Great. She is said to have founded the monastery in A.D. 327 in order to protect one of the fragments of the Holy Cross which she had brought from Jerusalem while on her way to Constantinople. Hence the name of the monastery: Stavrovouni means "Mountain of the Cross." This was one of the most important Christian sites of pilgrimage from earliest times.

The monastery was destroyed many times over the centuries, by Saracen raiders in 1426 and by an earthquake in 1492. It lay in ruins after being burned by the

Turks in 1570. They are said to have carried away a solid gold cross with their captured booty.

The monastery as it is now, with its patchwork of domes and pillars, dates from the 17th and 18th centuries, when it was rebuilt. Only the foundations, constructed of great stone blocks, are reminders of the original structure.

Walk up the steep stairs to the monastery itself, and through the courtyard to the 18th-century church opposite. The faithful have no doubt whatsoever that a piece of wood in the monastery's chapel, which is embossed in gold and set into a larger cross encased in beaten silver, is part of the True Cross. It hangs next to the iconostasis.

Lefkara

A picturesque village off the main Nicosia-Limassol highway (and old road as well) is Lefkara, situated in the Troodos foothills in the western part of Larnaca District. The village, split into **Pano Lefkara ⓫** and the smaller **Kato Lefkara** to its east, is famous for its cottage industry of handmade lace, known as *lefkaritika*, a local specialty produced here since the Middle Ages.

It is said that on a trip to the island Leonardo da Vinci bought lace here for the altar cloth of the Cathedral of Milan, although some skeptics claim he never set foot on the island of Cyprus. Indeed, there are some people who claim the term "lace" is incorrect and that it is actually nothing more than embroidery on linen. Whatever it is called, it is lovely and a graceful addition to any household. It is made by women of Lefkara who can be seen in the narrow village lanes clustered in groups, intently embroidering the intricate geometric patterns.

In the village you will also find silversmiths who create fine filigree work, as well as a small producer of Turkish Delight (Greek: *loukoumi*).

In any event, a visit must be made to the **Folkloric Museum** in the restored Patsalos House. The museum shows what life was like on the island of Cyprus a hundred years ago. On exhibit are the household furnishings of a wealthy family of the time, local traditional costumes and, of course, examples of the famous lacework.

Vacationers who are traveling by car can make a side trip to the Ayios Minas Monastery, in which a number of nuns paint splendid icons.

Khirokitia

*Khirokitia ⓬, one of the oldest Neolithic sites on the island, overlooks the Nicosia-Limassol highway further south (on most of the newer road signs it is spelled Choirokoitia). It probably dates from between 7000 and 6000 B.C. Settlers were farmers who cultivated wheat and barley, judging from flint sickle blades and analysis of carbonized seed materials. The bones of animals found here also provide evidence of early livestock breeding as well as hunting. From a later period of settlement, around 3500 B.C., fragments of pottery have been unearthed. The finds from Khirokitia are now in the Cyprus Museum in Nicosia.

The archeological site is close to the dry Maroni riverbed. It is situated atop a hill that was once covered in dense vegetation. When first excavated in 1934 by Porphyrios Dikaios of the Antiquities Department, a succession of *tholoi*, or beehive-shaped houses of single round rooms made of mud and stone, were uncovered.

French archeologists are digging here now. Excavations have shown four main inhabited areas. The hearths were on the house floors along with the benches and tables. The dead of these early people were buried beneath the floors of the dwellings. They were interred in a squatting position, with their knees drawn up

world through the erection of a "city wall," which was up to three meters high in places – something not found in Neolithic settlements of the Near East. Tools were made of flint, bone and stone; of containers only stone bowls survive. Some of these show a surprising degree of skill for such an early period.

Study of skeletal remains shows the people were short (1.61 meters in height was the average for men; 1.50 meters for women). The average life expectancy was 35 years for the men and 33.5 years for the women.

To the southwest of Khirokitia lies another Neolithic settlement worth seeing, that of **Kalavasos-Tenta ⑬**. Its perhaps most interesting find, a depiction of a human figure etched in red paint, is the oldest portrait discovered on Cyprus and is estimated to be over 5,000 years old. It is now on display in the Cyprus Museum in Nicosia.

to their chins. Apparently each hut that fell into disrepair was flattened, forming the foundation for a new one which was erected on top of it. In one hut there is evidence of 26 burials under eight superimposed layers of floor.

A good idea of what these houses would have looked like is provided by the reconstruction of four of them in 1996, according to specifications furnished by archeologists. They can be found just behind the entrance to the excavation site and can also be entered.

Many questions remain about this primitive society, such as where they came from and what their beliefs were. On the other hand, quite a bit can be deduced from the evidence discovered. For instance, significant communal effort would have been necessary to make use of natural resources in order to purposely isolate their living space from the outside

Above: An old, dignified monk from Stavrovouni. Right: Remains of the mud and stone houses of Khirokitia.

NORTHEAST OF LARNACA

Beachfront hotels line the road that leads out of Larnaca along the northeastern part of Larnaca Bay, with its dark sand – and sometimes rock – beaches. It teems with holiday apartments, restaurants, cafés and nightspots. The road continues to the eastern coast of the island and the famous beaches of Ayia Napa, then passes through the British military base area of **Dhekelia ⑭**. Shortly before this lies Tourist Plage Beach, a sand beach which is also easily reached by bus from Larnaca. A right turn beyond the tourist area takes you through the garrison and beyond.

Take the coastal road three kilometers northeast of Larnaca past the town of Livadhia. About two kilometers after that a left fork leads to **Voroklini ⑮**. Like Livadhia, this is a center of basketweaving; nowadays, however, this craft is only practiced by a few of the older residents. Those who like French literature

might be interested in visiting a nearby abandoned quarry, where the French poet Arthur Rimbaud worked in the winter of 1878/79.

Another two kilometers farther along, a road bearing left leads to **Pyla** ⓰, situated in the UN-controlled buffer zone and inhabited by both Greek and Turkish Cypriots, the latter of whom elected to stay rather than resettle in the North. In the harmonious hamlet of 700 Greek and 400 Turkish Cypriots, shops sell international clothing and other goods duty-free. A word of caution when shopping, though: It is illegal to buy from Turkish shops, and purchased goods may be confiscated by the authorities.

FAMAGUSTA DISTRICT

Famed more than anything for its beautiful beaches and clear waters, the Famagusta area to the northeast of Larnaca – a part of which lies to the south in the Republic of Cyprus – is one of the most popular tourist destinations on the island. **Varosha** (Greek: *Varósia*), the once bustling tourist resort to the south of Famagusta, has been a deserted ghost town since its inhabitants fled to the British military base of Dhekelia when Turkish troops advanced in 1974. It still remains under the control of the Turkish military. Yet the area to its south, centered around the town of Ayia Napa, has rapidly developed over the past few years.

The road from Larnaca hugs the coast after the Dhekelia power station, but turns inland before Xylophagou.

The circular remains of a Venetian watch tower can be seen three kilometers south on **Cape Pyla**. Also on the cape is the large **Cave of the Forty Martyrs** ⓱. The petrified bones that can be found throughout the cavern are thought by locals to be the remains of Christian martyrs, though they are more probably those of pigmy hippopotami. The red soil of the area is some of the most fertile on the island, providing for excellent potato and vegetable crops.

A turn to the right, about three kilometers out of **Xylophagou**, leads down to **Potamos** ⓲. The town lies at the mouth of a river, along the shore of which innumerable small fishing boats are moored over a 200-meter stretch. Two simple tavernas here serve good and inexpensive fish. Beside the road some six kilometers before Ayia Napa lies the small sandy beach of **Ayia Thekla** ⓳, near a small modern chapel of the same name.

From here a string of magnificent beaches continues almost to the rocky promontory of Cape Greco to the east, and then picks up again past the cape along the southeastern coast of **Famagusta Bay**. The beaches, with their fine white sand and translucent waters, are considered to be the best on the island and are favored in particular by Scandinavian tourists. Approaching Cape Greco, the beaches are silvery white, taking on a more golden hue beyond the cape. The whole coast is lined with luxury hotels, tourist apartments, tavernas and discotheques. A wide spectrum of water sports is offered, ranging from windsurfing and scuba diving to boating and parasailing, which looks terrifying, but is said to be easy to learn.

After Ayia Thekla comes the Makrinosos region, with three well-defined bays adjoining the **Golden Sands** beach and the famous **Nissi Bay**. On the **Makronissos Peninsula** ⓴, 19 **rock tombs** from Roman and Hellenic times can be seen about 250 meters east of the Hotel Dome.

Ayia Napa ㉑ does not have many sights to speak of, but offers a number of activities to compensate for this. There is, for example, an aquatic center with a giant water slide, a "dolphinarium," the country-fair-like Luna Park, and even a place to go bungee jumping. Anyone interested in sea shells can check out the small **Malacology Museum** in the Town Hall.

Also worth a look here is the modern main church of Ayia Napa, dedicated to St. Mary, with its murals in traditional Byzantine style. It stands on a broad square below the only building of historical interest in the town, the **Ayia Napa Monastery**. The monastery was erected about 1530 by Venetian noblemen around an earlier cave church from the eighth or ninth century.

The monastery is enclosed by a high wall. A beautiful octagonal fountain, sculptured in high relief and shaded by a dome resting on four pillars, graces the center of the courtyard. It is surrounded by a cloister with a cobblestone floor. A second fountain, on the north side of the courtyard, is in the form of an ornamental boar's head. A giant sycamore tree outside the south gate is over 600 years old and stands some 24 meters tall.

Up the hill, Ayia Napa spreads out in a maze of streets, with its open-air tavernas, restaurants and nightspots. Beaches on the far side of **Cape Greco** ㉒ can be accessed through Paralimni – Cyprus' proverbial "bread basket" – but the coastal drive along the rocky cape is well worth the effort.

The tip of the cape, now a protected area, is dominated by a radio-relay station that stands on a plateau which in antiquity was devoted to Aphrodite. Unfortunately, the narrow winding road that leads to the tip of the cape is blocked off to traffic before the end.

For the adventurous, the area is full of rocky coves, sea caves, and some sandy bays that embrace crystal-clear waters. A dirt track leads to the highest point on the cape, which offers breathtaking views of the surrounding bays. The main beach areas on the far side of the cape are in **Protaras** ㉓, of which **Fig Tree Bay** is the most famous, taking its name from a mature fig tree that is a well-known land-

Right: The romantic Venetian Monastery of Ayia Napa, built by the Venetians in the 16th century.

Larnaca

mark. Adjoining Fig Tree Bay are **Flamingo Bay** and the shallow **Pernera Bay**, and somewhat further up the coast is **Kalamies**.

Just off the main road between Protaras and Paralimni is the **Church of Ayios Ilias ㉔**, sitting on a rocky outcrop. The church itself is modern and not especially notable, but the view from it is lovely. **Paralimni** was damaged by an earthquake in 1941, but has long since recovered from its effects. The inhabitants once had a wide reputation for hunting *beccafico*. Nowadays they can boast not only possessing the largest village square on the island, but also of being the wealthiest farmers in Cyprus. Parlimni's prosperity, and that of Ayia Napa, can be directly attributed to the Turkish invasion; for both communities took over the former role of the now-occupied Famagusta as the agricultural and touristic center of the country.

In Parlimni there is a viewing tower, from which you can see all the way to Famagusta. Of the three churches located on the village square, the **Panagia**, of Franconian origin, is especially worth mentioning.

The countryside around Ayia Napa is dotted with hundreds of windmills, especially around the Protaras area. But after years of drawing from underground water supplies, sea water has filtered through, making much of the water too salty for either domestic or agricultural use. Today the main source of water for the area comes from an ambitious project called the Southern Conveyor, which transports water from dams along the relatively rainfall-rich southwest side of the Troodos Mountains to the east of the island and provides the capital with water as well.

North of Paralimni is the village of **Dherinia ㉕**, with three churches from the 15th to 17th centuries of interest. Dherinia is the closest point from which one can view the ghost town of **Varosha**. In the village itself, turn right at an old road sign that still points the way to Famagusta.

Further along, the road ends abruptly at a checkpoint. A café-restaurant with a flat roof and other establishments advertise views in which the high-rise skyline of Varosha is clearly visible. It is hard to imagine that the giant tourist resort has been deserted since 1974, when 45,000 Greek Cypriots were forced to leave their town by the Turkish army.

NATURE WALKS

Nature walks in the Larnaca District are mainly in the extensive southeasterly foothills of **Troodos**. The lava hills of this range extend in a southeasterly direction to **Stavrovouni** and beyond. The **Kornos Forest** provides extensive pine cover in the lowlands.

Several main tracks starting from **Kornos ❽** and **Lythrodontas ㉖** lead to

Above: A jubilant crowd greets the reconstructed Kyrenia boat on its arrival at Protaras. Right: Fascinating rock formations on the unspoiled coast of Cape Greco.

Lefkara ⓫. They are especially interesting in the spring, particularly during the months of February and March, when the flowers begin to blossom.

The Lefkara area's limestone hills, which are crisscrossed by thousands of paths and trails, are primarily popular for their flora. Untilled land in this region holds many surprises for hikers, and one might be lucky enough to see some of the rare orchids that grow here, such as the *Orchis punctulata*.

Giant fennels are characteristic of the area, as are many bee- and spider-orchids. Evergreen oaks (*Quercus coccifera*), remnants of older forests, have survived here. Tracks from the village of Lefkara itself, as well as those from **Kato Dhrys ㉗**, are worth exploring from a botanical point of view.

A walk on the coastline from the quarry area off **Xylophagou** at **Cape Pyla** extending eastward to **Potamos ⓲**, a natural and picturesque fishing harbor sheltering many boats, is perfect for quiet contemplation as one takes in the awe-

inspiring views. In springtime, especially in February and March, wild narcissus and cyclamen are in bloom.

Nature Walks in the Famagusta District

A good part of this district in the souhteast of Cyprus is primarily a tourist area with few undeveloped coastal stretches. The main area worth exploring is that of **Cape Greco ㉒**. Part of it still holds the remnants of old maquis forests with juniper trees.

A path following the southern coast of the peninsula is of some botanical interest, and provides for a number of attractive views. It is best to start out from the village of **Ayia Napa ㉑**, or else on the outskirts of town near the **Sunwing Hotel**. The road swings to the left, and the walk continues close to the sea. You will pass rocky coves, sandy beaches, and the rocky sea grottos of **Kermia Beach**, fascinating gnarled formations at the sea's edge.

After the beach is a difficult area with sharp rocks, and once past this, the headland leads away from the sea. Here you can turn inland and head towards Cape Greco itself, with its lighthouse and the relay station of Radio Monte Carlo. Keep to the right of this area and climb down a hill through farmland to a path leading toward Cape Greco. The tip of the cape is blocked by a gate.

The east coast of the Cape also has some smaller paths through an area reforested mainly with acacia. The area, especially the southern coast, is extremely rocky and has numerous vantage points offering stunning views of the cliffs plunging to the sea.

The sea on the eastern side of the cape is usually dead calm, especially in summer, since it is sheltered from the prevailing westerly winds. In spring, it is well worth looking for the stunning varieties of orchids which grow on the higher parts of the cape. Further along the cape, *Orchis pyramidalis* and *Orchis morio* grow, as well as wild gladiolus and narcissus.

LARNACA

Area Code 04

☎ Information bureaus of the **Cyprus Tourism Organization** can be found at Vasileos Pavlou (in the city center), tel. 654332, as well as at the airport, tel. 643000.

🛏 ⑤⑤⑤ **Golden Bay**, Larnaca-Dhekelia Road, P.O. Box 741, tel. 654444, fax. 623451; **Sandy Beach**, Larnaca-Dhekelia Road, P.O. Box 857, tel. 646333, fax. 646900; **Sun Hall**, Athens Ave., P.O. Box 300, tel. 653341, fax. 652717.

⑤⑤ **Flamingo Beach**, MacKenzie Beach, Piale Pasha Street, P.O. Box 733, tel. 650621, fax. 656732; **Four Lanterns Hotel**, 19 Athens Ave., P.O. Box 2592, tel. 652011, fax. 626012.

⑤ **121 Cactus**, 6-8 Shakespeare St., P.O. Box 188, tel. 627400, fax. 626966; **Parion**, 11 Faneromeni St., Ayios Lazaros Square, P.O. Box 558, tel. 656688, fax. 658165.

HOTEL APARTMENTS: **Acropolis**, corner Gr. Afxentiou Ave. and Ermou St., P.O. Box 758, tel. 623700, fax. 620319; **Pasithea**, Salt Lake, 4 Michael Angelou St., P.O. Box 309, tel. 6658264, fax. 625848. *YOUTH HOSTEL:* 27 Nikolaou Rossou St., near the Church of Ayios Lazaros, tel. 621188, open year round.

🍴 Most of Larnaca's restaurants are situated along the waterfront, as well as along the Larnaca-Dhekelia Road.

EXPENSIVE: **Al Halali**, at the Salt Lake near the Hala Sultan Tekke Mosque; **La Gourmandise**, Larnaca-Dhekelia Road, tel. 624100, elegant, delicious French cuisine.

MODERATE: **Marina Pub and Restaurant**, at the marina, tel. 627104; **Psarolimano**, 118 Piale Pasa, tel. 655408, seafront fish restaurant; **Scala Taverna**, Artemidos Ave., typical taverna.

BUDGET: **Megalos Pefkas**, at the south end of the harbor, Greek dishes; **Astrapi**, St. Lazarus Square, tel. 625088; **Cyprus Sky**, 1st April St., serves great gyros in pita bread.

🍸 *DISCOTHEQUES* can be found above all along the Larnaca-Dhekelia Road. *ROCK CAFÉS* are located along Watkins Street and the bordering Laika Yitonia. A good tavern with live Greek music is the **Black Turtle Tavern** at the Ayios Lazaros Church, 11 Mehmet Ali St., tel. 627872 (live music from 9:30 pm).

🏛 **Archeological District Museum** and **Kition Archeological Site**, open in summer Monday through Friday from 9 a.m. to 2:30 p.m., and in winter Monday through Friday from 9 am to 1:30 pm, Saturdays until 1 p.m.

Larnaca Fort and **Museum**, at the southern end of Athens Street, open in summer Monday through Friday from 9 a.m. to 7:30 p.m., in winter Monday through Friday from 9 a.m. to 2 p.m., Saturdays until 1 p.m.

Hala Sultan Tekke, mosque open daily from 7:30 a.m. to 7 p.m., in winter from 7:30 a.m. until dusk.

Municipal Art Gallery, Europe Square, open in summer Tuesday through Friday from 10 a.m. to 1 p.m. and 5 to 7 p.m., Saturdays 10 a.m. to 1 p.m.; in winter Tuesday through Friday from 10 a.m. to 1 p.m. and 4 to 6 p.m., weekends 10 a.m. to 1 p.m.

Pierides Foundation, 4 Zenon Kitieus St., open Monday through Saturday from 9 a.m. to 1 p.m.

Museum of Paleontology, Europe Square, open Tuesday through Friday 10 a.m. to 1 p.m. and 4 to 6 p.m., weekends 10 a.m. to 1 p.m.

Khirokitia Excavation Site, open daily 9 a.m. to 5 p.m., in summer (June-August) until 7:30 p.m.

Folk Art Museum of Lefkara, open Monday through Thursday from 9:30 a.m. to 4 p.m., Fridays and Saturdays from 10 a.m. to 4 p.m.

✝ *PLACES OF WORSHIP* (for denominations other than Greek Orthodox): **Greek Evangelical Church of Cyprus**, Gregoris Afxentiou St., services Sunday at 11 a.m.; **International Evangelical Church**, Apostilidou St., services Sunday at 9 a.m.; **Terra Santa Catholic Church**, Terra Santa St., tel. 652858, masses held daily at 8 a.m., Saturdays at 6 a.m. and Sundays at 7:30 a.m.

📅 **January 6**: Epiphany, on this day a priest throws a cross into the sea, and young men of the town dive in and try to be the first to retrieve it.

A variable holiday, usually in **February**, is the Carnival or *Apokreos*, with festivities, parades and masqued balls leading up to the Lenten period. In Paralimni, there is a squash competition.

Second to the last Saturday before Easter: Saint's Day of Lazarus, Procession of St. Lazarus' icon in Larnaca.

May or **June**: *Kataklysmos*, coinciding with Pentecost, includes games, boat races, swimming competitions, song contests and folk dancing. One day is set aside for the sole purpose of throwing water at anyone nearby, resulting in a good-spirited free-for-all.

July: Larnaca Festival, in the court of Larnaca Fort, includes concerts, theater and dance performances as well as art exhibitions.

Mid-September: Week-long open-air Film Festival in Larnaca Fort.

✚ For police, fire or medical emergencies dial **199**.
Hospital: New Hospital, Mystras St., tel. 630312. **Police**: One block north of the tourist office, on Arch. Makarios III Ave., tel. 630200.

📞 **Post Office**: King Paul Square, next to the Tourist Office, tel. 630180, open summer Monday through Friday 7:30 a.m. to 2 p.m. and 4 to 6 p.m., Saturdays 9 to 11 a.m., closed Thursday afternoons; off-season daily 7:30 a.m. to 2 p.m. and 3:30 to 5:30 p.m., Thursday afternoons 3:30 to 6 p.m., Saturdays 9 to 11 a.m.

Telephones / Telegrams (CYTA): 7 Zenon Pierides St., tel. 652337, daily 7:30 a.m. to 7:30 p.m.

🚌 *BUSES:* All buses to **Ayia Napa** and **Paralimni** (tel. 03-721321) and to **Nicosia** and **Limassol** (tel. 654890) depart from the bus stop opposite the Four Lanterns Hotel on the Phinikoudes shore promenade. The No. 19 city bus makes hourly trips to the airport weekdays from 6 a.m. to 6 p.m., departing from Ayios Lazaros Church.

CAR RENTAL: **Astra**, 3 Leoforos Artemidos Ave., tel. 624422; **Hertz**, in the International Airport, tel. 643388; **Petsas**, Karydes Court, Grig. Afxentiou Ave., tel. 623033, at Larnaca Airport, tel. 657850.

SERVICE (GROUP) TAXIS: **Makris**, 13 King Paul St., tel. 652929; **Acropolis Vassos**, across from the Tourist Office, tel. 655555; **Kyriakos**, 20 Hermes St., tel. 655100.

TAXIS: 24-hour service from: **Akropolis**, Gladstone St., Acropolis Sq., tel. 652531; **Pentafkas**, 2 M. Nikolaides St., tel. 656984; **Omonia**, 24 Pierides St., tel. 652800.

🛍️ The **main shopping streets** in Larnaca are Ermou Street and Odos Zenon Street, as well as their side streets.

The little **Cyprus Handicraft Service Shop** on Kosma Lyssioti Street offers a good overview of Cypriot handicrafts.

Hem-stitch embroidery and silver filigree work can be found in Lefkara. Hand-painted icons are offered for sale in the monasteries of Ayia Varvara and Ayios Minas.

AYIA NAPA / PARALIMNI PROTARAS

Area Code 03

ℹ️ Information bureau of the **Cyprus Tourism Organization** in Ayia Napa, 12 Leoforos Kyrou Nerou, opposite the monastery, tel. 721796.

🏨 🅢🅢🅢 **Vrissiana Beach**, Protaras, P.O. Box 29, tel. 831216, fax. 831221; **Nissi Beach**, Ayia Napa, P.O. Box 10, tel. 721021, fax. 721623.

🅢🅢 **Nissi Park**, P.O. Box 400, tel. 721121, fax. 722196; **Pernera Beach Hotel**, Pernera Beach, P.O. Box 5, tel. 831011, fax. 831020.

🅢 **Pambos Magic**, Ayia Napa, P.O. Box 30, tel. 721214; **San Antonio**, Paralimni-Protaras Road, P.O. Box 57, tel. 821561.

HOTEL APARTMENTS: **Farkonia**, Pernera, P.O Box 108, tel. 831180, fax. 831812; **Happy Days**, Protaras Road, P.O. Box 30, tel. 831010, fax. 820756.

YOUTH HOSTEL: 23 Dionysios Solomos St., tel. 723113.

CAMPING: **Ayia Napa Camping**, tel. 721946, CTO (Cyprus Tourism Organization) licensed, west of Ayia Napa, just a few meters from the beach. Room for 150 tents/caravans.

🍴 Restaurants and bars abound on the main roads in both Ayia Napa and Paralimni, too numerous and changeable to list thoroughly. Some reliable establishments are: **Mersinia**, outside Ayia Napa on the road to Paralimni, tel. 722640, Greek and continental cuisine; **Patio Mazery**, Ayia Napa, on the village square, tel. 721094, steaks and traditional Greek dishes; **Taylors,** Dherinia (4 km north of Parlimni), excellent food, reasonable prices. **Famagusta Beach View Restaurant**, Dhernia, best view of the ghost town of Varosha from here.

🍷 **Weekends from March through November**: *Ayia Napa Festivities*, concerts and traditional dancing in the Ayia Napa Monastery.

May: *Anthesia* flower festival, with folkloric show and floral parade, on a Sunday in the Paralimni stadium.

Early August: Week-long folkloric *Paralimni Festival*.

🏛️ **Ayia Napa Monastery**, open daily to visitors from sunrise to sunset; Malacology Museum in the Town Hall, Ayia Mavra St., open Monday through Saturday 9 a.m. to 2 p.m., Mondays and Thursdays also open 4 to 6:30 p.m.

📞 **Post Office**: Ayia Napa, 8 Dionysou Solomou St., tel. 721550, open Monday through Friday 7:30 a.m. to 2 p.m., Thursday afternoons 3:30 p.m. to 6 p.m.

Telephones / Telegrams (CYTA): Tel. 652337, open daily 7:30 a.m. to 7 p.m.

🚌 *BUSES:* **Paralimni Bus**, tel. 821318, Paralimni Church – Protaras Hotel District – Larnaca, Monday through Saturday 6:30 a.m. to 4 p.m. (seven trips), in summer until 5:30 p.m.; Paralimni Church – Nicosia, Monday through Saturday 7 a.m.; Paralimni Church – Protaras Hotel District – Ayia Napa, in summer hourly from 7 a.m.

CAR, MOTORCYCLE AND BICYCLE RENTAL: **Petsas**, Ayia Napa, 20 Leoforos Nissi Ave., tel. 721774; **Happiness Tours and Rentals**, Tefkrou Anthia 20, tel. 722580.

TAXIS: **Makronissos**, tel. 721777; **Emman**, 1A Loukas St., tel. 721379; **Paralimni**, tel. 823110.

🛍️ In Ayia Napa there are plenty of items on offer for tourists, though nothing original.

THE LITTLE PARIS
OF CYPRUS

LIMASSOL
LIMASSOL DISTRICT
KOURION
PITSILIA
NATURE WALKS

Limassol

LIMASSOL

Limassol is a district of contrasts, encompassing the entire spectrum of Cypriot life. **Limassol ❶** itself is a lively modern city, dubbed "The Little Paris of Cyprus" by local boosters because of its output, nightlife and joie de vivre. Much of this is centered on wine making and the enjoyment of its output, since Limassol is the center of the major wineries in Cyprus. But Limassol, unlike Paris, has not protected its architectural and cultural heritage. Instead it has concentrated its energies in the last two decades on constructing modern buildings, mainly catering to tourism and trade with the Middle East.

When visitors have had enough of the bright lights of the city and its madding crowds, it is time for them to head for the hills – in this case the foothills of Troodos known as Pitsilia, which are almost due north of the city of Limassol. The little villages nestled in the gently undulating landscape of the region retain a unique charm, making them one of the main attractions of this district.

Preceding pages: An enchanting sunset at the Roman Theater of Kourion. Left: A friendly chat in a neighborhood café in the Turkish Quarter of Limassol.

Much of the growth in Limassol has occurred because of mercantile development. Because of a liberal tax structure, favorable climate, and high quality work force, Cyprus has rapidly expanded as an offshore center for financial trading, and for shipping companies doing business outside the domestic market. Cyprus has the fastest growing shipping register in the world, numbering 2,500 at present, and many of the offices of these lines are in Limassol.

The municipality has come to realize the limitations of placing its emphasis solely on commercial and modern development. It has recently sought to compensate for its past errors by focusing on saving the areas of Limassol that reflect its ancient history.

The population of greater Limassol is about 175,000 today, more than double what it was in 1974 at the time of the division of the island, and triple what it was in the 1960s. Limassol is the second largest Cypriot city, and its population swelled as the result of refugees from the north of Cyprus and the Middle East, especially Lebanon. Limassol is now Cyprus' biggest port and also plays host to the largest number of tourists each year. The city has expanded on all sides, with the level of construction of hotels and apartments in the easterly Potamos Yermasoyias and

Map p. 83, City Map p. 79, Info pp. 96-97

75

Above: The Castle of Limassol houses the Medieval Museum.

Amathus areas being particularly astounding. Limassol doesn't offer much of historic interest, though its outskirts have some good beaches and interesting monuments.

History of Limassol

Although ancient remains have been found in the vicinity of Limassol, including tombs from about 1600 B.C. in a cemetery in the suburb of Ayia Phyla, the community of Limassol itself was not important until the Middle Ages, when Amathus declined. The name Limassol (the Latin form of the Greek *Lemesós*) is said to have developed from the word *nemesos*, Greek for "in-between," referring to the ancient city's position between its more illustrious neighbors of Amathus to the east and Kourion to the west.

Limassol first gained importance after the arrival of the crusaders. Richard the Lionhearted of England landed here on his way to Jerusalem during the Third Crusade in 1191. In another ship was his betrothed, Berengaria of Navarra, accompanied by his sister Joanna, Queen Dowager of Sicily.

According to legend, they were shipwrecked at Amathus. The two women were allowed to come ashore by the tyrannical Isaac Comnenos, but they distrusted his motives. They requested permission to send ashore for food and water, but Comnenos forbade this and instead sent four armed galleys to force them and their entourage to disembark and to take them prisoner. At the last minute, King Richard came to their rescue. He was so infuriated at the treatment of his fiancée and sister that he went into battle against Comnenos.

Eventually Comnenos was defeated, and Richard and Berengaria were married on May 12, 1191, probably in the chapel of the castle of Limassol. Immediately afterwards, Richard had Berengaria crowned Queen.

Although a great deal of Limassol's history is associated with the crusaders, none of them had come to Cyprus in order to conquer the island; they acquired it more or less by chance. After the fall of Acre in 1291, Limassol passed into the guardianship of the Knights Templar. But the wealth and power of the Knights gave rise to envy and distrust. Philippe IV of France finally had them declared heretics, and by the beginning of the 14th century the order was disbanded.

The property of the Templars was handed over to the Knights of St. John of Jerusalem. They then built the fortress at Kolossi, west of Limassol. In a dissertation entitled *Greeks and Latins in 13th Century Cyprus: A Study of Churchmen and Crusaders*, Basil Efthimiou Miltiades concluded: "Protected by the surrounding seas, the island became an ideal retreat for crusaders, for whom the possession of Cyprus allowed them to prolong for another century their occupation of the Syrian seaports."

And, he continued: "After 1291, planners of future crusades still looked upon Cyprus as their advance base, but the emphasis among crusaders and their churchmen changed from crusading zeal and ecclesiastical reform to lust for commercial profit."

After Queen Alice (1229-1237) had granted exclusive commercial privileges to the Genoese, they firmly established themselves in Famagusta, replacing Limassol as the principal port by the end of the century.

The vineyards were cultivated by the Knights of St. John of Jerusalem, who in 1291 moved their headquarters to Kolossi, to the west of Limassol. This area was a center of sugar production, which was a valuable export during Lusignan and Venetian times, especially the fine-grained form. The Turks continued the operation of the factories until demand for sugar dwindled when the West Indian industry began to thrive.

After the order of the Knights Templar was dissolved in 1312, Limassol suffered various setbacks. It was severely damaged by earthquakes, then set on fire by the Genoese in 1373, and sacked by Egyptian flotillas and the Saracens in the 15th century. In 1539, the Turks devastated the city.

Between the late 15th century and the 19th century, the town had a poor reputation, which might have been somewhat exaggerated in the reports on it made by a number of visitors. The German pilgrim Felix Faber, for example, mentioned in 1480 that "only one wretched church remains standing and that without bells." In 1815, the English painter Joseph Mallord William Turner described it as "a miserable town, consisting of 150 mud houses, of which 100 are inhabited by Greeks and 50 by Turks."

At the same time, Turner mentioned the 50 shiploads of wine exported each year from Cyprus, 20 of which came from Limassol. Wine production and carob cultivation aided Limassol's economic recovery in the 19th century. The fruit of the carob tree – also known as St. John's bread – is a dark pod containing hard seeds and a sweet pulp, from which John the Baptist is said to have sustained himself, along with wild honey and locusts. Carob is often used in a powdered form in the preparation of sweet foods, similar to chocolate.

Limassol's fortunes began to rise again in the 1880s, assisted by economic developments such as the building of a pier in 1881.

The Old Town of Limassol

By far, the most picturesque part of the city is the Old Town in the area of the medieval castle. The Limassol Municipality has secured a loan of about US $20 million from the Council of Europe for two projects, one of which is to spruce up the Churchill Hotel Reclamation Area off

28th of October Street, halfway between the town center and Potamos Yermasoyias.

The other project is concerned with the renovation of the buildings in the area surrounding the old covered market, extending to Ankara Street, where several mosques and a *hamam* (Turkish bath) attest to the city's Ottoman heritage. Plans are to aim for a neighborhood similar to the successfully renovated Laiki Yitonia in Nicosia.

City planners from the University of Marseilles are collaborating on recreating the residences and businesses in the same style as the original buildings, some of which are from the turn of the century, others of which are older. The city will be financing these renovations – and collecting the property rentals – until the loan is repaid. After that, the buildings will be returned unconditionally to their original owners.

Above: All the fixings for a fine picnic lunch at the Limassol Market.

The best place to start a visit to the Old Town is the **Castle ❶**, on a side street off Irinis Street between Ayia Thekla and Ankara streets.

The present building dates from the 14th century, although part of the west wall originated in an earlier Byzantine fortification in which Richard the Lionhearted and Berengaria might have been married. The pillar supporting the vaulted Great Hall collapsed, and part of the fortress was demolished in 1525. The Turks rebuilt it at the end of the 16th century, using wooden beams instead of stone pillars. During the Turkish period it was used primarily as a prison. It was again used as a prison as recently as 1940, and then as military headquarters.

The castle underwent further restoration and now includes a very interesting and well laid out **Medieval Museum**. The collection is a fine representation of military and civilian life during Medieval times. Well-preserved suits of armor and weapons, including blunderbuss rifles, are displayed in glass cases. Cannons are a reminder of the defensive nature of the structure, which was so often under siege by foreign invaders.

Outstanding among the museum's marble reliefs is one of *Daniel in the Lions' Den* (seventh century A.D.), of unknown origin. Close by are three silver plates with scenes from Daniel's life, including his marriage attended by two flute players. Among the bronze pots is a bowl for water in the *hamam* or Turkish bath. Ceramic plates include both Cypriot and Italian examples. Some ornate woodcarvings are fine examples of this well-developed craft.

A wooden staircase leads to the rooftop, a good place to get a view of the harbor and surroundings of the Old Town. Downstairs in the cellar are carvings from the Famagusta and Nicosia Districts, and photos of the majority of the medieval buildings now lying in the occupied north of the island.

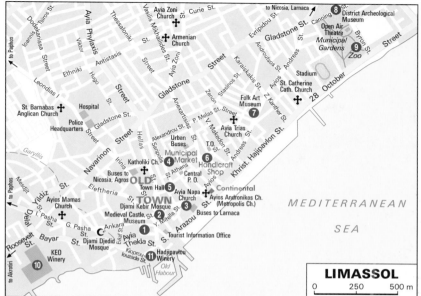

The museum is surrounded by gardens and pine trees, with a lone Turkish tombstone decorated with a head sporting a fez among them. It's pleasant to walk through the Old Town neighborhood and do some window-shopping before the little establishments in this area, one of the few retaining the flavor of Old Limassol, and now earmarked for renovation.

On the side streets surrounding the museum are iron and copper workshops. The streets such as Ankara, Evkaf and Safi are reminders of the former Turkish Cypriot inhabitants who lived in this district, many of whom relocated to Kyrenia after the division of the island in 1974. To the northeast of the castle is the **Djami Kebir Mosque ❷**, and at the end of Ankara Street is another mosque overlooking the **Turkish Cemetery** next to the usually dry Garyllis River. The entrance to the cemetery is walled in.

On Yenethliou Mitella are more metal-working shops, also small stores selling village wine and vinegar. Some of these still have signs written in Turkish from pre-1974 days. A small **hamam** or Turkish bath, called *loutro* in Greek, is still functioning on a little cul-de-sac between Mitella and Araouzou Street, but at this time it is neither clean nor in good repair.

The 1903 **Ayia Napa Church ❸**, a massive stone building, is east of the mosque on Ayios Andreas – or Saint Andrew – Street. The **Market ❹** behind the central post office north of Athens Street and west of Anexartisias Street is a good place to buy fruit, cold cuts and bread; add a bottle of local wine and you have the makings of a memorable picnic lunch. Interspersed between the produce stalls inside the cavernous old market hall, with a separate fish market, are makeshift shops selling baskets, weavings and other local handicrafts. In the back courtyard are shops with a large selection of cheeses and local sausages, plus natural yoghurt.

South of Droushiotis Street, east of the handsomely-restored **Town Hall ❺**, is **Iroon Square** (Heroes Square), once a notorious red-light district which has since been somewhat "gentrified."

Many modern shops and offices are located on or near Anexartesias Street – including the **Cyprus Handicraft Service Shop** ❻ at 25 Thermidos Street. South on Ayios Andreas Street are a number of tailor shops near the Old Town, which can whip up a suit in short order. Several modern shopping centers are along the street heading east – and a number of art galleries are in the vicinity surrounding the Folk Art Museum.

The Folk Art Museum

The **Folk Art Museum** ❼ at 253 Ayios Andreas Street, which first opened in the 1980s, has a delightful collection of tradtional costumes, farm and household tools, and examples of local handicrafts including the *sandoukia*, or carved wooden dowry chests, and *anathrika*, sturdy reed footstools from the Paphos District.

Above: Samples of the folk crafts of Cyprus in the Limassol Museum.

The collection features displays of many different styles of weaving and embroidery, and shows distinctive materials developed on the island over the centuries. A visit to the museum is not only interesting, it can also serve as an introduction to authentic Cypriot handicrafts for those who want to buy authentic products as souvenirs.

The District Museum

The **District Museum** ❽ on Byron Street across from the **Curium Palace Hotel** has a good collection of finds from the area's excavations, and is generally open every day, including weekends. The most striking displays here contain artifacts from Kourion and Amathus, the two prominent ancient cities. Labeling, in both English and Greek, is unfortunately rather vague.

A wide range of pottery, examples of which have been found ranging from 3000 B.C. to the 13th century A.D., has proved to be quite valuable in dating settlements. Bronze Age ceramics are especially notable. Jewelry on display includes delicate gold headdresses, shell necklaces and amulets. Coins include some minted under Emperor Caracalla showing the Temple of Aphrodite at Palea Paphos. A lovely marble head of Aphrodite from this temple is also on display. The most exotic objects come from Amathus and bear a definite Egyptian influence. The huge stone statue of Bes, the grotesque dwarf-like Egyptian fertility god, seems somewhat menacing. The erect penis on some of the smaller statues of the god is almost as large as he is. The Hathor-headed columns show the countenance of the Egyptian Goddess of the Sky and Patroness of Music and Dance. The various representations of the goddess who preceded Aphrodite are very graceful, with intricately carved Oriental-style headdresses.

The nearby **Municipal Gardens** bordered by Byron Street and 28th October Street are the home of a small **zoo ❾**, in which a pair of mouflons, a variety of wild sheep found only on Cyprus, can be seen. Out in the wild they live in the western section of the Troodos Mountains. They are extremely shy creatures, though, and catching a glimpse of one is a rare event indeed.

Limassol's annual wine festival, a 13-day-long Dionysian celebration with an abundance of locally-produced nectar of the gods, samples of Cypriot food, and lively folkloric performances, is held here each September.

Those interested in wine should make a side-trip to the **KEO Winery ❿** south of Franklin Roosevelt Street (Paphos Road) to the west of the Old Town. The company gives tours of its winery and adjoining brewery every weekday morning. Nearby **Hadjipavlou Winery ⓫**, at the Old Port, which is noted for its brandy production, does the same. Both places allow time for a sampling of the products at the end of the tour.

To the west of the industrial quarter is the new port of Limassol, which was constructed after 1974, and at which today nearly all the freight and ferry traffic to Cyprus is handled.

Nightlife

Limassol hosts a number of theatrical and musical performances in the winter, while in the summer season it works hard to maintain its reputation as a party town. Most of the nightlife centers around the hotels of Amathus and Potamos Yermasoyias to the east of town, which have a number of discos. The **Roussos Beach Apartment Hotel Disco** stays open till the wee morning hours for those who want to boogie the night away. Some of the large hotels also feature folk-dancing programs in the evening.

The **Porta** restaurant on Yenethliou Mitella in the Old Town has guitarists who sing traditional songs, and some of the other restaurants also feature music during the peak season.

Favored by locals is **To Peintari,** on Irinis Street in the Old Town, a smart *boite* with a large courtyard in which sophisticated popular music is regularly performed. Recommendable tavernas with live Greek music are **Vassilikos**, at Ayios Andreas Street 252, and the **Klima Tavern**, on the main street in Potamos Yermasoyias.

It is actually possible to take a tavern tour in Limassol for those inclined. Start at the **Cuckoo's Nest** at 228 Ayios Andreas Street. The interior is a clutter of memorabilia and kitsch, with business cards stuck in every available nook and cranny. Friendly chef Adamides is always ready to whip up either a tasty sandwich (grilled ham and local *haloumi* cheese is good), a snack such as stuffed vine leaves, or a hot dish to accompany your beverages.

After this, you can stroll west along the shore promenade to the Old Port. A row

Limassol

of cafés and pubs await you here. The most original – and most British – of all of them is the **Swan Inn**, at Ayias Thekly Street 44 right near the Old Port, where you can select a nightcap from an array of no fewer than 36 different whiskies.

Beaches

Many of Limassol's better beaches belong to the hotels on the east side of town near the ancient archeological site of Amathus, and in the Potamos Yermasoyias area. For an entrance fee, the Amathus Beach, Le Meridien and other hotels will allow non-guests to use their beaches, which are mostly sand with a few pebbles.

The Cypriot Tourist Office (CTO) beach of **Dassoudi** ❷, on the east end of town, is very long and well-equipped, with tennis and volleyball courts and playgrounds for children. Many areas are shaded by pine trees and the water is quite clean. Snack bars and restaurants offer a full range of food and drinks.

Lady's Mile Beach ❸, southwest of town on **Akrotiri Bay**, is a long sandy stretch of shoreline next to the British military base. It is named for the favorite mare of a British officer who used to exercise her here.

The long sand beaches below the ancient site of **Kourion** (see page 88) are fairly isolated, but they do have restaurants. **Pissouri**, farther west along the coastal road, has been developed as a small resort community with several hotels, pensions and apartment hotels in different price ranges.

On the nearly one-kilometer-long sand beach of **Avmidou** ❹, between Kourion and Pissouri, you will find the Melanda Beach and Kyrenia tavernas, but will see nothing at all of chaise longues, beach umbrellas, pensions or hotels. This beach is located on the grounds of the British military base of Akrotiri; even so, it is open to the public.

LIMASSOL DISTRICT

Amathus

The city of **Amathus** ❺ is about 11 kilometers east of Limassol, just past the Limonia Bay Hotel. Along the seashore are the protruding walls of the lower city, now submerged in the water.

Amathus has an illustrious history, but imagination is required to envision what must have once been a splendid sight. Only scant remains are left and these are not well identified. A visit to Limassol's District Museum to see the Oriental-influenced statues of Egyptian deities and ornate capitals will convey the exotic flavor of the original settlement, and is recommended before visiting the site itself. Excavations continue on what was one of nine original city-kingdoms of Cyprus and promise to yield many more significant finds.

Amathus was first settled in the 11th century B.C. and prospered through trade with both Greeks and Levantines. It remained independent, and was never taken over by the Greeks. Yet it was one of the most powerful states of the Cypro-Geometric Period. In the revolt of 499/98 B.C., Amathus went against all the other Cypriot kingdoms and sided with the Persians. Capital of one of the four districts of the island under the Romans, Amathus declined in Byzantine times. Richard the Lionhearted is believed to have landed here in 1191, shortly before marrying Berengaria.

Amathus had a temple to Herakles, called Melkarth here, and a joint temple to Adonis and Aphrodite. The annual *Adonia Games*, including boar hunts, athletic competitions, and performances of songs and dance in honor of the god Adonis were held here. Much of the ruins of Amathus were used for later construction over the centuries, and many artifacts from here have found their way into foreign museums.

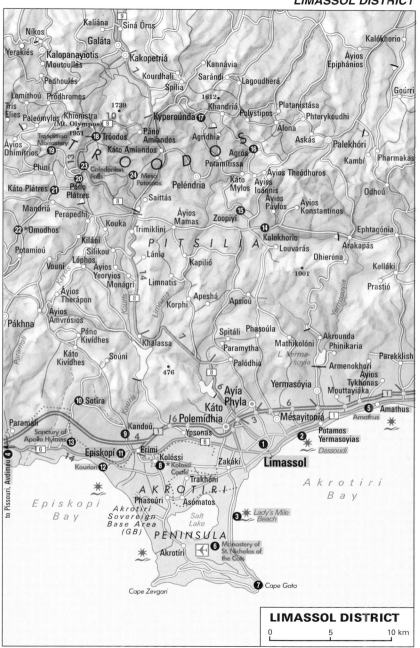

LIMASSOL DISTRICT

0   5   10 km

Info pp. 96-97

The French quarried the stone, sending much of it off by boat to Larnaca for their buildings there. The neighboring village of Ayios Tykhonas is largely built from the ruins. A stone vessel with bull-headed handles was hauled off to the Louvre in 1866. A few years later, the notorious General di Cesnola sent tomb offerings and sculptured panels to the Metropolitan Museum in New York.

A long hike up a steep barren hill scattered with stone fragments and pieces of walls leads to the **Forum**, revealing flagstone floors and remains of pediments and carved capitals. Excavations in 1990 and 1991 under the direction of Michalis Loulloupis of the Cyprus Museum in Nicosia brought to light remains of a sidewall of shops, a circular building, and an early Byzantine workshop. Continuing excavations will eventually unearth the entire agora. The circular building was

probably a *valaneion*, or public bath house, similar to those found at Kition in the Larnaca District. The workshop could have been used as a dyeing house or tannery. Attention has been focused on the sea-pebble mosaics at the bottom of three rectangular water tanks found near the south of the site. Pottery, coins and inscriptions describing Amathus' inhabitants have been found here.

The major portion of the site lies up the hill to the north of the main road before the **Amathus Beach Hotel**, which has a **7th-century-B.C. tomb** on display, just down the stairs next to the tennis courts. The first discoveries of this site were houses of the Hellenic Period still inhabited in the first century A.D. The paved **lower city** has been the source of capitals, columns and entablatures.

Akrotiri Peninsula

After the New Port area in town, head left towards the long sandy stretch known as **Lady's Mile Beach ❸**. Thick eucalyp-

Above: Two pelicans join the sunbathers on a sandy beach in Limassol. Right: The dignified keep at Kolossi Castle, Limassol.

Limassol

tus groves shade the road leading through landfill in the former marsh developed by the Cyprus Palestine Plantation in the 1930s. Permission from the Tourist Office is needed to visit the citrus farms and vineyards. A dirt track runs along the Akrotiri Peninsula, once renowned for boar hunting, leading past the **Monastery of St. Nicholas of the Cats** ❻.

This monastery, beautifully set amid orchards and vineyards, was founded in the year 325 by a group of monks sent to Cyprus by Emperor Constantine. Its name is derived from the cats that were brought here, supposedly by Constantine's mother, St. Helena of the Cross, to control the snake population. A few descendents of the ferocious felines, who eventually accomplished their task after centuries of effort, wander about the vicinity freely. The stone building standing here today, built between the 13th and 15th centuries, was abandoned shortly after Turkish rule began in 1570. It has several carved shields on the lintel of the north entrance.

The road from the monastery continues past the cliffs of **Cape Gata** ❼ (*gata* is "cat" in Greek), site of over a hundred tombs and more than 50 sarcophagi. It continues around the **Salt Lake**, a resting place for migrating birds.

*Kolossi Castle ❽, about nine kilometers west of Limassol, is one of the most attractive of the Lusignan monuments and can be reached most quickly via the Limassol-Paphos road. For those coming directly from Limassol, a more picturesque drive passes through the **Phasouri Plantations**.

During the Lusignan period, Kolossi was the seat of a small group of Knights of St. John of Jerusalem. After the fall of the last crusaders' fortress in the Holy Land, the order found temporary sanctuary on the island of Cyprus. In 1310, they relocated to the Greek island of Rhodes. To guarantee their rule, the Lusignans presented them with land and 60 villages in the Limassol District. The villagers had to cultivate sugar cane and vineyards for the Knights. The sugar cane

was refined in a hall beside the castle, which still exists today. The wine was exported by the Knights to Rhodes and other places under the name of *Commandaria*. This wine is still produced today by a number of vineyards in Cyprus, and is enjoyed both as an aperitif and a dessert wine.

The present dignified four-square **keep** was rebuilt by the Knights in 1454, on the foundations of an earlier structure. Although small, it looks nonetheless like a typical Gothic fairy-tale castle, with three-meter-thick walls and a drawbridge, surrounded by attractive grounds. The entrance leads to the east side of the three-storied fortification with a crenelated terrace.

Above the entrance is the coat of arms of Louis de Magnac, the Grand Commander of Cyprus who rebuilt the fortress. Above it are the royal insignia of Jerusalem, Lesser Armenia, Cyprus and

Above: A living roadblock, slowly moving along a country road.

the Lusignans, and in between those of Rhodes. On the wall on the right side of the first floor is a mural. A second-floor fireplace is decorated with carved chains and leaves. Beside the round arched windows, seats are built into the walls. A spiral staircase leads up to the roof, from where there is an excellent view of the Salt Lake of Akrotiri Peninsula and the surrounding countryside. In the cellar are three chambers that once served either as cells or storerooms.

In the garden is an aqueduct supplying cool water from the hills. The water which once poured over the end of the aqueduct was used to power a mill in which sugar cane was pressed.

Sotira

Just past Erimi, a road to the right leading to Kandou-Troodos is the turnoff for the site of Sotira. **Kandou ❾** was deserted by its original Turkish Cypriot inhabitants in 1974, and is now occupied by refugees from the north. A sign saying

"Sotira 3 miles" just outside Kandou points to a left turn ascending northwest to Sotira.

The village of **Sotira** ⑩ itself, which is made up of only a few stone houses, is quite picturesque. The **Metamorphosis Church** located here contains a damaged 16th-century icon of the Virgin Mary and a 17th-century icon of St. George. An inscription over the south portal records a restoration in the year 1553 by one Theodore Contarino.

The threshing floor (called *aloni* in Greek) opposite the school is interesting. If you are traveling by car or have taken a taxi, you have a choice of hiking from here up the dirt road on the steep hill to the west to the southern foot of Teppes, or else of driving there via the Chalcolithic site of Kaminoudhia.

The archeological site of the **Teppes** Neolithic settlement, situated on a 322-meter-high hill, offers a splendid view of the surrounding countryside (which was once probably heavily wooded), the sea and the Troodos Mountains. Its strategically advantageous position made it easy to defend in its early years. This factor, combined with a plentiful water supply from two springs, attracted ancient settlers. Foundations of the single room subrectangular and oval habitations of the Aceramic Neolithic period indicate they had flat roofs, circular platform hearths and benches.

Sotira's history, along with that of the other settlements on the southern side of the island, was abruptly terminated around 3900 B.C., probably by a series of earthquakes.

The oldest pottery, painted combed ware with surprisingly elaborate wavy banded decoration, tools of chipped stone, and bone implements which were found here can today be seen on display in the Nicosia and Limassol District Museums.

Kaminoudhia (meaning "kilns"), just north of Sotira village, belonged to the transitional Chalcolithic-Early Bronze Period. In some ways it represents a radical break with the earlier Chalcolithic, primarily notable for remains of a number of large multi-roomed houses; small rock-cut burial chambers containing pots and copper weapons and stone and shell ornaments, and entered by a *dromos* (entranceway). Comparisons between the pottery and metal types of Anatolia and those of Cyprus indicate that an immigration from the northern mainland must have occurred. The excavation of both of these archeological sites, which was begun in 1981, has been conducted since then by the American School of Oriental Research in Cyprus under the direction of Dr. Stuart Swiny.

Episkopi

Archeological finds from the entire area are displayed in the **Kourion Museum** of **Episkopi** ⑪. East of here, on the west bank of the Kouris River, is **Phaneromeni**, an excavation of a Middle to Late Bronze Age settlement and cemetery which yielded many of the objects now on display in the museum. Nearby **Bamboula**, to the west of Erimi, is the other major source of exhibits. It was a prosperous Bronze Age settlement that was the home of the ancestors of the population of Kourion. It was engaged in active trade, as is evidenced by imported jewelry and pottery, as well as by local products showing a strong Levantine influence. One memorable grave furnishing from Bamboula's cemetery, now on display at the Cyprus Museum in Nicosia, is the Mycenean *Window Krater,* with a simple but evocative drawing of a woman holding a flower, reminiscent of Cretan artwork.

The Kourion Museum is located in the private house of the late George McFadden, the assistant director of the University of Pennsylvania's excavations at Kourion and environs until his death in

Limassol

tified manor known as the **Sarayia**, containing sections of a chapel with marble reliefs from the Kourion basilica, and an area that was once a sugar mill, where hundreds of cone-shaped clay pots were found in 1979. This was a sugar producing center, a lucrative business during the Lusignan and Venetian Periods.

KOURION

Kourion ⑫ (Latin: *Curium*) is a great site, enjoyable most of all because of its dramatic setting overlooking the sea, as well as the aesthetic pleasure enhanced by knowledge of its significant history. A number of guides to the site exist but the most thorough one, written in a well-organized fashion understandable by the layperson, is *An Archeological Guide to the Ancient Kourion Area and the Akrotiri Peninsula*, edited by archeologist Helena Wylde Swiny.

Interesting chapters on Sotira Teppes, Kaminoudhia, the Temple of Apollo Hylates, the Stadium, earthquakes, and ancient theater were written by the editor and other experts. The illustrated pottery index is especially useful.

Kourion can be reached from Limassol Castle via bus, which also stops at the Episkopi Museum, or you can take the Limassol-Paphos service taxi and request a stop there.

The Kourion area has been inhabited since Neolithic times, as finds in Sotira and Erimi show, and from the Early Bronze Age as illustrated at Phaneromeni. The original settlement on the site is believed to have been founded near the Temple of Apollo in the 16th century B.C. by Dorians from Argos in Greece. Herodotus mentions it as their home in 1200 B.C. Its name may come from Koureus, son of a Greek immigrant. Achaeans settled here in the 14th and 12th centuries B.C.

The tomb of one of the early kings has been found in the Kaloriziki area. It is ev-

1953. In the garden outside the museum are inscriptions from the Temple of Apollo Hylates, sculptures and tombstones.

In the main exhibition halls are extensive finds from Kaloriziki, a site with no further visible remains one kilometer southwest, including terra cotta figurines and lamps, highly decorative vessels, faience seals and scarabs. From Kourion there are artistic fragments from the basilica and a marble head of Aphrodite from the second century A.D. Some of the many terra cotta votive figures of the Temple of Apollo are here, as well as a Roman marble fountain. Another exhibition room contains finds from prehistoric sites in the area. Especially interesting is a reconstruction of a Middle Bronze Age tomb at Phaneromeni, which contained a cache of ivory, glass, bronze and gold.

South of the main intersection in the center of the village are the ruins of a for-

Above: Elegant remains of the Temple of Apollo Hylates at Kourion. Right: Detail of a mosaic at Kourion.

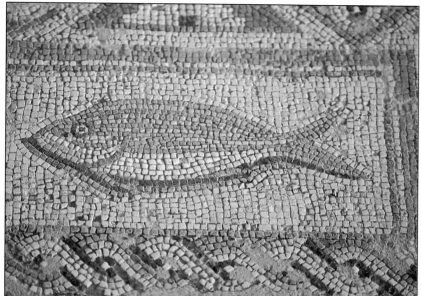

ident from a tribute list of Sargon II that Assyrians dominated the Kourion dynasty around 700 B.C.

Kourion initially sided with Greece in the revolt against the Persians in 499/98 B.C., but vacillated at the last minute, providing the edge Persia needed to take control of the island. Pasicrates, Kourion's last king, once again switched loyalties and supported Alexander the Great by leading his fleet in the attack on Persia at the Siege of Tyre in 332 B.C.

Kourion prospered under the Romans. Like so many other coastal cities, it was besieged by Arab raids during the mid seventh century. It sank into complete insignificance when the population moved inland to Episkopi (meaning "bishopric") after the bishop transferred his residence there.

The gold and silver hoard of objects plundered by Consul di Cesnola, known as the "Treasure of Curium," is now on display in the Metropolitan Museum in New York. Rumor has it that the ubiquitous consul gathered his treasure from the dozens of graves he bragged about ransacking in other areas of the island, rather than at Kourion.

The Theater and the Eustolios Complex

The excavation grounds of Kourion can be accessed by car. The paved road leading here ends at a parking lot beside the Eustolios Complex and the neighboring **Theater**.

This is impressive structure with a breathtaking view of the sea and the surrounding countryside. It is now used for the Shakespeare Festival in summer, as well as for other performances.

Theater was one of the most popular entertainments in Greek and Roman times. Most likely, the original form of drama can be found in the fertility rites of Dionysian festivals. The Theater of Kourion was built from massive limestone blocks in Hellenistic form in the late second century B.C. Its orchestra was completely circular, and classical tragedies of Euripides and Sophocles, along with Aristophanes' comedies, were performed on a small raised stage. Audiences sat in the fan-shaped auditorium and enjoyed the colorful performances featuring masked actors and a chorus, which functioned as both a sympathetic listener and spiritual partner.

In the first and second centuries A.D., during the Roman Period, the Theater was remodeled. The chorus had lost much of its significance and the orchestra was reduced to a semicircle. The projecting wings of the auditorium were shortened and the whole structure was roofed over and walled in, cutting the audience off from the wonderful view. An oblong stage and a new scenery building were added, with later construction featuring imposing marble columns and cornices. Finally, the auditorium was again enlarged to seat 3,500 people, the same number as today.

Pantomime and water ballet were especially popular with audiences, along with plays using women without masks, a radical innovation considered shocking in Roman times. In the third century A.D., the structure was rearranged for the spectacle of hunters pursuing wild animals. Natural caves underneath the theater were probably used to keep the unfortunate beasts.

Higher on the slope to the east is the **Eustolios Complex**, a palatial private building that was probably used later as a public recreation area. It houses a bath complex constructed after the destruction of the Theater in the fifth century A.D. The Roman baths were an integral aspect of daily life, and this one features the usual three sections: the *tepidarium*, or warm baths, *caldarium*, or hot baths, and *frigidarium*, or cold baths.

A mosaic in the vestibule greets the visitor with the Greek words, "Enter and

Right: The fascinating complex of Hellenistic ruins at Kourion, Limassol.

bring good luck to the house." The central room of the bathhouse has an outstanding mosaic with four scenes. The panel with birds and fish, featuring a partridge in the middle, is especially appealing. The most famous mosaic is that of *Ktisis*, the founding spirit, depicted as a pensive woman holding a measuring rod almost exactly the length of a Roman foot. The mosaics with intricate geometric patterns of Greek keys, crosses and multi-colored motifs are especially prominant in the northwestern and southwestern halls. In the southeastern hall, animals including Christian symbols of fish and birds are introduced into the usual geometric carpet design.

The Basilica and the House of Gladiators

After visiting the Theater and Roman Baths, go back a few steps towards the entrance, and then take the broad path to the right, which will bring you to a fence. This secures an extensive excavation site, presently closed to the public, in which archeologists are still working. There they have so far uncovered, among other things, a so-called **Nymphaeum**, a splendid well house dedicated to water spirits.

The ruins of the early Christian **Basilica** (fifth century), on the other hand, is open to visitors. The transition to Christianity was gradual on this island, once so firmly entrenched in paganism. It seems the way was paved, in the truest sense of the word, by earthquakes in the fourth century for the erection of Christian buildings among the pagan ruins. The church appears to have had five naves. Acanthus capitals from Roman buildings graced four columns supporting a timber and tile superstructure over the altar.

From the Basilica a narrow path along the edge of the excavation site leads to the extreme northwest corner of the fenced-in area. Here you will see a complex identified as either an aristocratic house with

private bath or public Roman baths: the House of Gladiators. A mosaic here depicting gladiatorial combat that might have taken place in the Theater has lost one of its three panels. The central panel shows two gladiators with the Greek names *Margareitis* and *Ellinikos* dressed in full armor, ready to strike with blunted swords. The second panel shows two armed gladiators, one named *Lytras*, separated from his opponent by *Dareios*, probably a Persian referee. The complex has been dated to the fourth century A.D. by coins found here.

On the path from the excavation site to the beach of Kourion is the little **Chapel of Ayios Hermoyenis**, set in a eucalyptus grove. Hermoyenis was a Turkish Moslem who converted to Christianity and was therefore martyred. Beside the chapel is an eponymous restaurant; a good place to take a midday break. Across from here, a large Mycenaean grave was discovered at the beginning of the 1990s. It can now be examined underneath its modern protective roof.

The Stadium

The U-shaped **Stadium**, two kilometers west of Kourion and just north of the Paphos road, was constructed in the second century A.D. It evolved for foot races, deriving its name from the distance covered, called a *stadium*, or approximately 186 meters. Athletes formed guilds honoring Herakles as their patron saint and toured the Roman Empire competing at meets. Only a few of the original seven rows of stone seats accommodating 6,500 people remain. Besides foot racing, the primary sport, boxing, wrestling and discus and javelin throwing were probably practiced, but the Stadium was too narrow for chariot races.

The Temple of Apollo Hylates

The worship of Apollo Hylates was most intriguing on Cyprus. The **Temple of Apollo Hylates ⓭**, one kilometer west of the stadium, was already functioning in the eighth century B.C. according to

evidence of terra cotta figurines. Apollo is a multi-faceted deity in charge of prophecy, music and archery, and is the protector of flocks. Trees, especially laurel, myrtle and the palm, are sacred to him, explaining the epithet *Hylates* or "Protector of the Woodland."

Remains of his sanctuary, surrounded by pines and cypresses, include the elegant Temple with steps and a portico leading to the Inner Temple, which is surrounded by two handsomely restored columns, the site of the rituals. Strabo mentions in the first century A.D. that anyone who dared to touch the altar in its center was flung from the cliffs at Kourion.

Revealing vignettes are provided from the terra cotta votive offerings of the seventh and sixth centuries B.C. found in the semicircular votive pit south of the

Temple. Especially charming are figures circling a tree while doing a ritual dance. The dancers sometimes wear bull masks, attesting to the continuing importance of the bull in pagan worship. Chariot groups and horsemen, sometimes armed, made their appearance later. North of the votive pit are remains of houses, including one with a front courtyard and columned hall that was most probably inhabited by the priest.

PITSILIA

The foothill region of the Troodos Mountains, known as **Pitsilia**, is a wonderfully refreshing area of unspoiled villages taking pride in both their traditional architecture and equally renowned hospitality. Many of them make local wines, rose water, honey and cheeses. Painted churches and restored houses are worth seeing, and cafés or restaurants are a good vantage point from which to savor everyday village life, which has hardly changed over the centuries.

Above: The "donkey express" is still a popular mode of transportation. Right: Preoccupied with details of monastic life high in the mountains at Trooditissa Monastery.

Public transportation is infrequent in Pitsilia, so renting a car is a good way of getting around the winding roads. But don't underestimate the danger of doing this if you are used to driving on the right hand side of the road. If you are at all uneasy about your safety, make arrangements to hire a taxi for the day. The route suggested here is a semicircle from the east side of Limassol, up through Pitsilia to Troodos, and then descending to the western side of Limassol. It makes for a long day trip, but really should be divided into two days.

The architecture in the hill villages is dense, utilizing every available space. Houses are often made of uncut hard stone called *sieropetres*, the spaces filled in with smaller stones and gravel, accenting the attractive textures and colors. The roofs of the hill dwellings are usually sloped and covered in red tiles, giving them a wonderfully rustic aspect when viewed from afar.

Heading north from the east side of Limassol, **Kalokhorio** ⑭ has the striking

Church of Ayios Yeoryios, a rustic gem containing interesting murals. **Zoopiyi** ⑮ farther north is noted for its mellow, nutty-flavored *Commandaria* dessert wine, which can be sampled and purchased in local shops. **Agros** ⑯, situated more than 1,000 meters above sea level and laid out in a semicircle over terraces, is the main village of Pitsilia and the location of the best hotel in the region, the Rodon. Roses grow in the area, and their petals are distilled into rose water in the springtime. Agros is known for its meat products: *loundsa*, a type of smoked pork, *chiromeri*, air-cured ham, and *loukanika*, richly-spiced sausages.

In the village church, Panayia Eleoussa (19th century), hangs an icon of the Virgin Mary, said to have been painted by the evangelist Luke.

Kyperounda ⑰ is noted for the murals in the **Stavros Church**. They were painted by Philippos Goul in 1466, and are considered to be some of the finest on the island. Beyond Kyperounda, the temperature drops rapidly and the vegetation

becomes more alpine. The road winds tortuously towards **Kato** and **Pano Amaniados**.

Troodos 18, at an altitude of 1,725 meters above sea level, is the highest inhabited area in Cyprus and is popular for winter sports and as a destination for a variety of summer activities. Troodos and environs has many trails for nature walks. The twisting road with lots of hairpin turns between Troodos and the **Trooditissa Monastery 19** goes through some spectacular scenery in areas shaded by huge pines and aspens. The central church was built in 1731 on the foundations of an earlier building from the mid 13th century. It has a sloped tile roof and a stable-like interior with walnut carvings giving it a rustic look. The miracle-working *Icon of the Virgin Mary* is now covered in silver gilt. The monastery only allows visits by Orthodox Christians; tourists are not welcome.

Above: A Troodos village. Right: Fruit and vine cultivation in the Troodos foreland.

Pano Platres 20, the setting for Seferis' poem *Helena*, is five kilometers southeast. It is the largest hill resort and has many hotels, cafés and restaurants, many with lovely views, set in the refreshing mountain atmosphere. In the summer, Pano Platres is a bit trendy, attracting many tourists and Cypriots who own vacation houses in the area. Charming **Kato Platres 21**, situated a bit lower, has quaint houses set among orchards, and is a more tranquil setting in which to rent a room.

Omodhos 22, a few kilometers further southwest, has winding streets set among vineyards. The church of the **Holy Cross Monastery** has a piece of the True Cross and ropes that bound the hands of Christ. Omodhos is famous for its beautiful lace. Samples of it can be purchased at the fair that takes place near the monastery each year on September 14.

The large village square of Omodhos is one of the loveliest on the entire island. A number of old houses in the idyllic village can be visited, as can a centuries-old winepress.

NATURE WALKS

The most interesting walks in the Limassol District start out from **Troodos 18**, at least in summer, when the cool fresh air of the mountains can be best enjoyed. There are four signposted nature trails. The **Artemis Trail** is a circular seven-kilometer-long trail around **Khionistra** (1951 meters) in the Black Pine region at about 1850 meters altitude. The flora of the area is very distinctive and includes many endemic species of plants characteristic of this summit, which may be considered a subalpine region. Vegetation includes the Troodos juniper *Juniperus foetidissima*, Cyprus crocus, Troodos alyssum, *Salvia willeana*, and many others. Orchids such as the spectacular *Limodorum abortivum* can be found under the pines. Several helleborines grow

in the area, including the rare *Epipactis condensata*. Bird watchers will occasionally sight the cross-bill, short-toed tree creeper, blue rock thrush and imperial eagle, among other species. The nine-kilometer **Atalanta Trail**, named for a mythological forest nymph, starts in Troodos. Like the previous nature route, it has rich plant life and spectacular scenery.

The four-kilometer ★**Caledonia Trail**, called the "Trail of Nightingales," follows the Kryo Potamo stream flowing from Troodos to Platres, winding down through pine forest with plane trees and alders. The walk is easy, but be sure to wear good hiking boots, as the stream has to be crossed quite often.

The walk to Platres begins 1.6 kilometers south of Troodos on the Platres Road, where a signpost reads "Caledonian Trail 500 meters" and the track begins under a wooden archway. It is a very beautiful area displaying luxurious growth with high forests, and many bushes and ferns. The trail leads to the **Caledonian Falls** ㉓, the island's only waterfall of note. This shady glen is perfect for a picnic, refreshingly cool even in the summer since the river never dries up. From here you can continue on the Caledonia Trail or via a wide forest trail to **Psilon Dendron**, a trout farm. In the restaurant here you can enjoy a delicious meal before you either take a room for the night, or else take a bus or taxi back to your hotel.

The **Persephone Trail**, named for the Goddess of Spring, is only about three kilometers long. Yet, it offers fine views and notable botanical growth, especially lichens and ferns. Forest roads and tracks near **Mesa Potamos** ㉔ also provide for interesting walks. The foothills of the Troodos Mountains, especially the Omodhos area, are richly endowed with paths and narrow roads. Walks beginning and ending on the main Platres to Omodhos road will often pass through areas with many rare plants. In winter Troodos shows its other face; the vegetation is dormant, and on the Khionistra there is even a blanket of snow.

LIMASSOL

Area Code 05

i **Cyprus Tourism Organization**, 15 Spyrou Araouzou St., tel. 362756, and George A St., Potamostis Germasogeias, tel. 323211.

▭ ⑤⑤⑤ Amathus Beach, Amathus, 9 km east of Limassol, P.O. Box 513, tel. 321152, fax. 327494, very elegant hotel with full services and excellent seaside location; **Elias Beach**, Amathus, 11 km east of Limassol, P.O. Box 4300, tel. 325000, fax. 320880, near ancient Amathus, has a horseback riding center; **Le Meridien Limassol**, 12 km east of Limassol, P.O. Box 6560, tel. 634000, fax. 634222, new luxury hotel, excellent location on the sea; **Churchill Limassol**, 28th October Ave., Ayios Athanasios, P.O. Box 1626, tel. 324444, fax. 323494, refined atmosphere.

⑤⑤ Adonia Beach, Amathus, 9 km east of Limassol, P.O. Box 4434, tel. 321111, fax. 310933; **Ariadne**, 333 28th October St., P.O Box 203, tel. 359666, fax. 357421; **Curium Palace**, 2 Byron St., P.O. Box 4800, tel. 363121, fax. 359293, elegant antique furnishings, convenient location; **Pavemar**, 28th October St., P.O. Box 263, tel. 324535, fax. 324743.

⑤ Continental, 137 Spyros Araouzos St., P.O. Box 398, tel. 362530, fax. 373030, a friendly, family-run hotel, close to Limassol Castle and the Old Town; **Sylva**, 124 Grivas Dighenis St., tel. 321660, fax. 327121; **Trans**, Amathus, 8 km east of Limassol, P.O. Box 4082, tel. 322268, pleasant, clean and reasonably priced hotel; **Aquarius Beach**, Amathus, 5 km east of Limassol, P.O. Box 1748, tel. 322042, small pension with garden.

CAMPING: **Kalymnos (Governors) Beach Camping**, Governors Beach, tel. 632300, 20 km east of Limassol, open year-round.

HOTEL APARTMENTS: **⑤⑤⑤ L'Onda Beach**, George A St., Potamos Yermasoyias, P.O. Box 2000, tel. 321821, fax. 320040, super-deluxe designer suites, horseback riding, squash, tennis, good Cypriot restaurant with orchestra music.

⑤⑤ Azur Beach, Potamos Yermasoyias, P.O. Box 1318, tel. 322667, fax. 321897, good location on the beach, spacious flats, friendly management, bar and restaurant; **Bertha**, Amathus, 9 km east of Limassol, P.O. Box 4017, tel. 322324, fax. 356286; **Lime Gardens**, 4 Tinos St., Potamos Yermasoyias, P.O. Box 3166, tel. 320033; **Old Bridge**, 13 Kranos St., Potamos Yermasoyias, P.O. Box, 3207, tel. 321200, fax. 329421, charming location among citrus trees.

✕ Blue Island, 3 Amathountos Ave., Old Limassol-Nicosia Road, tel. 321466, reliable and popular eatery;

Ladas, 1 Sadi St., tel. 365760, on the Old Harbor, good *meze*, seafood at reasonable prices; **Churchill Limassol**, 28th October St., Ay. Athanasios, tel. 324444, French cuisine; **Maharaja Indian Restaurant**, corner of Rigas Phereos and Grivas Dighenis St., tel. 376451, authentic Indian cuisine; **Porta**, 17 Yenethliou Mitella, tel. 360339, good food, accompanied by guitar music, occasional folk dancing; **Vassilikos**, 252 Ayios Andreas St., tel. 375972, live music Monday through Friday starting at 8 p.m.

☗ Arkhontissa, 103 Makarios Ave., tel. 337788; **Roussos Beach Disco**, Potamos Yermasoyias, 5 km east of Limassol, tel. 322322.

▥ District Archeological Museum, Byron St., across from the Curium Palace Hotel, open in summer Monday through Saturday 7.30 a.m. to 5 p.m., Sunday 10 a.m. to 1 p.m., in winter Monday through Saturday 9 a.m. to 4 p.m., Sunday 10 a.m. to 1 p.m., closed Easter Sunday; **Folk Art Museum**, 253 Ayios Andreas St., open in summer Monday, Wednesday and Friday 8:30 a.m. to 1 p.m. and 4 to 6:30 p.m., Tuesday, Thursday and Saturday 8 a.m. to 12:30 p.m., winter 3 to 5:30 p.m., interesting collection of heirlooms, embroideries, implements and costumes giving the visitor a good idea of fashions and lifestyle in former years; **Limassol Castle**, between Ayia Thekla and Ankara St., near Customs House, tel. 330419, houses a fine **Medieval Museum**, open in summer Monday through Saturday from 9 a.m. to 7:30 p.m., and in winter 9 a.m. to 6 p.m. **Municipal Art Gallery**, tel. 343212, permanent and temporary exhibits, open in summer Monday through Saturday 8:30 a.m. to 1 p.m., Monday, Tuesday, Wednesday and Friday also 4 to 6 p.m., in winter Monday through Saturday 8:30 a.m. to 12:30 p.m.; **Kolossi Castle**, 8 km west of Limassol, reached by bus from Limassol, open daily; **Kourion**, 12 km west of Limassol on the way to Paphos, reached by service taxi from Limassol to Paphos or via bus, which stops in front of Limassol Castle; **Kourion Museum**, in the George McFadden House in Episkopi Village, north of the site of Kourion. The bus to Kourion from Limassol Castle also stops at Episkopi. Bus service Monday through Friday 7:30 a.m. to 2 p.m., Saturday 7.30 a.m. to 1 p.m. **Kolossi**, **Amathus** and **Kourion** castles and the **Temple of Apollo Hylates** are open daily in summer 9 a.m. to 7:30 p.m., in winter Monday through Saturday 9 a.m. to 3 p.m., Sunday 9 a.m. to 2 p.m.

☞ *PLACES OF WORSHIP* (denominations other than Greek Orthodox):
Saint Catherine's Church (Catholic), 2 Jerusalem Street.
The **Greek Evangelical Church of Cyprus**, 10A Platonas.

📅 **Throughout the year**: *Classical Musical Recitals*, in the Dr. Nefen Michaelides Music School.

Beginning of February: *Annual Skiing Competition*, on the slopes of Mount Olympos, Troodos, Cyprus Ski Federation, tel. 02-365340, fax. 02-448777.

8th and 9th week before Easter: *Apokria*, street carnival beginning on the last Thursday before lent.

May: *Anthestiria*, flower festival, Lanition Stadium.

First two weeks of June: *Annual Summer Festival*, an outdoor festival of music, dance, sports, games and plays focusing on a different theme each year.

End of June: *Shakespeare Festival*, at the Kourion Theater.

July and August: *Ancient Greek Drama Festival*, at the Kourion Theater.

July 25-26: *Ayia Paraskevi Day*, at the Ayia Paraskevi Church, Yermasoyias, 5 km east of Limassol.

Late August: *Yermasoyias Festival*, at the Potamos Yermasoyias hotel area, with music, dance and theatrical performances.

Beginning of September: *Limassol Wine Festival*, Municipal Gardens of Limassol, free Cypriot wine from the barrel, local specialities, music and dance performances.

➕ **Hospital**: Limassol Hospital, tel. 363111.

☎ **Central Post Office**, Archbishop Kyprianou St. For afternoon services and poste restante: 1 Gladstone St., tel. 330143.

Telephones (CYTA): Corner of Markos Botsaris and Athens Street.

🚌 *BUSES*: **Bus Station**: Urban buses, Andreas Themistokles St. near Anexartisias St., tel. 370592; **Kemek Station**: To Nicosia and Agros, corner of Irini and Enosis St., tel. 747532; **Kallenos**, to Larnaca from the Old Harbor, tel. 04-654850.

CAR RENTAL: **Chris Self Drive Cars**, 118 Archbishop Makarios Ave., tel. 371891; **Europcar**, 38-40 Omonoias Ave., tel. 316789; **Petsas and Sons**, George I St., Sea Breeze Court, near the Apollonia Beach Hotel, tel. 323672.

SERVICE *(GROUP) TAXIS*: **Akropolis**, 49 Spyrou Araouzou St., tel. 366766; **Kyriakos/Karydas**, 21 Thessalonikis St., tel. 360261, to Nicosia and Paphos; **Makris**, 166 Hellas St., tel. 365550, to Larnaca und Paphos.

🛍 Limassol is a great place for shopping and, if you have the time to compare prices, you can find some bargains.

Material, locally made or imported, can be bought at very reasonable prices. The tailors are known for their fast, high-quality work, and suits made to order are a good buy. Leather goods, such as jackets and handbags, can also be made to order.

PISSOURI

This is a quieter area than Potamos Yermasoyias, with nice sandy beaches.

🛏 🟢🟢🟢 **Colombia Pissouri Beach**, P.O. Box 4042 Limassol, tel. 221201, fax. 221505.

🟢 **Bunch of Grapes Inn**, P.O. Box 200, Pissouri, tel. 221275, fax. 222510.

HOTEL APARTMENTS: **Kotzias**, P.O. Box 120, Pissouri, tel. 221014, fax. 222449.

TROODOS AREA

Area Code 05

AGROS

🛏 🟢🟢 **Rodon**, tel. 521201, fax. 521235, nice view, swimming pool. 🟢 **Vlachos**, tel. 528930, cozy, family-style hotel.

❌ **Meteora**, a simple tavern on the village's main street, large selection of typical regional dishes, including soups and stews, excellent *meze*, tel. 521331.

Those who feel they might have drunk a little too much of the local wine can also get good basic lodging at the tavern.

PLATRES

ℹ️ Information office of the **Cyprus Toursim Organization**, main square of Pano Platres, tel. 421316, open April through October.

🛏 🟢🟢🟢 **Forest Park**, P.O. Box 18, tel. 421751, fax. 421875, with 80 rooms.

🟢🟢 **Edelweiss**, P.O. Box 35, tel. 421335, fax. 422060; **New Helvetia**, P.O. Box 111, Limassol, tel. 421348, fax. 422148.

HOTEL APARTMENTS: **Paul's**, tel. 421425.

❌ **Psilo Dendro**, large forest inn on the edge of the village beside a trout-breeding facility, tel. 421350. Only open until 4 p.m. except in August, lots of tour groups.

TROODOS

🛏 🟢🟢 **Jubilee**, tel. 421647, fax. 421628, situated in a pine forest, nature trails, close to the Sun Valley ski area.

YOUTH HOSTEL: Located 400 meters from Troodos Square on the Kakopetria-Troodos Road, tel. 422400, open April through October.

CAMPING: **Troodos Camping Site**, tel. 421624, licensed by the CTO, 2 km from Troodos, off the main Troodos-Kakopetria Road, open from May through October.

🎿 *SKIING*: Drag lift in service at the Khionistra from late December to late February, tel. 02-365340.

Limassol

APHRODITE'S HOME

PAPHOS
SOUTHEAST OF PAPHOS
PALEA PAPHOS
AYIOS NEOPHYTOS
AKAMAS PENINSULA
POLIS / PAPHOS FOREST
NATURE WALKS

Paphos

PAPHOS

Of the six districts of Cyprus, Paphos is the richest in historical sites, legends and traditions. The Paphos District, known for its stunning landscapes and varied flora and fauna, has beaches that curve lazily along the coast for kilometers. Some of the other outlying stretches, with their clear turquoise water, appear almost totally deserted. Many of the legends are connected with Aphrodite, the Goddess of Love, who is said to have risen from the sea off the Paphos coast. The city of Palea Paphos (Old Paphos) was already characterized as Aphrodite's residence in the Homeric period. It was the place where elaborate and sensual rituals were incorporated into her worship. According to Homer's *Odyssey* "...laughter-loving Aphrodite went to Cyprus and to Paphos, where is her precinct and fragrant altars."

Palea Paphos, 16 kilometers from Nea Paphos, was the original inhabited center of the Paphos District. It remained the center of worship for the cult of Aphrodite after the population was shifted to Nea Paphos in 310 B.C.

Preceding pages: Aphrodite is said to have risen from the sea near these rocks, called "Petra tou Romiou." Left: Taking a break from sightseeing at a café in Paphos.

Paphos is the general name now given to the large settlement divided into the twin cities of Ktima and Nea Paphos. Situated on a hill about 1.5 kilometers from the harbor stands Pano Paphos (Upper Paphos), called Ktima by locals, the center for administrative offices and public services.

Nea Paphos (New Paphos) is the Roman city, also called Kato Paphos (Lower Paphos), on the harbor. It contains most of the major historical sites, luxury hotels and upscale restaurants, and is the hub of nightlife. The picturesque coast outside Nea Paphos has become known as the "Cypriot Riviera."

Pano Paphos

Pano Paphos, also called **Ktima ❶**, is the capital of the district. Frequent buses make the trip uphill from Nea Paphos. If you are coming here by car, you should park in one of the town's five public parking lots and walk to the sights. It takes about 20 minutes on foot to reach the District Museum from the western lot. The bustling **Market Hall ❶** off Agoras Street, north of the western parking lot, is worth visiting.

Ktima is quite attractive and well-tended. It benefits from a properly-developed town plan, noticeably absent

in Nea Paphos, that provides for tasteful new construction fitting in with the older neoclassical buildings. The **Town Hall** ❷, for example, is surrounded by landscaped gardens. The **Central Post Office** ❸, the **Telecommunications Office (CYTA)** ❹, the **Tourist Information Office** ❺, most of the town's budget hotels, and many travel agents are here. The town, which lies on a plateau about 45 meters above sea level, is cooled by sea breezes that make it comfortable even in the height of summer. The panoramic vistas from up here are impressive, especially at sunset.

Ktima was probably inhabited from the time of the raids on Nea Paphos by Arab pirates, beginning in A.D. 647. For safety, the townspeople moved to their country estates, called *ktima* in Greek, on higher ground which was less visible from the sea but afforded them a bird's eye view of boats carrying invaders.

Above: Mulling over current affairs at the local "kafenion."

Few of the buildings in Ktima are especially old, the oldest of all probably being the **Djami Kebir Mosque** ❻ at the northwest end of town. It was built over the foundation of an earlier Christian church in 1584.

The ***District Museum** ❼ on Grivas Dighenis Avenue, on the right side as you enter the town from Limassol Road, is the most notable museum in Paphos, containing an eclectic and ever-expanding collection of archeological artifacts. Interesting objects in the collection, dating from Neolithic to Renaissance times, include Mycenaean stirrup jars and an assortment of jewelry from the 15th century B.C. to the third century A.D., notably exquisite winged cherub earrings and a playful early Hellenic lion getting ready to pounce. Coins dating from the sixth and fifth centuries B.C. are from the Kingdom of Paphos, while bronze Roman coins feature the Temple of Aphrodite at Palea Paphos.

The bones of a young woman found in Lemba-Lakkous indicate she was at least

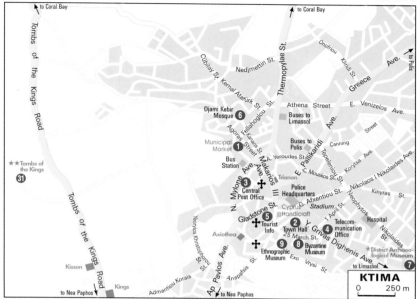

Paphos

1.70 meters in height, remarkably tall for the third century B.C., although other early settlements, such as Neolithic Teppes at Sotira, had inhabitants of about the same average height. Notable statues on exhibit include a marble Greco-Roman torso of Aphrodite dredged from the sea near Nea Paphos, a perfectly preserved statuette of Asclepius holding the staff and serpent, signs of healing, and a bust which might be a likeness of the owner of the House of Dionysus. The most amusing display perhaps is a set of Roman clay hot water bottles, which were molded to fit the shape of the body part to be heated, from the extremities to more intimate areas.

The smaller **Byzantine Museum** ❽ is housed in a section of the Bishop's Palace on Andrea Ioannou Street. On the way there you will pass by the classical Town Hall and the Municipal Park. Dating from the 15th to the17th centuries, especially notable artworks on display here include a *Virgin and Child* painted on a gold background, portraits of the apostles, a *Birth of John the Baptist* from Kedheres, paintings of the Ascension of Christ from Arminou and several nativity scenes.

Just a few steps away from the Byzantine Museum is the fascinating **Ethnographic Museum** ❾ on Exo Vyrsis Street. Privately owned and operated by Professor George S. Eliades and his wife Khrysso, the museum is in a traditional 1894 house with a magnificent oaken door. You have to phone in advance to arrange an appointment with Mrs. Eliades, who will enthusiastically explain the fascinating collection gathered over the last 50 years, which provides a glimpse into the rural households of many years ago.

The kitchen is furnished with pots, pans and various other cooking utensils. The charming bedroom is decorated with white lace and embroidered bed linen, and nightgowns, with some 18th and 19th century costumes on display, all of which were fastidiously made by the bride as part of her *prika* or "trousseau." A collection of *sandoukia*, or wooden chests in which the dowries were stored, is prominently displayed.

Other display cases have coins, seals and pottery, as well as fossils dating back millions of years. In the garden are massive olive-presses, grindstones, oxen yokes, ovens and a restored fountain, once the focal point of social activity in small communities. Also outside is a third-century B.C. tomb once used as a catacomb and later a prison.

Nea Paphos

Follow Apostolos Pavlos Avenue as it winds down the hill and ends up at the Nea Paphos Harbor. **Nea Paphos ❷** was a sleepy town with only a few hotels and pensions until the 1970s, following the partition of the island. The tourist boom that hit Paphos was facilitated by the 1983 opening of its own international airport. Today it is almost impossible to find undeveloped seaside close to Nea Paphos, yet building continues on almost every vacant patch of land.

In recent years, conservationists have intervened to halt further development of the largely unspoiled Akamas Peninsula to the north, and new construction in the town itself is more closely regulated in respect to aesthetic qualities.

Despite the sudden growth, tourism in Nea Paphos is conducted on a dignified and upscale level. Many Cypriot and foreign families choose Paphos for their summer holidays, often returning year after year. The town is relatively quiet, since all establishments except discos close at midnight at the inhabitants' request. In 1980, Nea Paphos was included in the UNESCO list of World Heritage Sites.

Nea Paphos was founded around 310 B.C. by Nicocles, the last ruler of the Kingdom of Paphos. It replaced Palea Paphos as the major settlement just before the Ptolemies abolished the Cypriot city-states.

Under the Ptolemies, Nea Paphos became the capital of the island, replacing Salamis. It was a natural choice for the seat of the government and for a ship-building center, with lumber supplied by nearby forests. The town was prosperous and mostly peaceful during Roman times (58 B.C. to A.D. 395). Remains of most of the main monuments, except for the Tombs of the Kings, are from the Roman Period. Nea Paphos was repeatedly damaged by earthquakes. After two seismic catastrophes in A.D 332 and 342, Salamis was chosen once again as the capital, and Nea Paphos declined.

Inhabitants began to move to Ktima, the estates located on the hill above Nea Paphos, after Saracen pirate raids started in A.D. 647. In that year, the first large-scale Arab naval operation led by Emir Muawiya of Syria against Cyprus took place. Moslem attacks on the island continued until 911. The political situation during these years seems hazy, but the island was probably never completely controlled by the Arabs.

The important Byzantine castle on the harbor was the site of Paphos' surrender to Richard the Lionhearted in 1191, ushering in the Lusignan Era. At the end of the 11th century the Lusignans built the castle of Saranta Kolones on the site, a well-fortified structure destroyed by an earthquake in 1222. Instead of restoring it, they built the less impressive fortress remaining on the harbor.

The population was gradually depleted during the brief Genoese rule (1372-74). Before the end of the Lusignan Period (1489), Nea Paphos was deserted by its inhabitants after it was almost completely destroyed by earthquakes. In 1608, the Venetian Victor Zembetos led an unsuccessful rebellion against the Turks in Paphos.

By 1800, the population of Nea Paphos was barely 1,000, but this had more than doubled by 1881. This growth was spurred by the greater economic prosper-

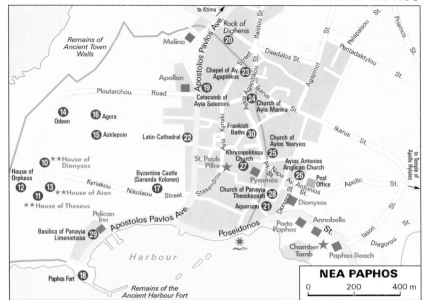

Paphos

istry during Roman times, when Paphos was the center of mosaic production. Inspired by master mosaic artists in Alexandria, Egypt, the striking mosaics found in Paphos were made with small cubes of marble and stone called *tesserae*, with glass paste added to give a wider range of color. The entrance to the site of the Roman villas, still being excavated, is at the end of Kyriakou Nikolaou Street, 300 meters from the harbor. On the right is a wooden reconstruction of the **★★House of Dionysus** ⑩, named for its representations of pleasure-loving Dionysus, God of Wine, in several of the main mosaics. The house, built in the late second or early third century A.D., was one of the largest Roman villas, with more than 2,000 square meters of floor space. Of these, 556 square meters in 14 rooms are covered with glorious mosaics. Over 40 rooms on two levels were built in an atrium style around a colonnaded courtyard with a rain cistern.

Many smaller rooms on the lower level, which had an advanced under-

ity caused by the dredging of the silted harbor in 1908. The population of the town has steadily increased since that time, and is now at about 24,000 and still growing.

The Mosaics of Paphos

One can walk to all the major archeological sites clustered in the same area on the harbor. For visitors who only have one day to cover Paphos' sights, the Tombs of the Kings, the fort on the harbor (mainly for its excellent view of the entire area) and the mosaics of Paphos are musts. The first stops should be at the Houses of Dionysus, Orpheus and Aion, and the Villa of Theseus, Roman Period villas a short distance from the harbor. In them are the finest mosaics of the eastern Mediterranean, mainly of mythological subjects which were discovered by chance during excavation work in 1962.

The mosaics, decorating both private homes and public buildings, are an indication of the wealth and high level of art-

ground sewage system, were used as kitchens, workshops, stores and offices. The house was located in the middle of a thriving residential area and was bordered by public streets.

All the mosaics in the House of Dionysus are in their original position except for the *Scylla Mosaic*, a black-and-white pebble design dating from an earlier building of the fourth century B.C. Scylla is an ill-fated nymph from Greek mythology, turned into a fish-like monster by Circe, with the the heads of serpents and dogs springing from her waist. The mosaic was lifted from its original setting and is now in the corner of another room.

The first mosaic seen upon entering the house represents Narcissus, the handsome youth who became so enamored of his own reflection in a pool of water that he pined away as a result of his unsatis-

Above: The famous mosaics in the House of Dionysos. Right: Detail of a mosaic depicting a nymph from the "Triumphal Procession of Dionysos."

fied desires and was ultimately transformed into a flower.

Four scenes from Greek mythology are vividly depicted in the **West Gallery** of the atrium. The first represents the poignant legend of Pyramus and Thisbe, the doomed young Babylonian lovers whose story is retold by Ovid in his *Metamorphoses* and also by Shakespeare in his *Midsummer Night's Dream.*

In the second panel, the mythological creation of wine and its tragic consequences are shown: After the legendary King of Attica, Icarius, extended hospitality to Dionysus, the god thanked him by teaching him to plant vines. In the left corner, a very serious Dionysus is shown sitting on a chair and holding grapes, and the nymph Akmi, naked to the waist, sits on the floor.

Icarius, the liaison between the gods and man, is seen proudly leading his ox cart laden with wineskins into town. On the way, he offers some of his product to two shepherds who get roaring drunk after sampling it. The two sodden tipplers

are depicted on the right under a Greek inscription meaning "the first wine drinkers." Icarius, unfortunately, was never able to get any feedback on his first batch because the friends of the crazed shepherds thought he had poisoned them and killed him.

The third mosaic depicts the meeting of the God of the Sea, Poseidon, and Amymone, one of the 50 daughters of Danaus, and the fourth is a wonderfully fluid illustration of the *Metamorphosis of Daphne* into a laurel tree (still called Daphne in Greek) as she flees the pursuing Apollo.

In the **Reception Hall** is the lively *Harvest Mosaic* with different panels depicting men gathering crops close to a variety of animals. Another memorable mosaic shows *Zeus and Ganymede*, with the god in the form of an eagle carrying off the Trojan youth Ganymede.

The *Four Seasons Mosaic* in the **Hall of Mother Earth** is remarkably expressive. The cubical designs and symmetrical proportions in the nine panels, with personifications of the four seasons represented in each corner, create an optical illusion that reveals a different aspect of their faces whenever the viewer shifts position. There are ten figures in the long panel of the *Triumph of Dionysus Mosaic*, including several exotic figures who hint at Indian origins and, of course, Dionysus himself, wreathed in grape leaves on a chariot that is being drawn by two panthers.

A wooden catwalk over unexcavated mosaics leads to the once enormous ****Villa of Theseus** ⓫, 150 meters to the southwest. First excavated in 1965 by the Polish archeological team of Warsaw University, it originally had more than 100 rooms and corridors, indicating it was once part of the palace of the Roman governor. Its name comes from the elegant circular mosaic of the battle in the Cretan Labyrinth between the celebrated Athenian hero Theseus and the Minotaur, made in the third century and restored after an earthquake in the fourth century A.D. Other mosaics show *Poseidon and*

Amphitrite riding on the back of a sea monster, and the *First Bath of Achilles* after his birth.

To the west is the **House of Orpheus** ⑫, systematically excavated since 1982, though only a three-paneled mosaic has been discovered. In one scene you see the naked *Herakles Fighting the Lion of Nemea*, in the second an *Amazon with Her Horse*, and the third has a wonderful scene depicting *Orpheus Playing the Lyre*, surrounded by transfixed animals.

The mosaics in the more recently discovered **★★House of Aion** ⑬ next door are considered to be the most significant late-Roman mosaic panels in Cyprus. These include the *Birth of Dionysus*, the *Triumph of Dionysus*, the *Judgment of Marsyas* and the beauty contest between *Cassiopeia and the Nereids* judged by Aion, the God of Eternity. Perhaps the most provocative mosaic and the one most often associated with Paphos on posters and postcards is *Leda and the Swan*, the shapely semi-clad Queen of Sparta being approached by Zeus in the form of a swan. The artistry of these panels is of an exceptionally high level, with rich colors and an outstanding grasp of expression. More importantly in iconographic terms is their identification with inscriptions.

A coin of Licinius I minted A.D. 317-323 imbedded in the pavement shows that the mosaics must have been made in the second half of the fourth century, when Christianity had become a recognized religion, though curiously these panels glorify paganism and ignore the former's influence.

The Acropolis

The ruins of a complex of buildings, the Odeon, Agora and Temple of Asclepius, are under the modern lighthouse,

Right: Today, Paphos Fort stands guard over peaceful Paphos Harbor.

probably the site of the town's acropolis judging from Hellenistic and Greco-Roman fragments unearthed there. To the north of the lighthouse are extensive remains of the ancient town walls, a ramp and a rock bridge leading across a moat. Southeast of the lighthouse is the inviting **Roman Odeon** ⑭, built in the second century A.D. A semicircle with 11 restored rows out of the original 25 provides seating for about 1,200 spectators. From the top rows of the theater, one has a clear view of the handsomely restored orchestra and stage, a pleasant setting for occasional summer performances.

To the south stood the **Asclepion** ⑮, the Roman Temple of Asclepius, the God of Medicine, used as a medical center noted for its fasts designed to purge the system. Those cured sacrificed a rooster in gratitude. Little remains of this large building, which had three rooms with direct access to the Odeon and Agora.

The Odeon, adjoining the **Agora** ⑯ (market and town square) to the east and the Asclepion to the south, represents the essence of the ancient civic center. They are grouped together in typical Greco-Roman fashion so that inhabitants could easily shop, meet, worship and go to the theater within the same day.

To get to the **Saranta Kolones Castle** ⑰, head east to Apostolos Pavlos Avenue and then south, turning right on Kyriakou Nikolaou Street. The castle's name, "Forty Columns," refers to the granite columns from destroyed Roman public buildings which previously lay scattered over the area and which were incorporated into the castle.

Built by the Lusignans in the early 13th century, probably on the site of an earlier Byzantine castle, it was surrounded by a three-meter-thick wall once defended by eight towers of various shapes. It was largely destroyed by an earthquake in 1222. Some exceptionally beautiful examples of glazed pottery have been found on the site.

Paphos

The Harbor

The most prominent building in the harbor is **Paphos Fort** ⓲. The harbor promenade is the main gathering place for residents of Paphos and their vacationing guests. A tame and photogenic pelican also feels at home here, and is regularly fed by the waiters of the nearby seafood restaurants.

The history of the fort reflects much of that of Paphos. Originally built as a Byzantine citadel to protect the harbor, it was reconstructed by the Lusignans in the mid 13th century to replace the **Saranta Kolones Castle**. Dismantled in 1570 by the Venetians, who found themselves unable to defend it against the Ottomans, it was restored and strengthened by the Turks after they occupied the island. In 1580-92, as inscribed over the entrance, the Turks under Governor Ahmet Pasha rebuilt the west tower.

During British rule it was used for salt storage. It was finally declared a protected monument in 1935. The fort was damaged by an earthquake in 1953. Beyond the vaulted central hall, rooms lead to the cells used when the castle was a prison, with dungeons below. Walk up the steps to the roof to get an excellent panoramic view of the entire setting. To the northwest is an oval depression which could be the site of another theater. Submerged remains of an ancient extension of the fort lie to the southeast towards the Moulia Rocks.

The Catacombs

Undoubtedly the most unusual monuments of Nea Paphos are the Catacombs of Ayia Solomoni and Ayios Lambrianos. To get to them go north on Apostolos Pavlos Avenue past Ploutarckou Road, and on the right, opposite the Hotel Apollon, you will come to **Fabrica Hill**. The catacombs were carved into the hillside, just below the Roman city wall, in the fourth century B.C., and were later converted into chapels in the early days of Christianity.

At the entrance to the underground **Catacomb of Ayia Solomoni** ⑲ is a huge pistachio tree, *Pistacia atlantica*, a species from which is gathered the fairly bland *Pissa Paphitiki* gum that is sold in local shops. The tree looks very strange to the uninitiated because it is covered with bits of cloth left by the faithful as votive offerings to Ayia Solomoni, a custom of both Christians and Moslems in the eastern Mediterranean. According to one version of her story, Ayia Solomoni is a popular saint whose seven sons were martyred in the second century A.D. for their beliefs.

Her catacomb chapel, originally a Hellenistic chamber tomb and believed by some to have also been a synagogue, is lit only by a few flickering candles, so it is helpful to have a flashlight to light your way and to better view the ninth-century frescoes, partially damaged by graffiti at

an early date and later by visiting crusaders in the 13th century. A fresco fragment behind the former altar, *The Heavenly Communion of the Apostles,* was painted in the 12th century. Going from the forecourt and over a few steps, a well is reached, the water of which pilgrims once drank as a cure for eye problems. Today the water would more probably make you ill.

The large rock to the northeast is called the **Rock of Dighenis** ⑳. According to legend, the local hero Dighenis threw it at the Queen of Paphos when she reneged on her promise to marry him if he supplied fresh water to the city.

She retaliated by throwing her spindle at him, which was transformed into a large granite column, a nearby landmark. This spirited courtship apparently rekindled the couple's love affair, for they married after all.

A brand new tourist attraction in Paphos is the **Aquarium** ㉑ on Artemidios Street, which has displays of Mediterranean aquatic life.

Above: Votive offerings left at the Catacomb of Ayia Solomoni. Right: Khrysopolitissa Church beside the remains of its predecessor.

Churches of Paphos

Most of the churches in Paphos are clustered on the east side of town. The scant remains of the late-13th-century **Latin Cathedral** ㉒ consists of the south-western corner with part of the ribbed vaulting on the right going down to the harbor. It was restored by Francesco Contarini, the last Bishop of Paphos, who was killed during the fall of Nicosia.

Rocks overhanging Apostolos Pavlos Avenue were favorite hermit retreats. One of the caves carved from sandstone was the honeymoon hideaway for Dighenis and his royal bride. It has since been converted into a tiny chapel dedicated to **Ayios Agapitikos** ㉓, the Patron Saint of Lovers. It is said that lighting a candle here and dedicating it to someone will win his or her affection. Nearby is a chapel named for the far less popular **Ayios Misitikos** or the Saint of Hate, a corruption of the name of the original inhabitant Themistos, just as Agapetos is said to be the model for Ayios Agapitikos.

The ruined 15th-century **Church of Ayia Marina** ㉔ lies south of here. In its interior is a white marble column with a Greek inscription recording the gift of Deacon Isidoros. The ruined **Church of Ayios Yeoryios** ㉕ farther south is notable because of the medieval tombstones of the Beduins, one of the earliest Latin families to settle in Cyprus. Thomas Beduin is mentioned as having a position in the court in A.D. 1223.

Ayios Antonios ㉖, just southeast, has been restored for use by the Church of England. It was a double nave Byzantine-style church, but the southern nave was destroyed. A fluted marble Roman pedestal is its most outstanding artifact.

The **Church of Ayia Kyriaki**, better known as **Khrysopolitissa** ㉗, to the southwest, was built after 1571 on the site of an early Christian basilica of the fourth century. Sections of a delightful mosaic pavement, uncovered between the road and the apse, are remains of the earlier huge seven-nave basilica, the main structure of which was 53 meters long and 38 meters wide. Four pink granite columns must have supported the roof of the eastern wing. Partially covered acanthus capitals of green and white *Cipollino* marble imported from the Greek island of Evia, as well as a few tombstones, lie on the grounds. The item attracting the most attention is a rounded white marble pillar under a tree at the west gateway. According to local tradition, this is the place at which Saint Paul is said to have been bound and flogged by Romans with a special 39-tailed whip for daring to preach the new religion.

The **Church of Panayia Theoskepasti** ㉘ to the south is named the "Church of Our Lady Veiled by God," from a legend stating that Arabs planning to sack it under the command of Abu-Alur in the seventh century were thwarted when a thick mist shrouded it so that they could not find it. Eventually the original church was destroyed. It was replaced in 1923 by the current one.

To the west of the Pelican Inn, close to the harbor, is the **Panayia Limeniotissa Basiclica** ㉙ (Our Lady of the Harbor), originally an early Christian basilica severely damaged by Arabs in 653. According to the monk Neophytos, it was destroyed by an earthquake in 1153. The **Frankish Baths** ㉚, substantial Lusignan remains north of the Khrysopolitissa Church, are near Ayios Antonios Church, to which they were once connected. Built in the late 14th to early 15th century, they are easily overlooked because they are partially subterranean. Its typical Ottoman-style domes were added in the early years of the Turkish occupation.

Tombs of the Kings

The intriguing burial area known as the ★★**Tombs of the Kings** ㉛ (see map page 103) is almost two kilometers northwest

Right: "Tombs of the Kings," the final resting place of the Ptolemaic aristocracy.

of Paphos Harbor, just off Tombs of the Kings Road heading towards Coral Bay.

Despite its name, the more than 100 graves serving as the town's necropolis from the third century B.C. to the third century A.D. were originally the final resting place of Ptolemaic aristocracy, not royalty. The area is known as *Paleokastra*, "Old Castles," and to the north is the *Paleoekklisia*, the "Old Church" which has traces of Byzantine frescoes.

Excavations continue at the Tombs of the Kings under the direction of archeologist Sophokles Hadjisavvas of the Cyprus Department of Antiquities, and treasures are often unearthed.

The tombs carved into the reddish rock overhanging the sea are barely visible from afar. These elegant funereal monuments, especially those in the north with frescoed walls, were no doubt inspired by tombs in the Hellenistic necropolis of Alexandria, since no prototype for the design existed in Cyprus.

A map at the entrance notes the location of the most interesting tombs, including **Tombs 3** and **4**, the latter being the best preserved. **Tomb 5** is very grand with its 12 elaborate Doric columns surrounding a spacious peristyle courtyard and rock-carved entablatures in the style of the dwellings of the time.

In **Tomb 7**, bones of a horse and its owner once buried together are preserved under glass. **Tomb 8** was originally thought to be a royal tomb because the courtyard near it is decorated with a limestone falcon, the Ptolemaic royal symbol, but it is now assumed it held the remains of an affluent Ptolemy.

Some of the tombs, marked by a cross, were reused during Christian times, others were inhabited by gypsies in modern times. A well carved into the walls of most of the darkened rooms off the courtyards is symbolic of the purification and expiation of the deceased's soul.

A rock-cut chamber tomb lying below the Annabelle Hotel, just behind the Mu-

nicipal Gardens on the eastern seaside, may be visited by applying at the reception desk.

The municipal beach on the east side of Nea Paphos is crowded and unimpressive, while many hotels in Nea Paphos have their own, far more appealing private beaches and pools. Some hotels will let non-guests use them for a small fee added to a bar or restaurant tab.

Funeral Customs

From ancient Greek authors, we learn that the belief in life after death was very strong, so much so that in Athens it was incorporated into Solon's laws. A vast array of funeral customs also existed in the ancient Hellenistic society of Cyprus, varying from place to place.

The body – or ashes and bones, if the person died far from home – was always put into a family necropolis. The deceased's possessions, such as jewelry, plus jars filled with olives, were placed around the body bound in woven mate-

rial. If the deceased had committed suicide, the corpse's right hand was cut off and the funeral was carried out without a public ceremony. A coin, sometimes placed in the corpse's mouth, was for the boatman Charon's fare, collected to ferry the deceased across the River Styx to face his or her final judgement in the Kingdom of the Dead.

Vestiges of ancient customs can still be found today in Cyprus. After the *necrodipna*, a meal eaten by the relatives of the deceased gathered around the tomb, a small amount of wine was spilled for the gods' health, and the leftovers of the meal, including the ashes, were thrown on the grave, a custom known as *pyra*. Judging from offerings found buried in a stratified manner, this was observed on a yearly basis.

In some places, such as the village of Argaka in the Paphos District, a modified version of this custom honoring the dead is often still celebrated, although the funerary meal is usually eaten in a restaurant these days.

SOUTHEAST OF PAPHOS

To delve into the legend of Aphrodite, take an excursion from Nea Paphos to Yeroskipos, and then to Kouklia, ending up at Petra tou Romiou, the seaside where the goddess emerged.

Two roads lead to Yeroskipos from Nea Paphos, the first directly from Ktima (Upper Paphos), the other built along the ancient pilgrims' path from the harbor. The latter route starts from the small road in front of the SODAP Wine Cooperative plant at the east end of the harbor. It climbs gently through recently cultivated peanut crops, source of the tasty roasted snack known as *kounes*, a favorite Cypriot treat. To the left of the road between Nea Paphos and Yeroskipos stands a small sanctuary, the **Temple of Apollo Hylates**, dedicated to the god Apollo Hylates according to inscriptions in the Cypro-syllabic script carved into the rock

over the entrance. This is evidence of the blending of a local cult of Hylates (God of the Woodland) with the god Apollo, as was also the case in Kourion. This unique temple from the fourth century B.C. has one circular and one rectangular subterranean chamber carved into rock. According to some sources, they might have been the chambers of an oracle who uttered prophesies to the guardian of the sanctuary, a counterpart of the famed Oracle of Apollo at Delphi.

Yeroskipos ❸ (from the Greek *Ieros Kipos*, meaning "The Sacred Garden"), was a resting place for pilgrims on their way to the springtime celebrations at the Temple of Aphrodite. On the south slopes of the village, amid the flowering fruit-tree orchard with doves cooing in the background, the pause no doubt included some of the sensual activities so closely associated with the Goddess of Love. The garden no longer exists.

Yeroskipos was one of the silk manufacturing centers active on the island, as its many mulberry trees suggest. Between

Above: An idyllic cove on Coral Bay. Right: The Church of Ayia Paraskevi, Yeroskipos.

Map p. 116, Info pp. 134-135

1925 and 1950 a silk factory operated here. Today its claim to fame is the manufacture of the sweet grape-flavored jelly known as *loukoumi* or Turkish Delight, created four centuries ago during the Ottoman Period and served in Istanbul's Seraglio in the Topkapi Palace.

Along the main road of the town, children and their black-clad *yiayiades* (grandmothers) lurk under parasols protecting them from the scorching sun, waiting for customers to buy boxes of the traditional sweets.

Most of the remaining buildings date from Byzantine times. The most outstanding Byzantine building in town is the five-domed **Church of Ayia Paraskevi**, similar to the only other one of this type left on the island in Peristerona. It was originally cruciform, but was altered by unfortunate enlargements in the 19th century and again in 1931, yet it still retains its ageless charm. The church contains some fine ninth to 15th-century frescoes, including *Jesus Entering Jerusalem*, *The Resurrection of Lazarus,* and a fragment of *The Betrayal* beneath the dome, which in itself is notable for its details of the soldiers' medieval armor and weapons. An icon depicting the Virgin and Child is unusual because it has a crucifixion painted on its reverse side. If the church is closed, ask the shoemaker next door for the key.

The 18th-century **House of Hadji Smith**, now a folk museum, is to the east. It was the residence of Andreas Zimboulakis, named British Vice-Consul in 1799 by William Sydney Smith. To honor his benefactor, Andreas assumed the name of Hadji Smith (*Hadji* was attached to the names of Christians who had made the pilgrimage to Jerusalem). The upper story of the museum has wooden balconies which impart the elegance of villas of the time. Its collection includes farming and domestic implements, Cypriot costumes, carved gourds, and a quaint painted grandfather clock.

Opportunities for swimming can be found on the beach of the Cyprus Tourism Organization, located about three kilometers southwest of Yeroskipos. A grassy strip borders the sand beach, upon which it is very pleasant to sit on windy days. There are chaise longues, beach umbrellas, showers and snack bars here.

The former Turkish Cypriot village of **Koloni** ❹ is the site of government shelters built in 1974 for refugees from the northern part of the island. Koloni is famed for its pottery; red earthenware painted in natural colors. The **Savvas Shop** on the left side of the road has a good selection of vases, bowls and plates, and a small workshop in which you can actually watch the potters creating this authentic handicraft. Two kilometers from here on a small road forking to the left is the abandoned **Anatolikon Monastery** and its interesting Medieval **Church of Ayios Kharalambos**.

Crossing the wide Ezousa River, which irrigates all of the experimental farms and greenhouses in this area where the bulk of

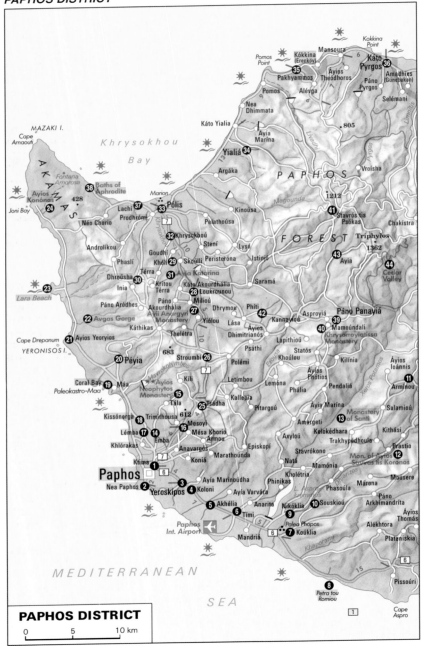

PAPHOS DISTRICT

0   5   10 km

Paphos' vegetables and fruits are produced, one enters the village of **Akhelia** ❺. Its name is derived from the French *L'Échelle*, meaning "ladder," though most likely the name of the Lusignan owner. Its importance during the Middle Ages stemmed from it being one of the bailiwicks of Paphos Province. The area was also part of the thriving sugar industry along with Kouklia, Lemba, Kolossi and Episkopi. Akhelia is mainly an agricultural center now, but has a few interesting churches. The **Church of Ayios Theodosios** from the 12th century was built in a cruciform plan with a cupola and is decorated with astonishing frescoes painted three centuries later. Its altar was made of Roman marble.

Historian Rupert Gunnis describes a delicately colored Virgin and Child icon in the **Church of Ayios Yeoryios**, dating from the early 16th century when the church was built. Sadly enough, the remarkable Renaissance iconostasis was sold by the See of Paphos in 1889, and is now in the Victoria and Albert Museum in London. The **Ayios Leonidos Chapel**, which has been restored, is close to the sea. It was once surrounded by Roman pillars and capitals, now displayed in the Paphos District Museum.

The new road to the **Paphos International Airport** leads to **Timi** ❻, meaning "honor," possibly founded by Greeks from the Peloponnese in 1200 B.C., a story given credence by the discovery of a Bronze Age site within the village. The Byzantine **Church of Ayia Sophia** was used as a mosque until 1975. Its frescoes, said to have covered the walls, are coated in whitewash.

This village and **Anarita**, only a few kilometers to the northwest, are renowned for the distinctive flavor of their *haloumi* cheese made from the milk of both sheep and goats, which are fed thyme. Anarita has a cheese festival in May, a festive time to visit and taste the delicious *anari*, the creamy whey which

gives the village its name. Timi also makes excellent sausage. Buy samples of these here, add bread and a bottle of local wine, and you have the fixings for a splendid picnic in Timi's cool eucalyptus forest next to the sea.

Back on the main road, 3.5 kilometers after crossing the turnoff to the airport is a road on the left leading to **Asprokremmos Dam**, one of the three in the Paphos District at which fishing is allowed. **Mandria**, the vegetable-producing center with the largest farms of the Paphos District, is at the next turnoff to the right. Three kilometers further along, after crossing three rivers, you arrive at **Palea Paphos** ❼ (Old Paphos), the village now called **Kouklia**, surrounded by orchards and farms.

PALEA PAPHOS

Two possible founders of the **Temple of Aphrodite** emerged in ancient legend. According to Pausanias' version, it was built by Agapenor, the Arcadian King of Tegea, who was driven by storm winds onto Cyprus' shores while on his way home. The more likely founder, however, was wealthy King Kinyras, father of Adonis, who lived to a ripe old age while ruling Paphos during the time of the Trojan War. He was the first of the priest-kings, who developed religious rites adapted to the worship of Aphrodite and later Adonis. He was said to be very wealthy, in fact even more than the legendary King Croesus. Kinyras' successors, called *Kynirades*, ruled until Ptolemy I replaced them with military governors in 295 B.C.

Kouklia was continuously inhabited from the 15th century B.C. until the end of the Middle Ages. During the Mycenaean migrations of the late 13th and 12th centuries B.C., Achaean Greeks settled here. The wealth of this Late Bronze Age city must have been enormous judging from sumptuous artifacts found in the

Paphos

tombs of ancient cemeteries. The first historically authenticated king of Paphos was Ituander or Eteandros, whose name was recorded on an inscription of the Assyrian King Assarhaddon in 673 and 672 B.C. During the Cypro-Archaic and Classical Periods (seventh to fourth centuries B.C.), Paphos reached the zenith of its influence. In the Ionian Revolt of 499 B.C., Paphos sided with the other Greek cities against the Persians, who retaliated by attacking the city in 498 B.C. In 480 B.C., Paphos contributed 12 ships to the fleet of King Xerxes.

Nicocles, the last king of Paphos, named Nea Paphos as the new capital around 310 B.C., and it eventually overshadowed Palea Paphos. Although Palea Paphos' population shrank during the Hellenic Period and was further depleted after the serious damage caused by earthquakes in 15 B.C. and A.D. 323, the sanctuary continued to prosper until the fourth

Above: Quantity, rather than quality, sometimes rules the market.

century A.D. It was often visited by Roman emperors, and athletic contests were organized in their honor. Palea Paphos declined in the late fourth century A.D., after Emperor Theodosius ordered all pagan temples to be closed by decree. It only flourished once again during the Lusignan Period, when Kouklia became the center of the sugar industry. Extensive sugar plantations were reported in the area, and the fine crystal sugar produced in the factories of the district was highly valued on the international market.

Palea Paphos sits on the plateau of a limestone hill about 1.5 kilometers from the sea. The prize object unearthed here was a unique cone-shaped black stone. This fertility symbol was anointed with oil and worshiped at ancient festivals of Aphrodite. It is now on display in the Lusignan Manor Museum at the site. The worship of Aphrodite was in this amorphous rather than human form, similar to the worship of other fertility goddesses in the Middle East.

Many fragments of smaller marble versions of the original were discovered during the initial excavations in 1888 by the British School in Athens. In 1950, the British Kouklia Expedition began excavations, joined by a German expedition a decade later.

For those whose lively imaginations can mentally embellish the melancholy traces of the ravages of time, the site will be rewarding. For others, the few remains of the once-impressive sanctuary might prove to be disappointing and confusing. Archeologists speculate that the main buildings of the sanctuary lie under the nearby farm houses and only the central structures have been revealed. The Paphian Temple of Aphrodite never resembled a typical Greek temple, but instead was a sanctuary similar to those found in Asia Minor and on Cyprus at Soli in the northern part of the island. Roman coins are the only source of depictions of the original temple, and they show a remarkable similarity in the details.

The site actually consists of two sanctuaries. The southern one was rebuilt by Romans on a Bronze Age site, and it was divided into a *temenos*, or sacred enclosure, with altars and a covered hall. The northern sanctuary was rebuilt in A.D. 77. It has a couple of halls and an east wing with an open courtyard. Like all of Aphrodite's temples it is said to be cooled by gentle breezes perfumed with flowers and herbs. A spot near the south wall of the north stoa is marked by a limestone monolith to indicate the location of the holy fertility symbol. The most curious feature of this altar was that it was in the open air, yet the rain never fell upon it. Only wall foundations, column bases and sections of Roman mosaics remain, with more mosaics in the ruins of a house west of the north sanctuary. Some of the stone was quarried in the Middle Ages to construct a Frankish sugar refinery.

Although the buildings and rites of the worship of Aphrodite are referred to by a great many classical writers, they all remain shrouded in mystery because no precise information can be gleaned from them. The fame of the cult of Aphrodite is due to an oral tradition. In this manner, the orgiastic pagan rituals connected with the sanctuary captured the popular imagination and attracted visitors from all over the ancient world.

According to these reports, the annual Aphrodite festival, with its contests and games, was the most popular in Paphos. Pilgrims wearing myrtle crowns filed in a dignified procession, accompanied by music, along the 14-kilometer-long sacred path that started at the harbor and ended at the shrine of the Goddess of Love. On their first visit, worshipers had to give a coin to the priests, in return for which they received a small piece of salt, symbolic of Aphrodite's birth in the sea, and a ceramic phallus, a memento of the fertility cult.

Prudish writers disapproved of what they labeled "religious prostitution" that was practiced in strategically-placed pleasure booths and pleasure benches in lush gardens. The historian Herodotus, in his usual imaginative manner, wove a tale about the custom that every young Paphian woman, rich or poor, had to serve as a priestess and sit in the temple wearing a plaited rope headband until an admirer claimed her by throwing a coin at her feet and saying, "I invoke the goddess upon you." The coins went to the temple and the woman to the man. After he initiated her into sexual practices, she could go home.

"All those who are beautiful and well-built finished quickly," reported Herodotus. "But the ugly ones had to stay a long time. There are some who waited as long as three or four years." It seems that during the Roman Period the custom had degenerated and was an excuse for rampant prostitution.

Southwest of the temple is a **museum** in the former Lusignan Manor House,

Paphos

originally called the *Château de Covocle* and later called the *Çiftlik*, because it was the manor of a large farm (Turkish: *çiftlik*) during the Turkish Period. It was originally an administrative center for the sugar factories in the Paphos area. All that survives of the original Frankish structure is the stately Gothic hall in the east wing, with four bays distinguished by dramatic 13th-century French-style arches.

The manor is now a museum, the prize display of which is the fertility stone of Aphrodite. Besides this there are objects found in the area including terra cotta figurines, weapons, jewelry, and an epigraphical collection with fragments engraved in the still undeciphered Cyprosyllabic script. From the entrance of the fort a paved path leads to a replica of the mosaic of *Leda and the Swan* The original was recovered in London after being

Above: The Museum in the Lusignan Manor House of Kouklia. Right: Watching the ever-foamy water at Petra tou Romiou.

stolen. It is now on display in the Cyprus Museum in Nicosia.

The **Katholiki Church** to the east has changed names many times. It was first called Panayia Aphroditissa, later Panayia Khrysopolitissa or "Our Lady of the Golden City," and now Panayia Galatariotissa or "Our Lady Who Gives Milk." This attribute prompted recent mothers to light candles in the saint's honor. In the dome are 15th-century frescoes of the Pantocrator and saints, and on the west wall are the remnants of a huge *Last Judgment*.

Up the hill to the northeast are remains of a ramp built by the Persian army during the assault on Paphos in 498 B.C. Unearthed at the site were fragments from a sanctuary, including a distinctive sculpted head of a priest-king, along with vast amounts of iron and bronze arrowheads and a bronze helmet.

Four kilometers southeast of Kouklia is the legendary birthplace of Aphrodite, **Petra tou Romiou** ❽, meaning "The Greek's Rock." This refers to Byzantine

hero Dighenis Akritas, who is said to have flung several large rocks at the invading Saracen pirates which landed in the sea. These large boulders now mark the magnificent site at which Aphrodite is said to have emerged from the water.

It's worth a stop, either to sit on the pebbly seaside for some peaceful contemplation inspired by the sheer magnificence of the seascape, or to plunge into the foamy waters for a swim, which is said to enhance the beauty of the bather. The Cyprus Tourism Organization operates a pleasant tourist pavilion across the road with outdoor tables that have a clear view of the site, most dramatic at sunset. The restaurant has a somewhat corny reproduction of Aphrodite as a fountain.

Scenic River Valleys

A fascinating area for walkers is the **Dhiarizos River Valley**, running along the land route between Palea Paphos and the Troodos Mountains. It can be reached by turning off the road past Kouklia which leads to **Nikoklia ❾**. In the village, which is named after King Nicocles, the last ruler of Pahpos, stands the **Church of Ayios Dimitrianos**, built in 1768. It is especially notable for its icons, and for the toppled Corinthian pillar which lies before the building.

Following the river alongside the eastern fork of the road leads to fascinating geologic patterns in an area which once nurtured one of the earliest of Cypriot civilizations, as witnessed by the rock-cut Chalcolithic graves on the plateau southeast of **Souskiou ❿**. Judging from the richness of gifts accompanying the dead of the communities scattered southwest of the village, the inhabitants were prosperous, probably through agriculture and animal breeding. The pottery, mostly bowls and vases, shows a lively imagination. Unfortunately, most objects were unearthed in unauthorized excavations, and the largest statuette was illegally exported from Cyprus.

The village itself is a ghost town, its quaint stone buildings abandoned after

Map p. 116, Info pp. 134-135

the 1974 division of the island. A gilded icon depicting Christ on the cross is now in **Arminou** ⑪, a former Armenian village up the river. The villagers of Arminou claimed it arrived there on its own, a story the inhabitants of Souskiou found hard to swallow. Bloodshed could apparently only be averted by the people of Arminou giving Souskiou the small Chapel of Ayia Marina in exchange for the icon.

Also worth visiting in this area is the deserted **Monastery of Ayios Savvas Tis Koronos** ⑫ near **Prastio**. This picturesque little chapel has imaginative stone carvings and well-preserved icons.

Returning to Nikoklia, if you take the fork leading west, a whole new aspect of Cyprus lies waiting. The upper Xeros Potamos Valley, a flood plain running from the coast to the edge of the Cedar Valley Forest, is an area once thriving with agricultural activity but now devoid

of any inhabitants except for a few nomadic shepherds. A walk through the peaceful landscapes will provide a soothing contrast to the bustling activity of Paphos itself.

About five kilometers from **Kelokedhara** is the deserted **Monastery of Santi**, or **Sindi** ⑬ as the locals call it, built in 1500. It contains a few icons inside the **Panayia Eleousa Church** and three restored monastic buildings.

Also in this hauntingly beautiful setting is the **Church of Ayia Paraskevi**, just across the river. According to legend, the craftsman who built Ayia Paraskevi commissioned a young apprentice to build the Monastery of Santi. When finished, the monastery was so much more impressive that the older master was filled with a murderous rage and pushed the youth to his death.

AYIOS NEOPHYTOS

Above: The colorful frescoes of the Monastery of Ayios Neophytos.

An excursion to the **Ayios Neophytos Monastery**, nine kilometers from Ktima, requires about half a day. It can be reached by taking the new road to Polis and turning left at Trimithousa. The more scenic route is on the old road to the west which passes near Emba.

Emba ⑭ is an agricultural center which is at its best in spring, when the fields are blanketed in brilliant scarlet anemones. Notable is the **Panayia Khryseleousa Church**, whose frescoes were ruined by an inept restorer in 1886, except for the Pantocrator on the dome. Note also the two-paneled icon (17th century) showing the Venetian coat of arms with the 12 apostles.

The road climbs through citrus orchards to the small village of **Tala**, two kilometers before the monastery, a perfect place to spend a restful holiday in a rented apartment on a hilltop with fantastic views of the sea. Its domed late-Byzantine **Church of Ayia Ekaterina** is worth visiting. At **Spilia Tou Mavrou**, five kilometers to the northwest and reached by taking a poor dirt road which is impassable in winter, an early Cypriot cemetery was discovered.

The ****Monastery of Ayios Neophytos ⑮** is in a splendid setting on the 612-meter-high Charta Summit of the Melissovouno, or "Honey Mountain," which affords breathtaking vistas of Paphos and the sea below. It's easy to understand how the isolation attracted the extraordinary hermit Neophytos, who was born in Kato Dhrys, a small village near Kato Lefkara, in 1134. He ran off and hid in the Monastery of Ayios Khrysostomos near Buffavento rather than marry a bride chosen by his parents. When discovered, he was forced to go home, but soon convinced his parents it was best for him to "embrace a monastic life rather than a bride."

Neophytos then set off for the hills above Paphos and dug a cave with his own hands (to the left of the present 15th-century monastery) where he lived from 1159 on. The problem was that his fame

spread, and he was soon joined by a prelate named Basil who convinced him to join the priesthood.

This self-taught ascetic eventually attracted vast numbers of followers, and a monastery was formed. Feeling frustrated in his quest for solitude, although already quite old, he burrowed yet another cave higher than the first one. Neophytos resided there in his final years, emerging only on Sundays to preach to his followers. Over the years Neophytos wrote a number of scholarly theology books as well as an indictment against Richard the Lionhearted, calling him the "wretch."

Especially notable at the site are the well-tended gardens with olive and fruit trees, first cultivated by Neophytos, and an amazing cave, called the **Enkleistra**, in which he lived his Spartan life. A cupboard here was once filled with the skulls of his followers. A little **chapel** with a simple wooden cross is decorated in marvelous frescoes, some dark-blue based, others brighter with rich gold accents, begun under the supervision of Neophytos by a disciple named Apseudes and continued by others after his death. The icons show influences of both the more sophisticated aristocratic Constantinople school and the softer, more popular "monastic" school. Outstanding among them are *The Adoration of the Magi* and another Byzantine-style icon in which Christ, dressed in blue, is shown teaching his apostles and Neophytos, who is flanked by the archangels Michael and Gabriel.

Avoid coming here on the holy days of January 24 and September 28, in order to appreciate the calm beauty of the setting and evoke the spirit of the shy cleric Neophytos while listening to the church bells, monks reciting prayers, and birds chirping. At that time, religious pilgrims come in flocks to kiss the silver reliquary containing the skull of Ayios Neophytos and drink the refreshing water from the spring near the café, said to be a disease

Paphos

preventative. Religious books are sold at the entrance of the monastery, and you can get a permit from the abbot to visit the monks' workshop for the restoration and binding of ancient manuscripts. A few guest rooms facing the sea are available in the very hospitable monastery.

Take the alternative route back to Paphos via **Mesoyi** ⓰. This fertile village has springs that supply water to Paphos, and to the groves of fruit and nut trees here. Notable Mesoyi products are hemp, baskets, carob syrup, which is a well-known molasses-like island specialty claimed to aid blood circulation, and wine. Rooms can be rented in a few of the houses here.

AKAMAS PENINSULA

A pleasant day tour by rental car takes you from to Ayios Yeoryios and, if you get up early enough, on to the Akamas Peninsula. The first stop here is the artists' village of **Lemba** ⓱. The contemporary Cypriot artist Stass Paraskos organizes summer courses here for young painters and sculptors from around the world; a number of curious creations by the master and his pupils adorn the garden of his studio on the village's main square. From here, follow the narrow road down to the coast; along the way you will pass by the Lemba Pottery studios and other artisans' shops. Beyond the edge of the village, a sign points the way to the "Prehistoric Village," the nearby **Lemba Experimental Village**, always open to the public.

In the 1970s, archeologists from the University of Edinburgh excavated the remains of a Chalcolithic settlement, which was inhabited from about 3500 to 2500 B.C. Later, a number of the settlement's round houses were reconstructed, so that

Right: Villager wearing the traditional baggy trousers. Far right: What about exploring the remote Avgas Gorge?

today visitors are given a good idea of the appearance of such villages. It is possible to enter the houses for a better look.

For the continuing journey you either take the coastal road or else make a short detour through the large village of **Kissonerga** ⓲.

Kissongera is particularly worth visiting on the Orthodox Easter Sunday, which is when the popular "Easter Plays" take place in the municipal stadium below the main street. Visitors can also join in the fun without having to register in advance. Competitions include such things as sack races and Easter egg races. The Cypriots, at least, enjoy themselves immensely at this festival.

Just past Kissongera, the seaside road winds through lovely landscapes, many stretches surrounded by banana plantations, before reaching **Coral Bay** ⓳, a fast-growing holiday resort built without any apparent plan. It got its name for its lovely sand beaches, tinged pink by coral fragments. This is a great place for a swim in cool turquoise water, followed by a tasty fish dinner in one of the seaside restaurants. Unfortunately, the construction of many holiday villas in the last few years has somewhat marred the wild purity of the rocky coast.

On the 378-meter-long, 90-meter-wide and 17-meter-high peninsula of **Paleokastro-Maa**, which breaks Coral Bay up into two sections, remains of a Late Bronze Age settlement were discovered, which was probably only inhabited from 1230 to 1200 B.C. Land and seaward walls up to four meters in thickness and the foundation walls of dwellings are all that remain today. The military settlement was probably founded by Greek and Cretan emigrants who had already had contact with Cyprus and who planned to settle here temporarily and who, a generation later, became integrated into neighboring villages.

A small exhibition on the excavation grounds illustrates the epoch of the My-

cenaean settlement of the island through photographs and copies of archeological finds from Paleokastro-Maa and other sites; which are relevant today vis-à-vis the current political situation. Through the arrival of the Greeks around 1200 B.C., Cyprus became completely Grecized; which shows, as supported by archeological evidence, that Cyprus has always been a Greek island.

Three kilometers further along on a mountainside nestles charming little **Peyia ⑳**, an unspoiled village with well-tended traditional houses, surrounded by orchards and carob and olive groves. Peyia is supposed to be of Venetian origin, although its inhabitants claim it dates from Byzantine times. Villagers here still wear the typical baggy pants, *vraka* in Greek, and knee-high boots.

A road veering northwest through pine and juniper forests leads after seven kilometers to the seaside at **Ayios Yeoryios ㉑**. About three kilometers from Peyia is the modern **Church of Panayia Zalayiotissa**, built on the ruins

of a 17th-century monastery and distinguished by its unusual specialty of curing varicose veins.

Ayios Yeoryios is an only sparsely built up scattered settlement with wonderful rocky bays and sand beaches at **Cape Drepanum**. Near the modern main church lie the fenced-in remains of an early Christian basilica. Lovely mosaics portray birds and fish, among other subjects.

Close by is the simple Byzantine **Church of Ayios Yeoryios**, featuring two peculiarities often encountered on Cyprus: in front of the church is a tree with strips of cloth left hanging from its branches by the faithful – in this case in the hope of having a lost animal returned. The church itself has thick twine wrapped around it. This custom probably goes back to ancient times, though its purpose remains a mystery. Perhaps this "girding" has some connection to the girdle of Aphrodite. It is said that any man who set his eyes on it was eternally smitten by the beautiful goddess.

The paved road ends in Ayios Yeoryios. From here a dusty path leads through fields to the Akamas Peninsula. Soon you will come to a signpost pointing out a turnoff for the **Avgas Gorge** ㉒ (sometimes also called Avagas Gorge), which is a pleasure to hike through and for which at least two hours should be set aside.

Four kilometers farther north on the bumpy dirt road as you approach the coast is **Lara Beach** ㉓. This long sandy stretch is the nesting area of the protected green and loggerhead turtles which lay their eggs here in summer. Concerned conservationists have been patrolling the beach every summer since 1978 to protect the nests from being inadvertently destroyed by tourists. Cages protect the nests from the sea turtles' natural enemies, which include crabs, foxes, crows and goshawks.

Above: Blissful twilight time at Ayios Yeoryios, on the Akamas Peninsula. Right: Grapefruit being harvested at Peyia, Paphos.

Just about 13 kilometers further along, a side trip from the coastal road leads to the **Ayios Kononas Chapel** ㉔, only two kilometers inland. Here Danish archeologists have discovered the ruins of a large Greco-Roman settlement. The chapel is built above a simple Hellenic grave.

Five hundred meters after the fork leading toward the chapel, the dirt road, which can still be driven on here, ends at the **Bay of Joni**. From here it is best to head back to Lara Beach. From there you have a choice: either take the already known route back to Ayios Yeorgios or else, at a signposted turnoff, take the road toward Neo Chorio, thereby cutting across the Akamas Peninsula. In the process you will find yourself winding along stretches of road with many twists and turns, passing through beautiful pine forests as you climb upward. Soon you will have ascended to an altitude of approximately 300 meters, and the north coast of the peninsula will come into view below.

In the small mountain hamlet of **Neo Chorio** you can take a break in a taverna

before visiting the Baths of Aphrodite or heading into the small town of Polis.

From Ktima to Polis

To get to the remote area of Polis on the northern shore, take the road from the central parking lot of Ktima on Pallikaridis Avenue. Factories line the main road throughout the first lap of the journey as one passes the villages of Konia, Anavargos and **Mesa Khorio**, which has the modern **Church of Ayia Marina**. After **Mesoyi 16**, the landscape changes into farmland. The road meanders through olive groves to **Tsadha 25**, in feudal times known as Kourka, four kilometers further. In Tsadha, the 1908 **Panagia Church** has an icon of the Virgin Mary, with the priest Gideon and his wife shown kneeling at her feet, painted by "Titus the Sinner" in 1540.

About three kilometers away, in a high valley on the grounds of the Tsadha Golf Club, is the small **Stavros tis Minthas Monastery**, today occupied by a single monk. It has an interesting portal in Gothic-influenced style. Vineyards cover the hills around **Stroumbi 26**, five kilometers away. The otherwise not especially attractive village celebrates a three-day "Dionysia" wine festival every year in late August, at which not can the local wines be sampled, but presentations of Cypriot folklore can also be enjoyed.

In Stroumbi you can choose between two roads to take to Polis. The main road veers northeast through the Khrysokhou Valley. On this route is **Yiolou**, which celebrates its Onion Festival in July. To reach the **Ayii Anargyri Monastery 27**, take a road to the left to **Miliou**. The monastery was built in 1649 and is named for the brothers Cosmos and Damian, called *Ayii Anargyri*, meaning "Saints without Fees," because they gave medical treatment without payment. The monastery is next to a Neolithic site. The foul-smelling hot springs located nearby are said to cure arthritis.

Miliou itself has modest accommodations in a tranquil setting of scrub and trees. Stop at **Angelos Café**, just before nearby **Loukrounou** ㉘, to have a drink on its cool terrace overlooking the rich valley. Its unique supermarket, crammed with every imaginable household object and foodstuff, is a good place to stock up on supplies.

Six kilometers further, on the left side, is **Kholi** ㉙, notable for its 16th-century **Archangel Church,** which incorporates the base of a medieval watch tower. The remaining six kilometers to Polis are heavily cultivated with various crops, including bananas, carob and other fruits and vegetables.

The alternate route to Polis via the undulating western road affords some spectacular vistas of the sea, first from the west and later to the north. It passes through **Dhrousha** ㉚, a lovely little village with 400 year-round residents, perched high on the backbone of the Akamas Peninsula. The mountains of Turkey can be seen on a clear day from here. It is noted for its whitewashed traditional houses, some now owned by foreigners. In the spring, the rare *Orchis laxiflora*, a vibrant red tulip, blooms in the area. Baskets gaily interwoven with colored ribbons and rag weavings are made here. The industrious *Dhroushiotes* have migrated to all corners of the world, but maintain close ties through their association. It built the first-class Dhrousha Heights Hotel, an open-air theater, and now has plans for a senior citizens' day care center.

In **Terra**, about two kilometers to the east, is a large **Roman milestone** used as the support for the veranda on a private house. The most interesting church in the whole area (albeit in ruins) is **Ayia Katerina** ㉛, overlooking the Paphos-Polis road, which may be reached by a path running two kilometers east of Terra. It was once known as the "Seven-Domed

Right: Panoramic view of surf and solitude in Khrysokhou Bay, Paphos.

Church," though only three of the domes have survived. In the narthex there is a fresco of St. Catherine.

Heading back to the main road, one can enjoy the panoramic views of **Khrysokhou Bay** while descending the eight kilometers towards the sea to **Prodhromi**, a suburb of Polis.

Khrysokhou ㉜ itself was an enormous estate during Venetian times, and later, during Turkish times, was the capital of the area. The *konak*, or mansion, still stands. In the mid-1800s, the Sultan sent two stallions here for breeding purposes, and from this line the "Paphos Pony" descended.

POLIS

Polis ㉝, a pleasant seaside town, is still a quiet holiday retreat, despite a dramatic increase in tourism in recent years. This is an ideal location for beach lovers who crave the simple pleasures of sand, sun and surf. The sand beaches of Polis and neighboring Lachi can easily be reached year round by bus or service taxi from Nea Pahpos. Polis is an important center of citrus fruit production, but is now cut off from its sister city of Morphou located in the northern sector. Walnuts, almonds, carob and wheat are also harvested here in abundance. The small traditional houses of the town, with wooden balconies and staircases, are typical of early 20th-century Cypriot architecture.

To the northeast of Polis was the copper center of **Marion**, said to have been founded in the seventh century B.C. by Athenians, and destroyed in 312 B.C. by Ptolemy (the future King Ptolemy I of Egypt). It was succeeded some decades later by a new town known as Arsinoë. The area today is predominantly made up of a vast necropolis containing mostly Hellenic tombs in which imported Attic pottery was found, with some older specimens dating from the sixth to fourth cen-

turies B.C. Excavations here are ongoing, and it is extremely likely that new archeological finds will be brought to light. An archeological museum on the main street of Polis opened in 1998. Here objects found on sites in the region have been put on display.

The contemporary town of Polis is refreshingly relaxed, but no one has to do without the basic amenities, such as banks, a post office and several travel agencies, all of which can be found here. Just outside the town is a lively campground set in a seaside eucalyptus grove. Because most people head west to visit Lachi and the Baths of Aphrodite, some of the most deserted beaches of the Paphos District lie to the northeast of Polis in the direction of the Turkish enclave of Kokkina (in Turkish: Erenköy), eight kilometers from the Green Line, beyond which is northern Cyprus.

Yialia ㉞ is a picturesque little village, once totally Turkish Cypriot, creeping up a narrow valley covered in orange trees. Three kilometers to the east up the river lie the scant ruins of **Ayios Cornuto Church**, known locally as *Monastir*, an interesting structure probably dating to Frankish times.

Tiny **Pakhyammos** ㉟ is a few kilometers further and has a long sand beach below the village. On a broad paved square almost directly above the sea rises the edifice of the **Church of Ayios Raffail**, built at the beginning of the 1990s, the interior of which is painted with new, unusual frescoes. This is the destination of many pilgrims who hope to be cured of their illnesses by St. Raffail.

After Pakhyammos, the road veers into the mountains to avoid entering Turkish terrain at Kokkina. This requires about a 45-minute detour by car on a winding road. **Kato Pyrgos** ㊱, the very last Greek Cypriot village on the coast, is far off the tourists' beaten track, and is mostly frequented by vacationing Cypriots during the height of the summer season, but is fairly deserted at other times of the year. The main road stretches along the seafront of small pebble beaches, but is

warehouse. Diners are entertained during the evening with live music. Beautiful beaches stretch out on both sides of the harbor, and just about every kind of water sport can be engaged in here.

From Lachi you can continue driving west. Soon you will pass the **Anassa Luxury Hotel**, which opened its doors to the public in 1998. Interestingly, this establishment belongs to the family of a former Cypriot Foreign Minister. Despite the protests of many conservationists, which ultimately forced him to step down, he had this exclusive 60-million-dollar complex erected in what had been an area of completely undisturbed nature bordering the environmentally protected Akamas Peninsula.

Still in its natural state, by comparison, is **Takas Bay**, further to the west. Here the only building is a single rustic seafood restaurant. Just beyond this, the road ends at the parking lot of the **Baths of Aphrodite 38** (Loutra tis Aphroditis), to which a paved path leads on a two-minute walk. The idyllic, shallow freshwater pool surrounded by green primeval forest before a low cliff was, according to legend, one of the goddess Aphrodite's favorite bathing spots. It was here that she is said to have engaged in an amorous encounter with her lover Akamas.

Nowadays, unfortunately, bathing is forbidden here. The pebble beach below the restaurant on the lower edge of the parking lot, however, is a great place to go for a swim. From the restaurant's terrace there is a wonderful view of the Bay of Polis.

From the parking lot there is a trail – not suitable for driving – that leads along the north coast of the Akamas Peninsula to the perhaps unjustly famous **Fontana Amorosa**. From Lachi you can also come here by excursion steamer. The so-called "Fountain of Love" is in reality nothing more than a wretched well, the water of which imparts to the drinker not eternal youth, but severe diarrhea instead.

sometimes used for exercises by Cypriot soldiers or British forces from the neighboring military bases. This should not hinder your enjoyment of this virtual paradise, for it has enough space to comfortably accommodate both visitors and residents. Some of the simple hotels at the west end of the village have fantastic unobstructed views of the sea.

Whatever you do while touring Cyprus, don't miss a visit to **Lachi 37** (sometimes spelled "Latsi"), two kilometers west of Polis. This is the newest holiday resort on the island, and is most popular with younger tourists traveling individually. It has a special character thanks to its fishing harbor and the seafood restaurants along the shore promenade. The most unusual restaurant of all is located a few meters further west, directly on the shore road: **Porto Lachi** is housed in a centuries-old one-time carob

Above: Whitewashed church at Polis. Right: Preparing to take the plunge in the sparkling water near the Baths of Aphrodite.

PAPHOS FOREST

Nature lovers will be enchanted by the sites of the Khrysorroyiatissa Monastery and the Forestry Station of Stavros tis Psokas in the **Paphos Forest**. It is best to have a jeep or a Landrover with a full tank of gas. The last stretch of road leading to Stavros tis Psokas is on a tricky dirt road and should not be attempted during bad weather. To get to the Khrysorroyiatissa Monastery, take the Polis Road from Pallikardis Avenue in Ktima for 13 kilometers, take a right turn, and go another three kilometers to Polemi, a large grape-growing center, and then drive northeast about 10 kilometers to Kannaviou. From here you can proceed to **Pano Panayia** ❸❾, where Archbishop Makarios III, the first president of the Republic of Cyprus, was born in 1913. Here you can visit the simple birth house of the statesman, and see an exhibit dedicated to him near his memorial.

Just southwest is the **Monastery of Khrysorroyiatissa** ❹❶, meaning "Our Lady of the Pomegranate." It was founded by a monk named Ignatius in 1152 after he found an icon of the Virgin Mary. He was subsequently "visited" by her and was appointed the task of building a monastery to shelter it.

The icon, kept in a silver-gilt case in a distinctive triangular-shaped cloister, is strangely enough the destination of an unusual variety of pilgrim: it is visited by condemned criminals who come here to pray for mercy. The breathtaking view from the monastery extends all the way to the sea and overlooks lush forests and orchards.

Khrysorroyiatissa is surrounded by vineyards and has a widespread reputation for making the finest wine on the island, called *Monte Royia*. The monks left a few years ago. During the Turkish occupation, this was known as the "Monastery of the Bell," because the abbot here had managed to circumvent the prohibition against bell ringing.

It is slow driving on a narrow dirt road for about 12 kilometers to get to **Stavros**

tis Psokas ㊶, named "The Cross of Measles" because a spring here was reputed to cure the disease (Greek: *psokas*). The expansive forest, mainly of stately golden oak, Lebanon cedar and Aleppo pine, lends the landscape a sense of grandeur. Stavros tis Psokas has a taverna and a guest house with seven simple rooms, each of which has a kitchen and fireplace. The rooms can be rented for stays of up to three days.

This is the realm of the indigenous Cyprus moufflon, the horned sheep that are featured on Cypriot coins. They are a protected species, today estimated to number only about 2,000 after nearly being hunted to extinction around the turn of the century. The elusive animals are extremely shy and not easily sighted, but early birds who get up at the crack of dawn and wait quietly near a clearing may get a chance to glimpse one in the wild. Alternatively there is a small herd in

Above: "Strange encounter of the third kind" on a nature walk in the Paphos District.

the enclosure next to the forest rangers' station. The rangers are very helpful and informative, but are often not at their post on weekends. Invigorating hikes on nature trails in the fresh mountain air can be undertaken in the area. A monastery deserted in 1850 and a small church are also on the grounds.

You can return to Paphos via **Phiti** ㊷, a traditional weaving center, and then continue back on the coastal road.

NATURE WALKS

The Paphos District is by far the most interesting area for nature walks, especially in the springtime. The diverse geological features of the region bear witness to its history. **Paphos Forest** in the northwest of the district provides innumerable areas for solid hikes on forest roads and tracks. Worthy of special mention are trails east and northeast of **Panayia** ㊴ that lead into the igneous foothills of the mountains, and to the mountains themselves.

The environs of **Ayia** ④ and the trails towards the **Stavros tis Psokas Station** ④ provide refreshingly cool summer walks and are interesting in respect to the fauna and flora. Hunting is prohibited in Paphos Forest, which consists of mostly pine and golden oak trees. The area is rich in birds. The elusive moufflon may occasionally be spotted.

From the main road, cross the valley to **Tripylos Peak** (1,362 meters). From the summit, panoramic views extend north and south to ★**Cedar Valley** ④, which can be reached by descending from the peak. Cedar Valley has about 5,000 Cyprus cedar trees and many Troodos pines. The views are spectacular higher up, and the flora is rich and undisturbed.

The **Xeros River Valley** down towards Paphos has interesting walks with spectacular views of the stark desolate landscape from the tracks of the valley. This is a grassy flood plain with very few trees, no habitation and only a few creatures, such as the odd vulture or an occasional herd of sheep. Prepare well for the walks along these trails.

Exalt Tours in Paphos (24 Ayios Kyriakas Street, Ktima) organizes trekking trips in the Paphos and Troodos areas. Transportation is by jeep. Routes on the day trips include such spectacular regions as the limestone area of **Avgas Gorge** ㉒ near Ayios Yeoryios, Peyia, Xeros, Dhiarizos and Akamas. Tours with art historical and archeological themes follow an itinerary that passes by several isolated Byzantine churches and ancient sites such as the Chalcolithic Souskiou Cemetery.

The **Akamas Peninsula** itself is Cyprus' last coastal wilderness. Its extensive maquis forest of junipers and mastics (*Pistacia Lentiscus*) is crisscrossed with forest roads and tracks. Many provide good hiking in winter and spring; some in summer as well. The area is a geological mosaic with a lively variety of vegetation to match. It abounds in orchids and en-

demic species, as well as cyclamen, buttercups and anemones in early spring. The small white-flowered *Cistus monspelliencis* is characteristic of certain areas. *Alyssum akamissicum* grows on the serpentinite areas, while the pale pink *Citrus parviflora* can be found everywhere in the limestone regions.

The **Akamas Region** is in the process of being declared Cyprus' first national park. Regulations will very probably come into force in the not too distant future keeping in line with the regions status as a protected nature area. The turtle-nesting beaches on the west coast of Akamas are already protected by strictly-enforced regulations during the nesting season. Notices to this effect warn the public of the regulations that govern the area.

The most spectacular walks in Akamas are the trail starting from the **Baths of Aphrodite** and going west to Fontana Amorosa and the mountaintop track from Smiyes, west of Neokhorio, to the firebreak that crosses the peninsula, from Jioni to Fontana Amorosa. This firebreak is an interesting walk in itself. Camping and picking wildflowers are prohibited in the Akamas Forest.

Three nature trails in this area provide unique views of the north coast of Akamas with its crystal clear, calm waters. One of them starts practically from sea level at the Baths of Aphrodite and climbs steeply to about 450 meters at **Pyrgos tis Rigenas**. The area in early spring is extremely rich in wildflowers, cyclamen, orchids, buttercups and many others. Pines, junipers, mastics and strawberry trees (*Arbutus andrachne*) cover much of the region. The forest is denser in the valleys higher up, where the main nature trail curves back to the sea. A small spring and a giant oak tree (*Quercus infectoria*) greet visitors at the **Palati tis Rigenas** ruins, which are in the process of being excavated by the Department of Antiquities.

Paphos

PAPHOS

Area Code 06

i **Cyprus Tourism Organization**, 3 Gladstone St., Ktima, tel. 232841, and at the airport, tel. 422833.

🛏 😀😀😀 By the sea: **Alexander the Great**, Poseidonos Ave., tel. 265000, fax. 265100; **Annabelle**, Poseidonos Ave., tel. 238333, fax. 245502; **Paphos Beach**, Poseidonos Ave., tel. 233091, fax. 242818, surfboard rentals, diving school, discotheque; **Cypria Maris**, Poseidonos Ave., tel. 264111, fax. 264125, outside the town.

😀😀 **Melina**, Ay. Lambrianos St., tel. 244400, fax. 246834; **Dionysos**, 1 Dionysos St., tel. 233414, fax. 233008; **Porto Paphos**, Poseidonos Ave., tel. 242333, fax. 241341, by the sea, in town; **Paphian Bay**, Poseidonos Ave., tel. 264333, fax. 264870, outside the town. Close to the archeological site, out of town: **Kissos**, Vereniki St., tel. 236111, fax. 245125; **Land of the Kings**, Tombs of the Kings St., tel. 241770, fax. 245594. Four kilometers east of Paphos in Konia: **Paphiana**, P.O. Box 314, tel. 260252, fax. 261476.

😀 In Nea Paphos: **Agapinor**, 26 Nikodimos Mylonas St., tel. 233927, fax. 235308; **Pyramos**, 4 Ay. Anastasias St., tel. 235161, fax. 242939. In Ktima: **Trianon**, 99 Makarios Ave., tel. 232193.

YOUTH HOSTEL: In Ktima: 37 Eleftherios Venizelos Ave., tel. 232588, open year-round 7:30 to 10:30 a.m. and 4:30 to 11 p.m.

CAMPING: **Yeroskipou Zenon Gardens**, P.O. Box 99, Paphos, tel. 242277, on the beach, 3 km east from Paphos Harbor, open April through October; **Fegari Camping**, tel. 621534, Coral Bay, 11 km north of Paphos, open year-round.

🍴 **Pelican**, Apostle Paul Ave., tel. 232827, seafood restaurant on the harbor; **Mediterranean Tavern**, 3 Ayia Napa St., tel. 235684, delicious fish dishes; *Meze* and *klephtiko* (lamb baked slowly in a special earthenware oven) is served at the **Demokritos Tavern**, 1 Dionysos St., tel. 233371, with music and Cypriot folk dances several times a week; **Les Etoiles**, 1 Diagorou St., tel. 234083, delicious international and Greek cuisine, quiet, pleasant restaurant.

🏛 Unless otherwise stated, the summer period is from June 1 to September 30; the winter period from October 1 to May 31.

District Archeological Museum, Grivas Dighenis Ave., tel. 240215, open in summer Monday through Saturday 7:30 a.m. to 1.30 p.m. and 4 to 6 p.m., Sunday 10 a.m. to 1 p.m., in winter Monday through Friday 7:30 a.m. to 2 p.m. and 3 to 5 p.m., Saturday 7:30 a.m. to 1 p.m. and 3 to 5 p.m., Sunday 10 a.m. to 1 p.m.;

Aquarium, Artemidios St., open daily 10 a.m. to 8 p.m.; **Byzantine Museum**, Andrea Ioannou St., open Monday through Friday 9 a.m. to 5 p.m. (in summer until 7 p.m.), Saturday 9 a.m. to 2 p.m.; **Ethnographic Museum**, Eliades Collection of Folk Art, 1 Exo Vriysis St., tel. 232010, open in summer (May through September) Monday through Saturday 9 a.m. to 1 p.m. and 4 to 7 p.m, Sunday 10 a.m. to 1 p.m., in winter (October through April) Monday through Saturday 9 a.m. to 1 p.m. and 3 to 5 p.m., Sunday 10 a.m. to 1.00 p.m.; **Paphos Fort**, Nea Paphos, open in summer Monday through Saturday 9 a.m. to 1:30 p.m., in winter Monday through Friday 9 a.m. to 2 p.m., Saturday 9 a.m. to 1 p.m.; **Royal Tombs**, open in summer daily 9 a.m. to 7:30 p.m., in winter daily 9 a.m. till sunset; **Mosaics**, in the Villa of Theseus and in the House of Aion, Nea Paphos, tel. 240217, fine mosaics in Roman Period houses, open in summer daily 9 a.m. to 7.30 p.m., in winter daily 9 a.m. until sunset; **Folk Art Museum** (Hadji Smith House), in Yeroskipos, 3 km east of Paphos, tel. 240216, open in summer Monday through Saturday 9 a.m. to 1:30 p.m., in winter Monday through Friday 9 a.m. to 2 p.m., Saturday 9 a.m. to 1 p.m.; **Temple of Aphrodite** and **Paleapaphos Museum**, in Kouklia, 14 km east of Paphos, open in summer daily 9 a.m. to 7:30 p.m., in winter open daily 9 a.m. till sunset; **Paleokastro-Maa**, archeological finds, Coral Bay, open Monday through Saturday 10 a.m. to 4 p.m.; **Saranda Colones Fortress**, open to the public during the daytime.

Notice: On public holidays the major archeological sites remain open from 9 a.m. to 5 p.m., except on Greek Easter Sunday, when all museums in Cyprus are closed.

⛪ *PLACES OF WORSHIP* (denominations other than Greek Orthodox):

Anglican Masses, Chrysopolitissa Church, Nea Paphos, services are held every Sunday at 6 a.m.

Roman Catholic Masses are held at the same church every Sunday at noon.

🎭 Variable but usually in **February**: Carnival or *Apokreos*, a two-week period of parties ending on the Monday preceding Lent, with parades through the main streets of Paphos.

Monday preceding Lent: *Kite Competition* in the castle area, a colorful event followed by a traditional feast.

May: *Anthestiria*, flower festival with a colorful floral parade, various cultural events and exhibitions of Cyprus flora, particularly that of the Akamas Peninsula, takes place on a Sunday.

May or June: Coinciding with Pentecost, the variable holiday *Kataklysmos* (Festival of the Flood) is a religious festival celebrated only in Cyprus.

June through September: *Pafia Festival*, with theater, ballet, concerts and folk dancing in the Odeon and in Paphos Fort.

August: During the two-week-long *Pampafia* exhibition in the park on Messogis Avenue, craftsmen from the Paphos area display their work; folklore presentations and samples of Cypriot culinary specialties are also on offer.

Last weekend in August: *Wine Festival* in the village of Stroumbi on the road to Polis.

End of November: Half-marathon in Paphos, organized by the Cyprus Health Runner's Club, tel. / fax. 420559.

Central Post Office, with poste restante and afternoon service: Themidos St., tel. 232241; in Nea Paphos: Ayios Antonios St.

Telecommunications: Office located on Dighenis Avenue, Pano Paphos, closed Saturday afternoon and Sunday. Card phones can be found just about everywhere; phone cards are available at kiosks and many supermarkets.

In case of emergency dial 199 for **Paphos Hospital**, located on Neophytou Nikolaidi Street in Ktima, tel. 240100.

BUSES: There are buses within the city and to the nearby villages of Emba, Lemba, Kissonerga, Peyia and Yeroskipos, as well as to the Ayios Neophytos Monastery and the airport numerous times daily, leaving from the market hall and many other bus stops (Alepa Bus Co., 28 Nikodemou Mylona St., tel. 234410).

Buses run to Limassol and Nicosia 3 to 5 times daily Monday through Saturday (Alepa Bus Co. and Kemek/ Nea Amoroza Bus Co., 79 Pallikaridis St., tel. 236822). Up to 11 buses make the trip to Polis every day (Kemek/Nea Amoroza).

RENTAL CARS: **Andy Spyrou/Europcar**, Posseidon Ave., Natalia Court, tel. 241850; **A. Petsas & Sons**, 86 Apostle Paul Avenue, Green Court, tel. 235522; **Budget Rent a Car**, Tombs of the Kings Road, Dora Complex, tel. 253824; **Hertz**, 54A Apostle Paul Avenue, tel. 233985; **Leos/Thrifty**, Poseidonos Ave/Iason Street, tel. 233770; **Sea Island Car Rental**, 26 Tombs of the Kings Road, tel. 231456; **Sir Rentals**, 94 Ellados Street, tel. 242258; **Geko**, 10 Vladimirou Irakleous Street, tel. 232848.

SERVICE (GROUP) TAXIS: **Karydas/Kyriakos**, tel. 232459; **Kypros**, tel. 237722; **Makris**, tel. 232538.

Nea Paphos has many boutiques with fashionable resort wear and traditional handicrafts. Paphos District is famed for its basketry, once made in almost every village but now continued in only a few, including Mesoyi and Yeroskipos.

CORAL BAY

Queen Bay, Coral Bay Road, P.O. Box 416, tel. 246600, fax. 246777.

Cynthina Beach, Coral Bay Road, located 8 kilometers northwest of Paphos, P.O. Box 23, tel. 233900, fax. 244648.

Yeronisos, Ayios Yeoryios, Peyia, tel. / fax. 621078.

KISSONERGA: Located 6 km from Coral Bay: **Lobster Tavern**, tel. 243940, good fish restaurant; **John's Tavern**, tel. 234205, for *sephtalia* (grilled sausage) and meat.

PEYIA: Located 4 km from Coral Bay: **Vrissi Tavern**, tel. 621113, for *meze* and great fish.

POLIS AND LACHI AREA

Area Code 06

Cyprus Tourism Organization, 1 Agiou Nikolaou Street (on the main square by the market hall), Polis, tel. 322468.

Anassa, Neo Chorio, tel. 233550, fax. 231656; **Elia Lachi Holiday Village**, Lachi, tel. 321011, fax. 322024.

Droushia Heights, Drousha, tel. 332351, fax. 332353; **Lover's Nest**, Polis, tel. 322401, fax. 322440; **Souli**, Neo Chorio, tel. 321088, fax. 322474.

Aphrodite Beach, Neo Chorio, tel. 321001, fax. 322015; **Chrysafina**, Prodromi, tel. 321180, fax. 322465; **Latsi**, Lachi, tel. 321411, tel. 321468.

CAMPING: **Polis Camping**, tel. 321526, on the beach, in a eucalyptus grove, 500 meters from town, open March to November.

There are a number of good tavernas and restaurants concentrated around the village square in Polis, close to the market hall.

Good country fare is offered in the tavernas found a little way inland in the villages of Drousha and Neo Chorio.

For fish, it is best to head to one of the tavernas at the harbor of Lachi.

PAPHOS FOREST

The **Rest House** in Paphos Forest at Stavros tis Psokas, tel. 722338, has seven rooms and some suites with shower and fireplace (reservations are strongly recommended); **Oniro**, Panayia, tel. 722434, fax. 722929.

Birth House of Archbishop Makarios in Panayia: They keys can be picked up in the Makarios exhibit in the Cultural Center at the Makarios monument, open daily 9 a.m. to 1 p.m. and 3 to 6 p.m.

DIVIDED
CAPITAL

NICOSIA
NICOSIA DISTRICT
FROM NICOSIA TO TROODOS
MARATHASA VALLEY
MAKHERAS MONASTERY
FROM NICOSIA TO IDALION
NATURE WALKS

Nicosia

NICOSIA

Nicosia ❶ is the capital of Cyprus and its largest city. It is the center of government as well as business and cultural life. Greater Nicosia, which has already swallowed up what used to be outlying villages in the 1950s, has a population of 190,000 (1998 census), of which 160,000 live in the south and 30,000 in the north.

In historical terms, Nicosia is a comparatively new capital. The only remains of the Bronze Age ancient city called *Ledra* or *Lydra* are a supposed acropolis near the main government complex, and rock tombs which developers stumble across from time to time when digging foundations. Copper-producing and smelting centers such as Idalion and Tamassos nearby were far more important, as were the ports of Kition (present-day Larnaca), Paphos and Salamis. Lefkosia, as it is still called by the Greek Cypriots, became the administrative capital of the island in the 10th century when the Byzantine rulers moved the seat of government from Constantia (now Salamis) on the coast. After Richard the

Preceding pages: The old-fashioned charm of Nicosia's Old Town recalls an earlier era. Left: The younger generation looks to the future with optimism.

Lionhearted and his crusaders wrested the island from the usurper Isaac Comnenos in the 12th century, Cyprus came under the Frankish lords. They set up the Lusignan Dynasty which ruled Cyprus for nearly 300 years. For the Lusignans, and all Europeans or non-Greek speakers since, Lefkosia became known as Nicosie or Nicosia. Under the Lusignans it developed into a rich and lovely city of palaces, gardens and churches, and boasted, along with Famagusta, some of the most beautiful Gothic and Renaissance architecture outside Europe. Many of the buildings and gardens of the Lusignans, which stretched out on both sides of the Pedieos River, were razed by the Venetians in 1567. The threat of Ottoman attack on the last bastion of Christendom in the eastern Mediterranean had become very strong, and the Venetians made a last-minute attempt to fortify the island's main towns.

Venetian experts felt Nicosia was practically indefensible, sprawled as it was in the middle of a plain with weak city walls and eight gates, and would have preferred to abandon it and fortify only Famagusta. A scarcity of building materials led engineers to destroy many of the fine buildings for materials and reduce Nicosia to a tight walled city with a circumference of just five kilometers. The Venetian Walls, though hastily raised, were in fact a perfect feat of military engineering.

The city was now confined within a circular wall with 11 bastions and three gates, surrounded by a wide moat. But there was a large price to pay: 80 churches, Greek and Latin, three Greek monasteries and two convents, as well as the Cornelian Palace built by Marco Cornaro – the father of Queen Caterina Cornaro, the last queen of Cyprus – were destroyed according to a contemporary chronicler. Although this figure could have been an exaggeration, it is a fact that many buildings mentioned by chroniclers disappeared without a trace. Within the walls remained the most beautiful Gothic buildings of the time, the Cathedral of Saint Sophia, the Palace of the Provveditore, the churches of St. Nicholas, St. Catherine, St. George of the Latins and St. Mary of the Augustinians, the Convent of Our Lady of Tyre, and many mansions worth seeing.

The city fell to the Ottoman army in 1570, and many of the Latin churches were converted into mosques, though the smaller Greek churches were allowed to continue serving the Greek Orthodox population. In time, whatever was left of these destroyed buildings was used again in the repair and extension of other buildings, creating utter confusion for later historians who found inexplicable features, such as Gothic lintels or even sarcophagi, built into structures of a much later date. The Bairaktar Mosque set on the Constanza Bastion was raised at the place where the Turkish standard-bearer fell in the attack on Nicosia.

Nicosia, like the rest of the island, went into decline during the Ottoman Period. The governor of the island had moved into the old Palace of the Provveditore (Venetian: Lieutenant), now called the Konak or Saray, and many of the other mansions had been converted into dwellings with the addition of the Oriental-type covered balconies jutting out over the main door. On the whole, there was little attempt to rebuild or even maintain the once-splendid Gothic buildings.

When Britain acquired the island in 1878, some of the larger buildings were adapted for use for the civil and military administration, supplemented at first by simple wooden structures to house various officials. The first residence of the High Commissioner, later Governor, was a pleasant but unassuming wooden building between the villages of Ayii Omoloyites and Strovolos. It was eventually burned down in anti-British riots in 1931 and replaced by an impressive two-storied stone building with a giant British coat of arms dominating the entrance. This is now the Presidential Palace.

In the 1950s, Nicosia began spreading out towards the nearby villages and into the countryside. By the time of Cyprus' independence in 1960, many of these villages were suburbs. There were no clearly defined quarters where Greeks or Turks lived, though there were areas where one or the other community was dominant within the city walls. In 1960, Nicosia's Old Town was the main shopping and business center. Konak or Atatürk Square, as it had been renamed, had the central post office, banks and shops, and the law courts, with nearby offices rented by Greek and Turkish lawyers. Delineation of areas was more by trade than nationality: goldsmiths, carpenters and textile shops were all found on their own particular streets.

The main market near Ayia Sophia attracted whole streets of retailers, while Konak Square had the bookshops and car showrooms. Outside the walls, Nicosia was still mainly residential. Larnaca Road, now the bustling shop-lined Makarios III Avenue, is a broad street with townhouses set in gardens.

Right: The Berlin Wall of Cyprus – the Green Line remains an insurmountable barrier for nearly all Cypriots.

Nicosia

The Division of Nicosia

The division of Nicosia began in 1963 with the intercommunal trouble. British officers called in to supervise negotiations between the combatants drew a cease-fire line across Nicosia with a green pen. It then became known as the "Green Line." It ran from the Paphos Gate down Paphos Street and Hermes Street to just north of the Famagusta Gate, with a similar line across the northern suburbs. Due to the arbitrary delineation, the post office, law courts, the Kyrenia Gate police station, the land survey office, and many other government offices, hundreds of businesses and residences, a flour mill, factories and entire new housing developments in Kermia, Constantia and Neapolis, the suburb of Omorphita, and the Armenian Quarter, with its church, school, social clubs and family homes around Victoria Street were all in the Turkish sector. The main road to Kyrenia through Ortaköy and Gönyeli was also cut off.

Nicosia is in the center of the Mesaoria Plain, meaning it has hot dry summers during which most of the population moves to cooler areas. After August 15, a public holiday dedicated to the Assumption of the Virgin Mary, the city virtually comes to a standstill.

From medieval times onwards, the northern coast with Kyrenia and the castles of St. Hilarion and Kantara in the Pentadaktylos Range were popular summer retreats. Cutting off the road to Kyrenia meant the Nicosians now had to travel to their favorite seaside resort (until then a mere 25-minute drive away) by United Nations escorted convoy, which could take nearly an hour. Eventually, a new road to Kyrenia bypassing the Turkish enclave was built over the Pentadaktylos Range. In Nicosia itself, development now moved to the south.

It appeared that the Turkish invasion of 1974 had sounded the knell for Old Nicosia as a commercial and business center. The Green Line (cutting still farther into Greek areas) became the nucleus of confrontation with its armed soldiers and a wall of sandbags; this was a desolate area of no man's land surrounded by residential districts in which the prevalent feeling was tension. As Greater Nicosia grew, the Old Town seemed to shrink more and more into itself.

This trend was reversed in the early 1980s, when the progressive Mayor Lellos Demetriades and his Municipal Council set up a plan to revitalize the Old Town. Ledra and Onassagoras Streets still functioned as shopping streets, but there were a number of areas which had been completely abandoned, especially around the Famagusta Gate. The plan called for the Municipal Council to create several focal points in order to encourage people to return to live and work within the city walls.

Two focal points were the Laiki Yitonia, initially a tiny pedestrian area with a few old houses restored, and the Famagusta Gate, which was being used as a storeroom by the Department of Antiquities. Work had already started in the meantime on a unified sewage system for the city across the line, which took in the Greek and Turkish sectors and was backed by the United Nations Development Program.

The plan for revitalizing Old Nicosia was incorporated in another UN-backed project, the Nicosia Master Plan, in which the two halves of this unique circular walled city would be restored in a cohesive and homogenous style.

Laiki Yitonia was an immediate success, and now covers five times the original area, with more and more streets being turned into pedestrian areas every year. The Famagusta Gate, with its wide arched passage through the Venetian walls and adjoining stone guard rooms, was tastefully restored and turned into the

Right: The Archeological Museum (Cyprus Museum) in Nicosia contains treasures dating all the way back to the ninth millenium B.C.

Nicosia Municipality's Cultural Center, which hosts concerts, recitals and lectures, as well as art exhibitions. In time, other old buildings, such as the municipal garage and a small municipal bakery, were turned into arts workshops and exhibition areas.

The stagnant area, encompassing only a few small cottage industries and repair shops, now came back to life. Old houses, stores and shops were turned into piano bars, cafés, restaurants, art galleries and even a theater. This whole area offers a rich and varied nightlife for Nicosians and visitors.

Most places of interest in Nicosia are found either inside the walled city or just outside of it; all are practically within walking distance of each other. If you are staying in Nicosia, the location of your hotel will dictate your starting point. If you are driving in from another town, park your car in the municipal parking area in the moat below the Town Hall, the entrance of which off Stasinos Avenue is clearly marked. Steps at the far end of the moat will lead you onto the ramparts near the post office and into Eleftheria (Liberty) Square.

It is best to visit the Cyprus Museum, the Byzantine Museum, the Folk Art Museum and the House of the Dragoman in the morning. In the afternoons, the first three are open for only two or three hours, while the House of the Dragoman is closed.

Cyprus Museum

The *★Cyprus Museum* ❶ on Museum Street is the main archeological museum of the Republic of Cyprus. Housed in an unassuming building with a portico (erected 1908 to 1924 and dedicated to Queen Victoria), the museum was established both to display artifacts from all over the island and also to preserve, store and study them. The facilitation of research is another important aspect.

A first-time visitor to the museum may find it somewhat difficult to absorb so much history, but will still marvel at the beauty and artistry of works created up to 8,500 years ago.

Inside the entrance, to the left, is a shop with books, cards and slides. Enter Room I to the right and proceed counterclockwise around the ground floor. The arrangement of displays by chronology and type enables one to easily follow developments. Please keep in mind that objects may be on loan to another institution, or may have been moved to another room, so that the following description may not always match the current layout.

Room I: Aceramic and Ceramic Neolithic (7000-3750 B.C.) to Chalcolithic (3500-2500/2300 B.C.) Periods. Stone figures and implements of stone, flint and bone; human figures with simple features; pottery, jewelry and steatite cross figures from the Ceramic Neolithic and Chalcolithic Periods.

Room II: Early Bronze Age (Early Cypriot, 2300-1900 B.C.). Clay figu-

rines, plank figures, terra cotta models of plowing and a ritual scene.

Room III: Pottery from the Middle Bronze Age (Middle Cypriot, 1900-1625 B.C.) to the Hellenic Period. A faience rhyton (ancient drinking horn of pottery or bronze) from Mycenaean times is especially beautiful. In two of the three frieze panels lively scenes in inlay or enamal can be seen: in the upper panel two bulls, an antilope and a wild goat are racing past; beneath this, two hunters can be seen, each chasing a bull. A Cypriot speciality is the so-called "free field style" painted vase from the Cypro-Archaic Period (700-600 B.C.). On one of the loveliest of these vases, a mighty bull can be seen sniffing a lotus flower.

Room IV: Votive figures from Ayia Irini, Late Bronze Age (Late Cypriot, 1625-1050 B.C.). Warriors, bulls, centaurs, etc., miniature to life size.

Rooms V, VI, XIII: Sculpture from the Cypro-Archaic (750-475 B.C.) to Roman (58 B.C.-A.D. 330) Periods, showing development from monumental, stiff, styl-

ized works with Oriental and Egyptian influences, to classical Greek and finally Hellenistic styles. In addition there are Roman realistic portraits, the famous Torso of Aphrodite of Soli, and a larger-than-life bronze statue of Emperor Septimus Severus.

Room VII: In the front section of this long hall the most beautiful examples of Cypriot bronze casting have been gathered together. Tools, weapons, buckles, and even a large grilling spit can be seen here. The most valuable objects on display in this room, artistically speaking, are the famous statues of deities including one of the Horned God of Enkomi. In addition, there are a number of copper bars of varying size in the form of stretched animal skins.

In the middle of the long right wall of this room is a staircase leading to the basement as well as an upper floor, and to Rooms VIII and IX. For now, let us stay

Above: Marble statues, with Aphrodite in the center, on display in the Cyprus Museum.

in Room VII. In the mid and rear portions of the room are several Roman mosaics, including the well-known one of *Leda and the Swan* from the ancient Temple of Aphrodite in Kouklia near Paphos.

Furthermore, there are a number of display cases containing marvelous jewelry. One of the cases has a golden scepter, found in Kourion, with a cloisonné orb; on its tip a pair of bearded vultures are poised. An interesting necklace from the seventh century is made of dainty pearls, counterbalanced by a cylindrical agate pendant crowned by a golden bee and two serpents. Portions of the famous silver treasure of Lambousa from pre-Christian times can be seen here, too.

Basement Level, Rooms IX and X: In the dark cellar of the museum, several different types of graves, complete with skeletal remains and grave furnishings, have been carefully reconstructed. In Room IX gravestones from the sixth to third century B.C. are predominantly on display. In Room X you will see numerous inscriptions in Cypro-Minoan syllabic script; a script which has never been deciphered and which was in use until the Hellenic Age. Who knows, maybe you will crack the code!

Upper Level with Room XI: In Room XI you will find furniture with ivory inlay work, and bronze objects from a royal tomb in Salamis (eighth century B.C.). Photographs document the discovery and recovery of these objects. In an unnumbered side room the history and technique of copper mining and copper working are clearly documented.

Room XIV: In the last room of the museum plank idols and small terra cotta figures from the Middle Bronze Age can be seen.

Around Paphos Gate

Diagonally across the road as you come out of the museum is the neoclassical **Municipal Theater ❷**, built in 1967, home of the Cyprus Theatrical Organization. Behind the theater are the **Municipal Gardens**, pleasantly laid out with palm trees and various Mediterranean flowering bushes and trees, artificial ponds and walkways, benches, and an aviary with a pond for waterfowl, always an attraction for small children.

At the intersection of Museum and Homer streets, looking northwest, you can see the **House of Representatives** to the right and the **Nicosia General Hospital** to the left. Museum Street leads past the Municipal Theater to the **Paphos Gate ❸** roundabout, where there is a **Statue of Markos Drakos**, one of the heroes of the 1955-59 Liberation Struggle against British rule. The Venetian Walls and the **Roccas Bastion ❹** in front mark the limits of the Green Line in this area, with Turkish flags prominently displayed.

Keeping the walls on your right, walk up **Markos Drakos Avenue**, with several early-20th-century town houses set on terraces to your left. On the right side of

the street stands a United Nations observation post and part of the walled city, which nowadays lies in the Turkish-occupied sector of Nicosia.

At the crossroads, Markos Drakos Avenue bears right at the **Ledra Palace Checkpoint ❺**. This is the only point at which the Green Line can be crossed. A Cypriot Police checkpoint precedes the no man's land controlled by the United Nations in front of the Ledra Palace Hotel, and farther on, the northern Cyprus checkpoint. Just before the first checkpoint stands the **Residence of the Ambassador of Greece**, and just beyond it the **Goethe Institute**, the German cultural center.

On the right are some buildings with bullet holes and damage incurred during the fighting of 1974, and a social club and restaurant run by refugees from the Karpasia area. You can return the same way to Paphos Gate.

A quick route into town is through Paphos Gate. Called the **Porta di San Domenico** by the Venetians, the Venetian Passage is now practically below ground level. It was originally a tall narrow stone gateway with wide steps on both sides leading to the garrison building above it. The gate was closed by the British in 1879 and part of the walls next to it cut away to create an opening onto Paphos Street.

The Venetian garrison buildings were used by the Ottomans as an arsenal and then by the British as police headquarters. Heavy fighting took place here during the coup d'état against President Makarios and the ensuing Turkish invasion in 1974. The damage has been repaired, and the buildings house the Paphos Gate police station and the fire department.

As you come out of Paphos Gate, you will see a portion of the Green Line. The barricade near the Catholic **Church of the Holy Cross ❻** leads to Victoria Street and the Armenian Quarter. Paphos Street is blocked a little farther up. Turn to your

Nicosia

right and you will pass the **Maronite Café** and see the **Maronite Church** ❼ at the end of Favierou Street.

Opposite the Paphos Gate police station, at the corner of Favierou Street, stands the **Castigliotissa** ❽, the remains of the once fabulous Lusignan Palace, flattened by the Venetians when they built their walls and bastions. Now restored by the Department of Antiquities, it is used as a small cultural center.

Walk past the Paphos Gate police and fire stations and you will come to the main station for Nicosia's buses at Solomos Square.

Continue down Kostas Pantelides Avenue, with buildings on your left and the city ramparts and gardens in the moat below on your right. You will then reach Eleftheria Square, with the **Nicosia Town Hall** and the **Main Post Office** on the **D'Avila Bastion** ❾. Walk in front of the town hall to the post office and watch for a sign which will lead you into Laiki Yitonia.

The restored Old Town quarter of ★**Laiki Yitonia** ❿, with its pedestrian area, its attractive houses and its many tavernas and handicrafts shops – as well as one of the best bookstores on the island – is an inviting place to stroll and to pass the time in.

There is also an office of the Cyprus Tourism Organization (CTO) in the neighborhood, as well as the Leventis Municipal Museum and a private Jewelry Museum, which can be visited free of charge. In the latter museum's two small rooms not only are examples of typical Cypriot silver jewelry shown, but also articles of silverware such as can be seen in just about every living room on the island.

The Old Town

For orientation purposes, it is usually best to explore the walled city by starting at **Eleftheria Square**. This is where **Ledra Street** begins, Nicosia'a main

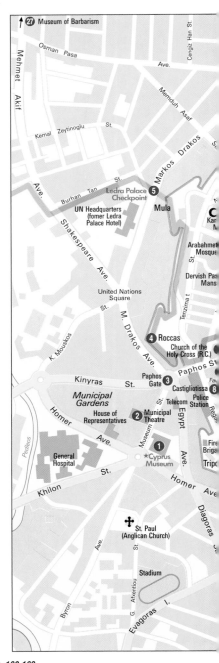

NICOSIA

0   100   200 m

shopping street. It is still packed with a wide variety of shops, many of them with their wares displayed outside the doors. Ledra Street ends in a cul-de-sac at a barricade.

Turn right up Nikokleous Street, which leads to Phaneromeni Street and the **Phaneromeni Church** ⑪. The present building dates back to 1872 and was erected on the site of an older Greek Orthodox monastery or convent, with stones taken from the ruins of Athalassa Castle outside the city.

At the back of the churchyard is a marble mausoleum dedicated to Archbishop Kyprianos, his bishops and other Greek Cypriot leaders who were killed on July 9, 1821, by order of the Turkish Governor Küchük Mehmet. They were all either beheaded or hanged. The reason: The struggle for freedom against the Turks had

Above: Market stands display the fruits and vegetables that are the staples of the Cypriot diet. Right: A crumbling reminder of former glory in Nicosia's Old Town.

broken out in Greece some three months earlier. The Governor wanted to set a brutal example for the Greek community so that Cyprus would not follow suit.

Outside the yard at the back of the church is the former Phaneromeni Girls' School, which is nowadays attended by both girls and boys. On the northeast side of the churchyard stands the **Araplar Mosque** ⑫. Built during the first half of the 16th century in a mixture of Byzantine and Gothic styles, it was originally a small church or chapel. Practically in its shadow is a small restaurant which has tables and chairs set outside in warm weather. It serves simple Cypriot food at modest prices.

Take Mouseon Street beyond the Phaneromeni churchyard to emerge at the top of Onassagoras Street, once lined exclusively with fabric shops, of which there are still a large number. Walking down Onassagoras Street towards Eleftheria Square, turn left on Pythonos Street and then right onto Solon Street to the Tripioti Church.

The **Tripioti Church** , built in 1695 on the site of an older Byzantine building, is an interesting work of architecture because fragments of other buildings have been incorporated into its structure. Both the south and west doorways have carved lintels which obviously belonged to older buildings or churches, most probably from the 14th century. This was once the society church of Nicosia, and its parishioners must have made many valuable donations since the iconostasis covers the entire width of the church and is beautifully decorated.

Continue down Solon Street and you will reach **Hippocrates Street** and Laiki Yitonia. Turn to your right on Hippocrates Street and you will come to the **Leventis Municipal Museum** (Laiki Yitonia). The museum occupies one of three houses built by a prosperous Nicosian in 1885 for his three daughters. The second one now houses the offices of the Nicosia Sewage Board, and the third was demolished in the 1930s. The museum is a good example of late 19th-century urban architecture.

The house was acquired by the Anastasios G. Leventis Foundation for the Nicosia Municipality in the 1980s. At the time it was in a state of disrepair, but a team of experts and architects lovingly restored it to its former glory. It was opened as the Municipal Museum in 1989. The history of the city is told through artifacts, jewelry, coins, maps, posters and costumes from prehistoric times to the present day. There is no admission charged, but a small donation is always welcome.

Coming out of Laiki Yitonia onto the ramparts, turn to your left and go down Konstantinos Paleologou Street to **Canning Bridge**. If it is market day (usually Wednesday), the area will be crammed with stalls selling fruit, vegetables and other goods, and the carts of traveling peddlers. On the **Costanza Bastion** stands the **Bairaktar Mosque**

built by the Ottomans in memory of the standard bearer who fell here during the attack on Nicosia in 1570.

The Eastern Old Town

If you wish to explore the eastern part of the walled city, it is best to start off in the morning from Eleftheria Square down Konstantinos Paleologou Street to Canning Bridge. Turn into the walled city down Trikoupi Street until you come to an open space to your right. Here you will see the **Omeriye Mosque** , formerly the 14th-century Church of St. Mary of the Augustinians. The Augustinian order had a monastery in Nicosia in medieval times to which this church belonged, as well as a hospice for travelers. A square chapel on the north side of the church was added later, and its octagonal turret and spiral staircase were extended by the Ottomans to form a minaret.

Continue along the side of the mosque, which still functions for Moslems resident in Nicosia, up Patriarch Gregorios

Nicosia

Street to the House of the Dragoman on the right side of the street. The ★**House of Hadji Georgakis Kornesios** ⑯, as it is officially known, is the most important example of urban architecture of the last century of Ottoman rule to be preserved in Old Nicosia. Hadji Georgakis Kornesios was the "Dragoman of Cyprus" (*dragoman* literally means "interpreter"), the highest rank held by a Greek layman from 1779/80 to 1809. The Archbishop, as ethnarch (leader of the Greek Cypriot nation), looked after the spiritual and temporal well-being of the Greeks of Cyprus, whereas the Dragoman was the liaison with the Ottoman authorities and was responsible for tax collecting and other administrative functions.

From the street, the house looks rather fortress-like with its thick walls and iron-barred windows. The main door is set in a pointed arch with carved decoration and an inlaid marble slab set above it. The slab is carved with a winged Lion of Venice and probably came from an old Venetian building. A second marble plaque set into the wall on the interior of the entrance above the main door bears the monogram of Hadji Georgakis and the year 1793, when the house was probably extended by the Dragoman.

Once inside the main door, the house takes on a completely different aspect. There are the colonnades and courtyard of a prosperous town house of the period, with auxiliary and service rooms on the ground floor and the living quarters above. At the bottom of the garden, beyond the courtyard with its fountain, is the *hamam*, the family's personal Turkish bath, complete with a heating system under the floor and a small garden with citrus trees.

A covered wooden staircase leads to the living quarters, which have been restored as exhibition areas or furnished in

Right: Statue of Archbishop Makarios III in front of the modern Archbishopric of Nicosia.

the style of grand town houses of the early 20th century. A long corridor to the right of the main hall leads to the decorated "divan room," the only one of the Ottoman Period still preserved in Cyprus. Here the Dragoman would receive his guests. They lounged on the lavish coverings and cushions of the low divans, talking and eating sweetmeats, sipping fruit drinks and smoking water pipes.

During the time of Hadji Georgakis, the entire ceiling and wooden panels between the windows were painted in vivid colors, some of which have been discovered under layers of dark green paint applied in later years. In the recess of the north wall between the built-in cupboards (one of which hides a secret passage to the roof), there is a wall painting of a city, possibly a conventional representation of Constantinople. The divan room also contains two portraits of Hadji Georgakis Kornesios, one of his son, and one of his son's wife.

On leaving the House of Hadji Georgakis, turn right where you can see **Ayios Antonios Church** ⑰ at the bottom of Patriarch Gregorios Street. This was renovated in 1743, but contains tombstones from the 15th century. It was an important church in the 19th century, attended by the Hadji Georgakis family in their own family pew.

Zenon Kitieos Street leads to another important center of Nicosia. Here are the two Archbishoprics, new and old, St. John's or Ayios Ioannis Cathedral, the Byzantine and Folk Art Museums, the National Struggle Museum, and the Pancyprian Gymnasium, the prime secondary school of the capital where most of the country's elite were educated. This square, now looking so peaceful, was the scene of many clashes between British forces and young demonstrators in the 1955-59 period. Schoolboys from the gymnasium used the roof of the Seferis Library on the corner to throw stones at soldiers and policemen below.

The Archbishoprics

The Byzantine-style **New Archbishopric** was completed in 1960. A gigantic **Statue of Archbishop Makarios III** (which was ordered by his successor Archbishop Khrysostomos) dominates the forecourt. Walk along the railings to the open courtyard which leads to the small ***Church of Ayios Ioannis** ⑱, which is the cathedral where the Archbishop officiates. Built in 1662, its interior was painted in the years between 1736 and 1756. Both Byzantine and Western elements are evident in Biblical scenes, and the story of the discovery in Salamis of the tomb of St. Barnabas, founder of the Cypriot Church, is in late-Byzantine style. Once again, parts of other buildings were used for this church.

Over the western entrance is a sculpted marble panel from some destroyed Gothic building, with three Lusignan coats of arms. Another coat of arms appears over the door, and another sculpted panel was inserted higher up on the same wall. The southern doorway has a carved lintel in Italian Renaissance style, and a 15th-century sarcophagus has been embedded in the back porch.

The Archbishop Makarios III Cultural Foundation, with its ****Byzantine Museum** ⑲, is in the courtyard behind Ayios Ioannis. One of the most exceptional collections of Byzantine icons and murals in the world covers the entire spectrum of Byzantine art in Cyprus from the fifth to the 18th centuries. The oldest objects in the museum are six early Christian mosaics from the fifth century, depicting representations of Mary and some of the apostles.

They were originally in the Panagia Kanakaria Church near Lythrankomi in the Turkish-occupied part of the island. They were stolen from there in 1974, and reappeared in 1989 through an American art dealer. The Church of Cyprus successfully sued the United States for the unconditional return of the mosaics.

The oldest icon in the museum hangs just beyond the entrance (No. 1) on the

right. It is a fragment of a painting of Mary executed in encaustic technique from the eighth or ninth century. In this early method of icon painting, egg yolk was not used as a fixer for the pigment – as was later common practice – but rather, honey was. Because of this, the texture of the colors is somewhat reminiscent of Impressionist paintings.

On the other side of the courtyard is the **Old Archbishopric**, which used to be the Benedictine Abbey of St. John the Evangelist. It passed into the hands of the Greek Orthodox Church when the Benedictine Order left the island after the Mameluke raid of 1426, and was a monastery until the 18th century. At that time it was renovated, incorporating the remains of the old abbey into the ground floor, and became the residence of the Orthodox Archbishop. It now houses the **Folk Art Museum** ⓴.

Above: Byzantine frescoes in Ayios Ioannis Church, Nicosia. Right: Grateful prisoners are freed in the bronze "Liberation of Cyprus."

The museum was set up in 1950 by the artist Adamantios Diamantis for the Cyprus Studies Society to preserve the folk art of Cyprus. Diamantis collected most of the exhibits from all over the island. His collection includes traditional handicrafts, such as weaving and embroidery, costumes from various parts of the island, hand-carved dowry chests and pottery. Over the years more items have been collected, and the museum offers a look at the domestic life of the Cypriot, in town and in the countryside, during the 19th and early 20th centuries. Further to the north is the **National Struggle Museum** ㉑, which contains various relics of the 1955-1959 Liberation Struggle, as well as a research library.

Between the church and the museum, a covered lane leads to the not especially interesting **Market Hall** ㉒ of Nicosia. On the short walk there you will pass, on your right-hand side, the old electrical works. Today, this building houses the **Municipal Arts Center** ㉓, with its somewhat avant-garde exhibition rooms.

Temporary exhibitions here present the works of leading contemporary Cypriot and international artists. There is also a pleasant café in the museum, as well as a well-stocked museum shop.

Around Famagusta Gate

From the Archbishopric, Korais Street leads to the city ramparts dominated by a monumental modern sculpture called the *Liberation of Cyprus* on the **Podocataro Bastion** ㉔.

Turn left down Nikephoros Phokas Avenue, which leads to **Famagusta Gate** ㉕. The Porta Giuliana, as it was once called, was the strongest and most elaborate of the three gates built by the Venetians. It has been restored and now houses the **Nicosia Municipality Cultural Center**. It has a vaulted passage which cuts through the thick walls to the moat, with a cupola in the center of the passage letting in the light. The central passage has proven to be an ideal site for lectures, music recitals and exhibitions.

Stone-built guardrooms on both sides of the passage have also been restored and transformed into exhibition rooms. In the moat on the other side of the gate is an **open-air theater** where performances take place in summer, and a small **park** with modern sculptures.

Numerous cafés, galleries and restaurants abound in the area of Famagusta Gate. Some of these are housed in spaces converted from storerooms set in the city walls, others occupy old shops and houses. The Green Line is again quite close by, but there are kebab shops practically on the line itself in a maze of narrow streets. Most of the restaurants and cafés in this lively area don't open for business until the evening, catering to Cypriots who prefer to go out for dinner or late-night snacks rather than for lunch.

To reach **Khrysaliniotissa Church** ㉖, the oldest Byzantine church in Nicosia, dedicated to "Our Lady of the Golden Flax," turn off Nikephoros Phokas Avenue down Theseus Street. **Antigonos Street**, the second little street to the right,

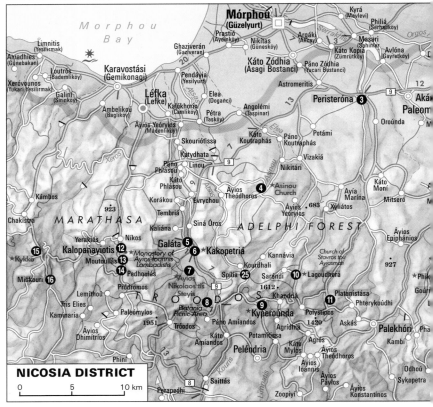

NICOSIA DISTRICT

0 5 10 km

leads you to this pretty church, which was built, according to local tradition, by Princess Helena Paleologa in 1450. It has some beautiful old icons, some of them dating back to the 14th century. Return to Famagusta Gate and take a leisurely walk along the street running on the ramparts until you return to Eleftheria Square.

NICOSIA DISTRICT

The Nicosia District, the largest of the island, includes all of the Solea and Pitsilia valleys, and parts of the Marathasa region, with mountain villages, fruit orchards, hill resorts and countless Byzantine churches and monasteries, a contrast to the villages and an-

cient sites in the plains. On a day trip from Nicosia or Limassol, either with a tour group or by rented car, it is possible to visit a number of the refreshing mountain villages and their unique painted churches, outstanding examples of a remarkable indigenous art form which incorporates foreign influences. This is an experience you should not miss if you want to truly appreciate Cyprus' rich folk heritage.

Staying the night in one of the hill resorts will give you more time to appreciate the beautiful scenery and explore further. Almost all the churches are kept locked, and finding the priest or caretaker who has the key can be a time-consuming process. However, it often leads to pleas-

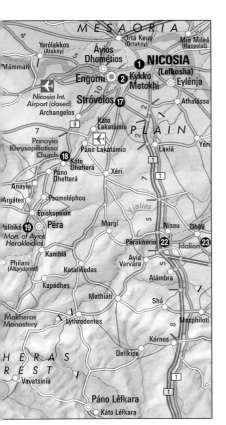

Troodos is at a sharp angle in a dip down a wide road and is easy to miss.

The road now skirts Nicosia Airport in a UN-controlled area and the original Nicosia-Troodos road, which now lies partly in the Turkish-occupied zone. You meet the road again at a sharp left turn at **Kokkini Trimithia**. You can also take the new highway from Nicosia to Kokkini Trimithia.

The road bypasses most of the villages. You will see on your left the villages of **Akaki** and then **Peristerona ❸**, where you can pull over and stop since the village appears on either side of a wide dry riverbed. You can clearly see the Byzantine **Church of Saints Barnabas and Hilarion**, built in the early 10th century with 17th to 18th century additions. It is one of the two surviving five-domed Cypriot churches (the other is in Yeroskipos). It was founded by Archbishop Nicephoros, whose tomb is in the narthex of the church. Its restored iconostasis, dating back to 1549, has a colorful 16th-century icon, the *Presentation in the Temple*.

An adjacent **mosque**, formerly a Latin church, shows this was once a mixed village in which Greek and Turkish Cypriots worshiped side by side.

Asinou Church

Astromeritis, the next village after Peristerona, is famous for its watermelons. The turnoff to Troodos to the left comes just at the entrance of the village. There are several cafés at this point, traditionally a coffee stop before the drive into the mountains. A few kilometers down the road is a signpost to ****Asinou Church ❹**, also known as **Panayia Phorviotissa**, with some of the finest examples of Byzantine mural paintings on the island. The church is normally open during the day; if not, stop at the small nearby village of Nikitari to find out about getting the key.

ant encounters with friendly villagers who are usually more than eager to show guests the notable aspects of their cultural heritage. After they have done so, you will often be invited to share some wine or food, a pleasant way to while away a few hours.

FROM NICOSIA TO TROODOS

The route from Nicosia to Troodos is down Grivas Dighenis Avenue to the traffic lights at **Kykko Metokhi ❷**, a dependency of Kykko Monastery built in 1890. Turn left and follow the road signs for Troodos through the straggling new suburbs of **Anthoupolis** and **Archangelos**. The turnoff to the right for

Asinou Church, now on UNESCO's list of World Cultural Heritage Sites, is dedicated to the Virgin Mary. It is a rectangular vaulted building with a second steep-pitched roof with flat tiles, and is completely painted on the interior in a brilliant Byzantine manner. Over the south entrance you can see a painting of the donor, identified as Nicephoros Magister, offering a model of the church (looking very much as it does today) to the Virgin Mary. From the various inscriptions, experts believe that the church was built between the years 1099 and 1105.

About two-thirds of the original decoration in the very sophisticated Comnenian style of Byzantine painting (1081-1185) survives, with some excellent examples of how the artists of the period portrayed various incidents in the lives of Jesus and the Virgin Mary, such as the

Above: Steep-pitched tile roof of the Asinou Church. Right: Typical houses of the hillside town of Kakopetria.

Annunciation, Christ's *Triumphal Entry into Jerusalem*, the *Last Supper* and the *Death of the Virgin Mary*, as well as the obligatory saints.

The *Communion of the Apostles* in the center of the apse is one of the most interesting compositions in this style, showing Christ offering wine to six of the apostles, with his gaze directed at Judas, who has turned away at the extreme right. The northwest recess is filled with an interesting painting, the *Forty Martyrs of Sebaste*, a scene from early Christian times. The martyrs were put on a frozen lake with tempting hot baths for those who wished to forsake their religion. The central section of the nave is covered with a series of paintings from the 14th and 15th-century revival, more rustic in style. Scenes from the life of Christ cover the vault and the north arched recess. On the left of the south door is the *Mother of God*, portraying Mary on a royal throne holding Christ before her, attended by two archangels. On the right of the same door is St. George.

Standing in the middle of the church, looking towards the sanctuary, is a painting of John the Baptist with the Virgin Mary on the northeast pillar interceding for mankind through Christ, depicted on the opposite side on the southeast pier.

The south side of the northeast pillar has a figure of St. Helena in imperial clothes, holding an orb and scepter. Saints Peter and Paul face each other on the west pillars. In the upper realms of the building is a painting of the Last Judgment, with a host of saints and donors in the lower parts. Also worth noting are the three outstanding paintings in the south apse of the narthex. These are: *St. George on a White Horse* in a hilly landscape, *St. Anastasia the Poison Curer*, holding a cross and a bottle of medicine with the donor beside her, in smaller scale, dressed as a lady of the upper classes of the period, and the *Mother of God Enthroned with Christ* and three kneeling patrons of the church.

Return to the main road by the same route. Just a few kilometers further on is **Koutraphas**, a small farming village. The road continues here through the foothills of the Troodos Mountains to a road junction offering drivers two choices: either Kakopetria and Troodos straight ahead, or Kalopanayiotis and Kykko to the right.

Galata and Kakopetria

Take the wide highway straight ahead, which winds up through the mountains to Troodos passing all villages. The first village you will pass through is **Evrychou**, followed by **Tembria** and then **Kaliana**, which can be seen on the other side of the valley. Turn off the highway at a signpost for **Galata** and **Kakopetria**, which are now for all practical purposes one village. The road through these villages is rather narrow, and in summer drivers need a great deal of patience to cope with the creeping traffic.

Nicosia

In the middle of **Galata** ❺ stands the **Church of Ayios Sozomenos**, dating back to the early 16th century. It has a steep pitched roof and a complete series of frescoes made up of several cycles. One cycle is devoted to the life of Christ, scenes from the life of the Virgin Mary, and episodes from the life of St. George, including the slaying of the dragon. Also inside are paintings of various individual saints and female martyrs, while the exterior north wall has two paintings: the *Seven Ecumenical Councils of the Church* and the *Triumph of Orthodoxy*.

The **Church of the Archangel Michael** was originally called Panayia Theotokos (Mary Mother of God). This timber-roofed chapel just below the village is completely painted in the post-Byzantine style of the early 16th century. Above the north door is a painting showing *Christ Enthroned*, with the Virgin Mary and St. John the Baptist on either side and a group of donors, the Zacharia family, at their feet. An inscription is dated January 17, 1514, and identifies the

artist as Symeon Axentes, who also carried out some of the paintings in the Church of Ayios Sozomenos. The other paintings include the Virgin Mary and various dignitaries, and scenes from the life of Christ.

Nearby is the larger **Church of Panayia Podithou**, which once belonged to a monastery. It was erected in 1502, and its paintings are of the Italo-Byzantine style which appeared on the island towards the end of the 15th century. The donors of the church were Demeter de Coron, a captain of the barony of Pendayia, and his wife Helena. Above the main entrance to the church is the *Descent of Christ into Hades*, and on either side of the entrance are the figures of the Virgin Mary and Christ. The painting of the *Communion of the Apostles* is an outstanding example of depicting movement

Above: The steep-pitched tile roof Church of Panayia Podithou. Right: Young scholars break into smiles during the serious process of getting educated.

and capturing detail in the clothing, so characteristic of this period in Cyprus. In the west pediment is a powerfully-painted *Crucifixion*, and in the east pediment a depiction of *Moses Receiving the Ten Commandments*.

The small **Church of Ayia Pareskevi**, between Galata and Kakopetria, was originally a cemetery chapel. Its paintings include a depiction of the Virgin Mary and of dignitaries, and fragments of an *Ascension* by Symeon Axentes, dated 1514.

Drive over the small bridge and you are now in ★**Kakopetria** ❻. In summer, the schoolyard behind the central square offers parking at reasonable rates. Return to the bridge on foot, and you will see a signpost for the Old Village pointing the way to the old village center. The upper path leads past the "bad rocks" which give the village its name (*kako* is Greek for "bad," and *petra* means "stone").

The alleyways between the balconied stone houses are cobbled and wind gently above the river below. On the other side of

Nicosia

the river you can see the picturesque **Mill Restaurant**, built into the rock with wide wooden verandas and tables set out near the original Old Mill on the riverbank. Here you can savor delicious fresh river trout prepared by a Cypriot chef who managed a restaurant in London for many years. Steps from the Old Village lead to the riverbank, and a bridge crosses to the Old Mill.

The many other restaurants and cafés in this area and around the main square offer a variety of local dishes with simple, satisfying food.

Ayios Nikolaos tis Steyis

The most beautiful church in the Solea Valley is ★**Ayios Nikolaos tis Steyis** ❼ (St. Nicholas of the Roof). It stands about five kilometers above Kakopetria and can be reached through the village (signposted from the square) or from the main Nicosia-Troodos highway.

The church was erected in the early 11th century, and a domed narthex was added a hundred years later. The distinctive steep-pitched roof with flat tiles was added on quite early as a protection against snow and rain, and thus gave its name to the church. The paintings date from the 11th to the 17th centuries and cover the entire interior, providing vivid examples of the changes in style and technique over these years. Some of the later paintings were removed by the Department of Antiquities to reveal earlier ones. The earliest paintings, such as the *Raising of Lazarus* and the *Triumphal Entry into Jerusalem*, are in the west vault. A *Virgin Mary with Archangels* is in the apse, the *Ascension* is in the vault, and busts of various dignitaries are on the pillars.

The next group of paintings of the early 12th-century Comnenian style are in the southwest compartment of the nave. Some of those are in the narthex, including the *Virgin Mary in the Temple*, the *Forty Martyrs of Sebaste* on the west wall, and various saints on the south wall and the pillar opposite. Parts of the *Last*

Judgment are in the dome of the narthex. A very fine large painting, *St. Nicholas*, was executed in the 12th century. The *Christ Pantocrator*, the "Ruler of the Universe" surrounded by twelve angels in the dome and twelve prophets in the drum of the dome were painted in the mid 14th century, as were a group of life-sized saints in some of the lower parts of the nave. On the east pillars supporting the dome are 17th-century paintings of St. Peter and St. Paul, with a small portrait of the donor, a monk called Philotheos, with the date 1633.

To Panayia tou Araka Church

The road now leads uphill through the inviting summer picnic area of **Platania ❽**, with its forest station and rustic tables and benches, to the Karvouna crossroads. The road down heads towards Saittas and Limassol, to the right to Troodos, and to the left to ★**Kyperounda ❾**. Here you can see the **Church of the Holy Cross**, a small chapel from the 16th century, with a series of paintings in and around the north and south arched recesses dated back to 1521, including a series of miniature paintings telling the story of the *Discovery of the Holy Cross.*

From Kyperounda, take the road to Khandria and ★**Lagoudhera ❿** for the **Church of Panayia tou Araka**. The 12th-century church stands just outside the village on the road to the village of Sarandi. Visitors can ask for the key and be escorted through the church by the priest, who may be found on the premises next door.

The interior of this church has the most complete series of paintings of the mid-Byzantine Period on the island. An inscription dates the painting to 1192, but the church itself is older. The *Christ* in the dome is one of the most beautiful ver-

sions of the subject and has been widely used both as a scholarly illustration of Byzantine art in Cyprus and – on a more mundane level – for charity organizations' Christmas cards.

Farther down are the *Twelve Prophets* between the rounded windows leading to the *Annunciation*, in which the Archangel Gabriel is seen stepping down from an elegant Byzantine building to deliver his message.

The paintings in the vaults and on the walls depict scenes from the lives of Jesus and the Virgin Mary. A warm and human representation of the *Birth of Christ*, on the south side of the western wall, shows the Virgin Mary resting at the entrance to a cave and a midwife washing the child.

The remaining surfaces are covered by representations of the apostles, martyrs, ascetics and hermits, as well as prelates of the church. St. Symeon Stylites, who lived on top of a pillar, is also portrayed, as is St. Mary of Egypt receiving communion from St. Zosimus. St. Lazarus shown in prelate's vestments in the southeast recess is one of the most dynamic paintings of the 12th century. The portrayal of the *Virgin Mary Enthroned* with Christ on her lap attended by the archangels is stately and powerful in the apse.

From Laguoudhera you can continue on to the village of **Platanistassa ⓫**. There you can inquire in the first café on the main street as to the whereabouts of the keeper of the key to the **Church of Stavros tou Ayiasmati**. Take him with you to this steep-pitched tile roof church standing in an idyllic setting (and don't forget to bring him back home after you've had a look at the church!). Inside there are some 40 frescoes from around the year 1500 to be seen.

MARATHASA VALLEY

The Marathasa Valley and the famous Kykko Monastery can be reached via the Nicosia-Troodos highway. At the road

Right: Ayios Ioannis Lampadistis is a treasure trove of Byzantine artwork.

Map pp. 154-155, Info pp. 168-169

Nicosia

junction after Koutraphas and just before Evrychou, turn to the right. A pleasant drive through wooded foothills with small villages to the right and left leads to a fork in the road a few kilometers up, with one road leading to Kykko and the other to Kalopanayiotis.

Kalopanayiotis ⑫, the lowest-lying of the three villages of the Marathasa Valley, is famous for its sulphur springs and the ***Monastery of Ayios Ioannis Lampadistis**, which can be seen clearly in a dip in the hills, just below the village. The monastery is no longer in use. Its church is a combination of several buildings of various dates: an 11th-century church dedicated to St. Herakleidios on the south; a barrel-vaulted church dedicated to Ayios Ioannis Lampadistis, a local saint, in the middle; a timber-roofed narthex which was attached along the west end of the two churches in the middle of the 15th century; and a tall vaulted building on the north, attached at the end of the 15th century, which might have been a Latin chapel. The whole building

is covered by a second protective roof of flat tiles.

In the **Church of St. Herakleidios** there are 13th-century paintings in the dome, the south vault and the western arm of the nave. The best preserved is the *Triumphal Entry into Jerusalem* in the western vault, with its vivid colors and a date palm tree with children among the dates. Other paintings show the *Raising of Lazarus*, the *Crucifixion*, the *Sacrifice of Isaac*, the *Ascension* – covering the whole of the vault of the south arm – and the *Christ Pantocrator* in the dome, as well as a colossal *Archangel Michael* on the right of the west door. The piers are also painted with images of the Virgin Mary, Christ and Christian saints. A cycle of over 30 scenes from the New Testament in late-Byzantine style dating back to about 1400 covers the remaining vaults of the church and is unique on the island.

The **Church of Ayios Ioannis Lampadistis**, in the middle of the complex, was rebuilt at the beginning of the 18th century retaining the northeast pier over

the saint's tomb. A narrow arch in the east which has fragments of two layers of paintings, suggesting a 12th-century date for the original church. The skull of the saint is preserved in a silver casket in a niche above the tomb and is believed to have healing powers. The fame of the holy relic increasingly brought more pilgrims. By the 15th century, the monastery was extended by a vaulted narthex. The vault later collapsed and was roofed again in timber, but the paintings, which included the *Miracles of Christ, Mary Magdalene and the Disciples at the Holy Sepulcher*, the *Resurrection* and the *Last Judgment* on the north, east and south walls, survived. An inscription identifies the artist as coming from Constantinople, most probably after the Turks captured it in 1453.

The **Latin Chapel**, as it is called – though there is no record of it having been used as such – has the most complete series of wall-paintings in the Italo-Byzantine style popular on the island at the end of the 15th and beginning of the 16th century. The artist has not been identified, but it is obvious he was trained in the West and was skilled in portraying the landscape backgrounds and architecture prevalent in Renaissance art, used in the portrayal of the *Akathistos*, the famous hymn of 24 stanzas in honor of the Virgin Mary sung in the Greek Orthodox Church during Lent. Other paintings include a *Virgin and Child* and several Old Testament subjects.

On the west side of the stream at the east edge of Kalopanayiotis is the **Church of Ayios Andronikos**, a small mountain-type chapel with a steep-pitched roof. It has a number of paintings from the 16th century. Less than one kilometer further up is **Moutoullas** ⑬ village, with its tiny 13th-century **Chapel of Panayia tou Moutoullas**. Built in 1280, it has the only dated series of wall-paintings of the 13th century on Cyprus.

Above: During a Greek-Orthodox baptismal ceremony. Right: The Kykko Monastery is situated in a verdant setting.

Visitors can obtain the key from the house next door. There is an interesting painting of the donors, Ioannis Moutoullas and his wife Irini, on the north wall. Many of the paintings have been badly damaged, but it is possible to make out the *Birth of Christ* on the south wall. It also has a 15th-century mural, the *Presentation of Christ in the Temple*. The *Raising of Lazarus*, the *Triumphal Entry into Jerusalem*, and the *Crucifixion* are to be found on the west wall, and the *Resurrection* on the north wall.

The third village is **Pedhoulas** ⓮, a summer resort famous for its cherries. The painted **Church of the Archangel Michael** stands in the lower part of the village and dates from 1474. Visitors can obtain the key from the house next door. The painting of the donors of this church is well executed. Of particular interest are the clothes worn by the women, which show traditional local woven embroidery on the mantles. The walls of the nave are divided into two areas, the upper one for the New Testament cycle and the lower

one for individual saints. The *Crucifixion* can be seen in the west pediment and the *Ascension* in the east one. The paintings have been attributed to a local artist. His portrayal of individual saints is particularly charming, notably Constantine and Helena supporting the Holy Cross between them, St. Kyriaki with the personifications of the days of the Holy Week on medallions inscribed on her front, and St. Barbara with her plaited hair falling onto her chest. The road from Pedhoulas leads up to Prodromos and eventually Troodos.

*Kykko Monastery

Kykko Monastery ⓯, the most famous and richest monastery in Cyprus, is reached either via Pedhoulas or via Yerakies west of Kalopanayiotis. The first President of Cyprus, Archbishop Makarios, served here as a novice, as did the present Archbishop. It owns land in the area and in Nicosia, where former olive groves near Kykko Metocki have become valuable items of real estate.

The monastery is of Byzantine origin, and was founded in 1100 during the reign of Emperor Alexios Comnenos. According to tradition, it was established by a monk called Isaias with the money he received for curing the emperor's daughter of sciatica. Whether the monk also brought the famous *Icon of the Virgin Mary*, which is ascribed to St. Luke, one of only three still surviving, is not certain. The icon, however, is greatly venerated. Covered in silver gilt and enclosed in a shrine of tortoise-shell and mother-of-pearl, it stands at the front of the iconostasis and is only brought out on special occasions.

The monastery also owns many other priceless icons and sacred objects, some of which are believed to have come from Russia, either with pilgrims on their way to the Holy Land or from Russian Orthodox churches with which the monastery had close relations.

Three kilometers west of the monastery is **Throni tis Panayias** (Throne of the Mother of God), where Archbishop Makarios was buried, at his own request, not far from his home village of Panayia.

There are important religious festivals that take place at Kykko on August 15 and September 8. Near the monastery itself is a tourist pavilion serving meals and drinks.

A short detour of four kilometers to the south of Kykko Monastery will take you to the village of **Milikouri** ⑯, famous for its grape products, most notably *soudjuko*, a sweet made of solidified grape juice, flour and almonds, and *zivania*, a potent spirit.

On the belfry of the medieval **Church of Ayios Yeoryios** is a crude painting of the "Siege of Milikouri," an incident in 1957 when the British occupied the village for 54 days because they had been informed that Colonel Grivas was hiding

Right: The dream of every recluse – Ayios Herakleidios Monastery.

here. Ayios Yeoryios has been remodeled three times, once in 1811 as is noted in an inscription over the door. Its 17th-century iconostasis is quite well preserved, but the old icons were for the most part destroyed by an inept restorer early in this century.

FROM NICOSIA TO THE MAKHERAS MONASTERY

Another pleasant drive starts from the village of Strovolos. In Nicosia, take Evagoras Avenue and Demosthenis Severis Avenue, past the Presidential Palace, around the roundabout, heading south down the broad highway through Strovolos and Lakatamia, following signposts to Dheftera and Pera.

Strovolos ⑰ was once notable for its resident healer, Dr. Stylianos Atteshli, who was called the "Magician of Strovolos." The "magician," who lived here until his death in 1995, wrote a book on his spiritual philosophy and was said to be gifted with special psychic powers. A cult following developed, with many northern Europeans making the pilgrimage to Strovolos in hopes of having a session with him.

Eleven kilometers out of Nicosia you will come to a signpost for **Panayia Khrysospiliotissa** ⑱ (Our Lady of the Golden Cave). This is more or less a catacomb, a natural cave which was enlarged to make a church in early Christian times. At one time the entire interior was painted, but the murals have been badly damaged and very little of the original artwork can now be seen.

Pass through Kato Dheftera and you will see a turnoff to your left to Pera and Makheras. At the village of Episkopeion you turn off to **Politiko** ⑲. This small pretty village now stands on the site of what once was **Tamassos**, a city-kingdom of ancient Cyprus and an important copper center. Excavations by a team of German archeologists uncovered the

Nicosia

Royal Tombs, where a magnificent sword and helmet were found, and a **temple** dedicated to a female deity, either Astarte or Aphrodite, as well as the remains of what have been identified as copper workshops.

About 500 meters away stands ★**Ayios Herakleidios Monastery**. It is said that when Saints Paul and Barnabas came to Cyprus they were guided to Tamassos by Herakleidios, whom they later ordained as Bishop of Tamassos. He was martyred at the age of 60 and was laid to rest in the cave where he had lived and preached.

The monastery was founded in the year A.D. 400. In subsequent centuries it was destroyed and rebuilt several times, until Archbishop Khrysanthos had the church and cells renovated in 1733. The church contains the relics of its patron (his skull), and is decorated with fine frescoes and icons. The nuns, who have resided here since 1962, sell honey and marzipan.

Return now to Episkopeion and continue on to Pera. At Kambia, take the road signposted to Makheras Monastery. This is a winding strip of tar which slowly rises through foothills and forests and then dips down to **Makheras Monastery** ⑳, 41 kilometers from Nicosia. There is a small café here and a parking lot. The monastery was founded by two monks in 1148, when an icon of the Virgin Mary was discovered in a nearby cave. The monks are not very fond of seeing non-Orthodox visitors; tour groups and those who are improperly dressed will not be allowed inside.

Nearby is a **Monument to Grigoris Afxentiou**, an EOKA fighter who was killed when he refused to surrender during the 1955-59 Liberation Struggle.

Continue down the road to the village of Lazania, where the road starts climbing again, and take the turnoff signposted for ★**Phikardou** ㉑. This is a remarkable small village which has been declared an "ancient monument" in its entirety. Its excellent examples of 19th-century folk architecture and woodwork are being carefully restored by the Department of Antiquities.

One takes a trip back into the previous century when strolling past the quaint two-story buildings on narrow cobbled lanes. Traditional activities such as threshing and the production of wine and *zivania* continue today. The mainly elderly community is almost completely self-sufficient, a rarity in the modern world. The **Katsinioros House** is an imposing house at the north end of the village, which is now a museum with typical furniture and implements.

Returning to the road, turn right, and a short distance after **Gourri** you will be back on the main road to Klirou and Nicosia.

FROM NICOSIA TO IDALION

The A1 highway leading to Limassol from Nicosia also passes through **Perakhorio** ㉒, 17 kilometers south of Nico-

Above: Fields of wildflowers signify that spring has arrived. Right: The Makheras Monastery is a famous site of pilgrimage.

sia. Far more interesting than the **Church of Ayia Marina** in the village is the older **Church of Ayii Apostoli**, on a hill west of town. The key to the church is kept in the house closest to it. Although damaged, the frieze of winged angels with perfectly painted hands in the Byzantine style is described by historian Rupert Gunnis as "one of the most lovely and satisfying things in all of Cyprus."

Three kilometers to the northeast is the undistinguished village of **Dhali**, and just outside it below two limestone hills is the site of ancient **Idalion** ㉓. Idalion was a Bronze Age religious center with at least 14 temples. It is rich in mythological implications, with the remains of a Temple of Aphrodite and another dedicated to Athena. Stone votary statuettes found here are now in the Cyprus Museum in Nicosia, and a statue of King Sargon II of Assyria was sent to Berlin. American archeologists are in the process of excavating a large public building. Adonis was said to have been killed here by a wild boar, and as a reminder of this the nearby hills turn crimson each spring when they are blanketed in poppies.

NATURE WALKS

Nicosia itself is a bustling city, but the Nicosia District is very large and encompasses vast mountainous regions of particular interest to nature lovers. Attractive areas for rambling and trekking within easy reach of Nicosia are in the **Makheras Forest**.

Starting from **Politiko** ⑲, a dirt trail leads through the deserted village of **Philani** along a steep gorge. The variety changes abruptly since the lava-formed foothills of the Troodos Mountains start near this village. In the chalk hills before Philani, orchids abound, including many *Ophrys fusca* varieties. Amid white rock roses and wild lavenders grow orchids such as *Orchis anatolica* and the rarer lemon yellow *Dactylorhiza romana*.

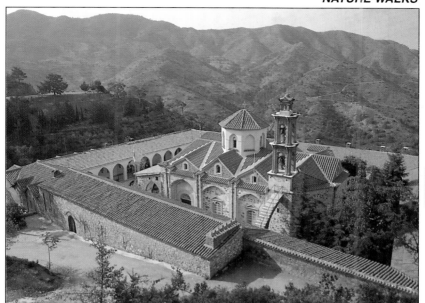

The trail to the Makheras Monastery leads to **Kionia** ❷❹ (1423 meters), a mountain peak with a splendid view stretching to Larnaca in the south.

Further west, past Palekhori and Polystipos on the road to Lagoudhera, a road through **Adelphi Forest** leads to **Spilia** ❷❺, or for the more adventurous, to the jagged **Madhari Peaks** overlooking the road. The forest here gets denser, with some trails and interesting flora, which includes the Cyprus endemic golden oak (*Quercus alnifolia*), many orchids and peonies in late spring.

Starting from **Ayios Nikolaos** ❼ near **Kakopetria**, a walk ideal for the athletic can be taken along a rapid stream that ends in **Troodos**. Alternatively, it can be done less arduously by descending in the opposite direction. The views of the stark steep-sided gorge and the surrounding forest are spectacular. In late spring and early summer it is of keen botanical interest, with rare orchids such as *Epipactis veratrifolia* and the endemic *Pinquicula cristallina* on the banks of the river. Trout

and fresh water crabs, both protected, can be seen in the river. Fishing for trout is allowed at some dams if you have a permit.

In the higher altitudes of this walk, the black pine is quite common, while the brutia pine is found lower down. Keep an eye out for butterflies which abound in the area from late spring onwards.

Further west, past the **Marathasa Valley**, the territory gets wilder and less populated, with very extensive areas of forest waiting to be explored. The main road leads to the Kykko Monastery and to Kambos. Few other actual roads exist, although a number of forest trails are in the area.

Exploring this region requires some preparation, as routes are long and facilities few. The flora is interesting and the morphology of this region quite varied. Moufflon, several reptiles, and many butterflies can be spotted in the area, as well as the occasional hare and hedgehog. Bird watchers are likely to see Cyprus jays, Scops owls, ravens and several birds of prey (Bonelli's eagles) and warblers.

NICOSIA

Area Code 02

 Cyprus Tourism Organization, Laiki Yitonia, east of Eleftheria Sqare, tel. 444264.

▦ ⑤⑤⑤ **Cyprus Hilton**, 116 Arch. Makarios III Ave., tel. 377777, fax. 377788, restaurants, pool, health club, jogging track and squash courts; **Holiday Inn**, 70 Regaena St., tel. 475131, fax. 473337, only luxury hotel in the city center, indoor pool.

⑤⑤ **Asty Hotel**, 12 Prince Charles St., Ayios Dhometios, tel. 773030, fax. 773311; **Best Western Classic**, 94 Regaena St., tel. 464006, fax. 360072, on the city wall; **Cleopatra Hotel**, 8 Florinis St., tel. 445254, fax. 452618, conveniently located, pleasant poolside bar and good restaurant; **Europa Hotel**, 16 Alkaio St., Engomi, tel. 454537, fax. 474417.

⑤ **Averof Hotel**, 11 Averof St., tel. 773447, fax. 773411, friendly family-style hotel in a quiet neighborhood; **Rimi**, 5 Solonos St., tel. 463153, fax. 452816 in the Laiki Yitonia; **Royal**, 17 Euripides St., tel. 463245, the most basic and least expensive hotel in town; **Venetian Walls**, 38 Ouzonian St. tel. 450805, fax. 47337, in the Old Town on the city wall.

YOUTH HOSTEL: 5 Hadjidaki St., tel. 442027, open year round 7:30 to 10 a.m. and 4 to 11 p.m.; **Cyprus Youth Hostels Association**, P.O. Box 1328, tel. 442027 (days), 446542 (evenings).

❌ **Laiki Yitonia**: A variety of restaurants, tavernas and bars serve local food and *meze*. **Archontiko**, 27 Aristokyprou, tel. 450080, outdoor seating when the weather is good; **Xefoto**, 6 Aeschylos St., tel. 477840, excellent Greek music every evening, which often inspires customers to dance. **Famagusta Gate Area**: A characteristic feature of this neighborhood is its idiosyncratic mixture of piano bars, theater-restaurants, tavernas with music and gyros restaurants, many run by artists and actors with their own local following. **Makedonitissa Area**: This area off Grivas Dighenis Avenue is bustling with tavernas, bouzouki nightspots and entertainment arcades. *EUROPEAN CUISINE:* **Scorpios**, 1 Stassinos St., Engomi, near the Europa Hotel, tel. 351850, exclusive restaurant offering haute cuisine, reservation essential; **Corona**, 15a Orpheus St., Ayios Dhometios, tel. 444223; **Mignon**, 38 Metokhi St., near the Churchill Hotel, tel. 781032; **New Yorker**, 1 Vereniki St., tel. 452753; **Navarino**, 1 Navarino St., tel. 450775. *EUROPEAN AND LOCAL CUISINE:* **Date Restaurant**, corner Khalkokondylos-Agathon streets, near the Hilton Hotel, tel. 376737, sophisticated *meze*, popular for business lunches, reservation essential; **Ekali**, 1 Ayios Spyridhon St., Pallouriotissa, tel.

433950, panoramic view of Nicosia from the rooftop restaurant. *FISH TAVERNAS:* **Astakos**, Menelaos St., Engomi, tel. 351917; **Kavouri**, 125 Strovolos Ave., Strovolos, tel. 425153, closed Sundays; **Psarolimano**, 55 28th October Ave., Makedonitissa, tel. 350990. *ARMENIAN / MIDDLE EASTERN CUISINE:* **Tsolias**, 44 Theofanou Theodotou St., tel. 449879, snack bar serving great Oriental *meze*. *CHINESE:* **Changs**, 1 Acropolis St., Engomi, near the Ledra Hotel, tel. 351350; **Pagoda**, 11 Loukis Akritas St., tel. 771000. *CYPRIOT MEZE:* **Mandri Tavern**, 27 Arch. Kyprianou Ave., Strovolos, tel. 497200, vast selection of local specialities. *ITALIAN:* **Italian Trattoria Romantica**, 13 Evagoras Pallikarides St., near the Hilton Hotel, tel. 376161, reservation essential; **Milano**, 41 Prodomos St., tel. 454156.

🍸 A number of bars and pubs are near the Laiki Yitonia area close to Eleftheria Square within the city walls. **Mythos Pub**, Theodotu St.; **Maple Leaf Pub**, 43 Kallipolis Ave., Lykavitos; **Antonakis Tavern**, 18 Germanou Patron St., tel. 464697; **Cellari**, 17 Korai St., tel. 41099, popular taverna with good *meze*, guitar music and Greek songs; **Mikis Night Spot**, International Fair Highway, tel. 353925.

🏛 **Cyprus Museum**, Museum St., tel. 302189, the island's most important archeological museum, open Monday through Saturday 9 a.m. to 5 p.m., Sunday 10 a.m. to 1 p.m.; **Byzantine Museum and Icon Museum**, Archbishop Makarios III Cultural Foundation, Archbishop Kyprianos Square, tel. 456781, open Monday through Friday 9 a.m. to 4:30 p.m., Saturday 9 a.m. to 1 p.m.; **House of Hadji Georgakis Kornessios**, Patriarch Gregorios St., open Monday through Friday 8 a.m. to 2 p.m., Saturdays 9 a.m. to 1 p.m.; **Jeweler's Museum**, 7-9 Praxippos St., Laiki Yitonia, open Monday through Friday 10 a.m. to 4:30 p.m.; **Ayios Ioannis Cathedral**, Arch. Kyprianos Square, open Monday through Saturday 8 a.m. to noon and 2 to 4 p.m.; **Leventis Municipal Museum**, Hippokrates St., Laiki Yitonia, tel. 451475, open Tuesday through Sunday 10 a.m. to 4:30 p.m.; **National Struggle Museum**, Archbishop Kyprianos Square, tel. 302465, open Monday through Friday 8 a.m. to 2:30 p.m. and 3 to 6 p.m.; **Omariye Mosque**, Tyrillias Square, open Monday through Saturday 10 a.m. to 12:30 p.m. and 1:30 to 3:30 p.m.; **Municipal Arts Center**, 19 Apostle Barnabas St., open Tuesday through Saturday 10 a.m. to 3 p.m. and 5 to 11 p.m., Sunday 10 a.m. to 4 p.m.; **Municipal Cultural Center in the Famagusta Gate**, Nikiphoros Phokas Ave., Arch. Kyprianos Square, tel. 463205, open Monday through Friday 9 a.m. to 5 p.m., Saturday 10 a.m. to 1 p.m.; **Folk Art Museum**, within the Archibishopric, Arch. Kyprianos Square, tel.

463205, open Monday through Friday 9 a.m. to 5 p.m., Saturday 10 a.m. to 1 p.m.

🎭 **March**: *Sports and Leisure Exhibition*, an exhibition of sporting goods and camping equipment held at the Cyprus State Fair Grounds; *Philanthes and Ikebana Club Flower Exhibition*, Japanese style, at the Hilton Hotel.

May: *Tourism Exhibition*, all segments of the tourist industry are on display at the Cyprus State Fair Grounds.

End of May: *Cyprus International Fair*, the largest trade fair with exhibitors from Europe, the Middle East, China and Japan.

Late June / Early July: *Cyprus Music Days*, week-long music festival with numerous big-name artists from all over the world, jazz or classical music every other year (1999: jazz).

End of September: *Cyprus Rally*, three-day car race with international participants, with points toward the European championship. Starts and finishes in Nicosia.

October 1: *Cyprus Independence Day*, military parade at 11 a.m. and public reception in the Presidential Palace in the evening.

📌 *PLACES OF WORSHIP* (denominations other than Greek Orthodox): **Holy Cross Church** (Catholic), Paphos Gate.

ART GALLERIES: **Apokalypse**, corner of Avlonos and Chytron Streets, tel. 766655; **Argo**, 64 E Dighenis Akritas Ave., tel. 754009; **Gloria**, 3a Sozos St., tel. 762605; **Opus 39**, 21 Kimonos St., tel. 424983.

THEATERS: **ENA**, 4 Athens St., tel. 348203; **Municipal Theater**, Museum St., tel. 463028; **Satyrico**, VI Kafkarides Cultural Centrer, tel. 421609.

CINEMAS: **Zena Palace**, Theodotou St., tel. 444 128; **Metropol**, 3 Theodotou St., tel. 444840; others.

CITY SIGHTSEEING TOURS: The Tourist Office organizes a twice-weekly two-hour tour of the Old Town from their bureau in Laiki Yitonia, Tuesdays and Thursdays at 10 a.m.

HORSE RACING: **Nicosia Racing Club**, Ayios Dhometios, P.O. Box 1783, tel. 379566 and 775791, races held on weekends.

➕ **Emergency Calls**: In case of fire, for police and ambulance dial 199. **Hospital: Nicosia General Hospital**, Homer Ave., tel. 451111 and 452760.

📷 **Post office** at Eleftheria Square, open Monday through Friday 7:30 a.m. to 2:30 p.m., Thursday also 3:15 to 6 p.m. **Cyprus Telecommunications Authority (CYTA)**, 14 Egypt Ave., tel. 450111, for international calls, faxes and telegrams.

🚌 *BUSES / SERVICE (GROUP) TAXIS*: **Kemek Transport** runs buses to other towns from 34 Leonidas St., tel. 463989; **Kyriakos Taxis** run mini-buses and service taxis to Limassol, Paphos and Larnaca from 27 Stassinos Ave., tel. 444141. A seat in a service taxi to other towns can be booked by phone, and passengers are picked up and dropped off wherever they wish. Service taxis run daily 6 a.m. to 6 p.m. (until 7 p.m. in summer). **Karydas**, 8 Homer Ave., tel. 462269; **Kypros**, 9 Stassinos Ave., tel. 464811; **Makris**, 114 Stassinos Ave., tel. 466201.

RENTAL CARS: **Andy Spyrou / Europcar**, 11 Armenias St., tel. 338226, fax. 338227; **Ansa**, Eleftherias Sq., tel. 472352, fax. 311293; **Carop**, Eleftherias Sq., tel. 472333, fax. 311293; **Hertz**, 66A Metochiou St., Engomi, tel. 477411, fax. 461428; **Petsas & Sons**, 24A/B K. Pantelidis Ave., tel. 462650, fax. 366002.

🛍 Traditional handicrafts, such as Lefkara lace and hand-woven table cloths and pillow cases, silverware, copperware and pottery can be found in the shops on Ledra Street and adjoining streets, in Laiki Yitonia, the main shopping area around Arch. Makarios III Ave., and at the **Cyprus Handicrafts Service Shop**, 186 Athalassa Ave, tel. 305024, or 6 Aristokypou in Laiki Yitonia, tel. 303065.

The most modern department store in town is **Woolworth's** on Ledra Street. Many shops in Nicosia are closed for a week to ten days around August 15.

TROODOS AREA

Area Code 02

KAKOPETRIA

🏨 😊😊😊 **Linos**, in the historic city center, tel. 923161, fax. 923181, traditionally-furnished rooms in a restored natural stone house (under preservation order), some bathrooms with whirlpool.

😊😊 **Hellas**, 4 Mammantos Street, tel. 922450, fax. 922227; **Makris Sunotel**, 48 Mammantos St. tel. 922419, fax. 923367.

😊 **Hekali**, 22 Grivas Dighenis Street, tel. 922501, fax. 922503; **Krystal**, 15 Grivas Dighenis Street, tel. 922433.

KALOPANAYIOTIS

🏨 😊 **Heliopolis**, tel. 952451; **Kastalia**, tel. 952455, fax. 351288; **Loutraki**, tel. 952356.

PEDHOULAS

🏨 😊😊 **The Churchill Pinewood Valley**, tel. 952211, fax. 952439; **Jack's**, tel. 952350, fax. 952817, highly recommended, friendly, clean and comfortable.

YERAKIES

🏨 😊😊 **Treetops**, Yerakies Village, tel. 952200, fax. 952230.

Nicosia

NORTH OF THE GREEN LINE

NORTH NICOSIA
MORPHOU / SOLI / VOUNI
KYRENIA
FAMAGUSTA
SALAMIS / ENKOMI
KARPASIA PENINSULA

North Cyprus

The Green Line

Most tourists who vacation on the island only get a chance to see the line between the Turkisho-ccupied north and the Republic of Cyprus in Nicosia; a barbed-wire line that cuts across the island, marked by rusty oil drums and mine fields. Many vacationers are not even aware of its presence.

Since the invasion, the Blue Berets oversee this "Green Line," so-called because it was first drawn across a map by a British general with a green pen. The Green Line is about 180 kilometers long and stretches from Kokkina and Kato Pyrgos in the northwest to Famagusta in the east. This no-fire zone takes up about three percent of the island.

UN peacekeepers first came to the island in 1964 as part of the United Nations Force In Cyprus (UNFICYP), when fighting flared between the two communities three years after Cyprus gained its independence from Britain in 1960. They quickly took up position, mainly in Nicosia, under what was originally a three-month Security Council mandate.

Preceding pages: The promenade of Kyrenia Harbor with fortress wall. Left: Lala Mustapha Pasha Mosque in Famagusta, the former St. Nicholas Cathedral.

Today, the 1,200-strong UNFICYP forces still monitor the no-fire line on a continuous basis, using 150 observation posts and mobile patrols with high-powered binoculars and night vision devices. At present, the largest contingent of peace-keeping troops comes from Great Britain, followed by Austria and Argentina.

Some 40,000 mainland Turkish troops are estimated to be stationed in the island's northern part, which Turkey invaded and occupied in 1974. Across the no-fire line the Turkish troops, in addition to some 5,000 Turkish Cypriot soldiers, face a total of approximately 10,500 Greek Cypriot and Greek regular soldiers in the south.

The UN has been successful in arranging for the unmanning of three sensitive areas inside Nicosia, an arrangement it would like to see extended to other posts in and adjacent to the capital, where opposing troops are still dangerously close to each other. The zone itself shrinks from seven kilometers at its widest to three meters at its narrowest point in the center of Nicosia, close enough for opposing forces to converse.

Some years ago, in Pyla, a village which borders on the buffer zone and where the original Greek and Turkish Cypriot inhabitants still live together, the

construction of a minaret caused some concern. Greek Cypriots expressed the fear that it could potentially be used as an observation post, but UNFICYP representatives met with village leaders from both communities. They determined that there was no objection from the villagers themselves to having the minaret erected, and negotiated a reduction of its height from 25 to 18 meters.

Along with its military tasks, the UNFICYP has undertaken a substantial humanitarian role. For example, they support the approximately 500 Greek Cypriots and 190 Maronites still living in the Turkish-occupied area by providing them with food and emergency medical services.

Insofar as the military situation allows, the UN forces also encourage farming and small commercial activities within

Above: UN soldier standing guard in the divided city of Nicosia. Above right: Greek Cypriot women staging a protest march on the Green Line.

and close to the no-fire zone. It has been responsible for slowly returning much of the buffer-zone land to its owners for cultivation.

In recent years, the number of the Blue Berets stationed in Cyprus has been nearly halved. Denmark and Canada have completely withdrawn their troops, while Austria, Argentina and Great Britain have reduced their contingents significantly. Thus, currently only about 1,200 soldiers patrol the Green Line. The primary reason for the withdrawal of troops lies in the fact that the sender countries have been increasingly reluctant to finance their UN contingents themselves.

Intercommunal talks on Nicosia often take place in the Ledra Palace, a once elegant hotel that now serves as barracks for the UN British contingent. Sitting as it does in the middle of Nicosia's no man's land, it is close to the only checkpoint where tourists can cross from south to north for a day trip. The Greek Cypriot government bars entry to tourists who try to cross from the Turkish-occupied northern sector into the Republic of Cyprus, considering them to have arrived on the island illegally.

Angered by the lack of progress toward achieving a settlement, Greek Cypriot women first organized a protest march on the Green Line, hoping to storm across the buffer zone. The demonstration, aimed at outlining the fact that nearly 200,000 Greek Cypriots cannot return to northern homes they fled in 1974, was quickly followed by more women's marches, as well as others organized by refugee groups.

During one demonstration, in 1989, nearly 100 Greek Cypriots, mainly women, were arrested and detained by Turkish Cypriot authorities after they clashed in Nicosia's buffer zone with troops and police from the Turkish side. There have been no marches recently. Serious incidents along the Green Line occur only seldom, and those that do are not a threat to tourists, but incidents do, indeed, occur from time to time.

The most critical situation so far was recorded in the summer of 1990, when several Greek Cypriot youths were arrested and jailed only for trying to pull down the flags of Turkey and the occupied northern zone flying over Nicosia's divide. Greek Cypriot soldiers who inadvertently stray across the line of demarcation are immediately shot at by Turkish forces without any warning.

In the capital's no man's land, trees now grow through the floors of crumbling, windowless buildings, and weeds thrive in the streets which are patrolled only by UN peacekeepers. On the Turkish Cypriot fringe of the capital's buffer zone lies a commercial street. On the Greek Cypriot side, the area has slowly started to crumble from neglect as its owners move out. Efforts, however, are underway to revitalize the neighborhoods next to the buffer zone, and music and laughter can be heard echoing down from a few nightclubs and pubs along deserted streets. In summer, one kebab house serves food at tables arranged in the middle of a narrow street that literally faces guard posts in the heart of the Old Town of Nicosia.

But while formal talks have not been successful, intercommunal meetings between the two sides, including visits across the line by party leaders and journalists, are on the increase. Greek and Turkish Cypriots have been cooperating to restore the old part of Nicosia that lies within its 16th-century walls, an area which has been described as a veritable treasure trove of Venetian, Ottoman and Byzantine architecture.

Ignoring the political divide, representatives of the Greek and Turkish Cypriot communities of the city plan with the thought in mind that Nicosia will one day become the capital of a federal Cyprus. From this point of view, both sides deemed it pointless to develop their halves of the city in isolation since they would then be left with road systems that didn't mesh, zoning that didn't match, and commercial districts that did not complement each other.

For this reason, architects, engineers, city planners, sociologists and economists from both communities have been meeting to develop a master plan that takes into account such things as traffic patterns and land use for a strategy to allow unified growth of the capital in the future. In addition to this scheme, both communities completed a joint sewage and water treatment system, started before 1974. In the words of the Greek Cypriot Mayor Lellos Demetriades: "We are building bridges. I wish more were built by others."

North Cyprus

Ledra Palace Checkpoint

The travel section on North Cyprus is arranged in day trips for people who have crossed from the Republic of Cyprus at the Ledra Palace Hotel checkpoint in

Nicosia. If one enters the island via the Republic of Cyprus, it is usually possible to cross to North Cyprus for a day trip – if your family name is not Greek. The checkpoint on the border may be closed without notice, however, due to unforeseen conditions.

Those who enter Cyprus via an airport or port in the Turkish-occupied north cannot enter the Republic of Cyprus. Even just having a stamp of the Turkish administration of North Cyprus in your passport will make you ineligible to enter mainland Greece as well. The viewpoint of the government of the Republic of Cyprus is that the harbors and airports in northern Cyprus are illegal points of entry into the country. There are no organized day tours to the occupied north of Cyprus. If asking a Greek Cypriot whether such a tour can be undertaken individually, his answer will generally be a firm "No." There is not

Above: The skyline of North Nicosia, with minarets of Selimiye Mosque (Cathedral of St. Sophia). Right: A shoeshine stand.

much point, therefore, in asking a Cypriot whether or not the checkpoint happens to be open at present or is temporarily closed because of political tensions. The Greek Cypriots are on the horns of a dilemma: since they do not recognize the Turkish occupied north as a state – in fact blatantly disavow its existence – they cannot very well forbid its being visited; it belongs de jure to the Republic of Cyprus. Still, they dislike it when vacationers visit the occupied north. After all, they themselves are not allowed to go there.

The checkpoint at the Ledra Palace Hotel usually opens at 8 a.m. and closes at 6 p.m. Crossings into the north are only allowed until 1 p.m. Inquire when you cross over what time you are expected to return, and try to get back a little earlier (making allowances for possible unforeseen events). It is not allowed to drive a rental car from the Republic of Cyprus into the Turkish area.

When you get to the Turkish Cypriot checkpoint, make it clear that you are en-

176   **City Map pp. 146-147**

tering for a day trip only. Your passport will not be stamped and you only need to fill out a short form and pay a small fee. If you are late returning to the Greek Cypriot checkpoint, you could be refused reentry. While on a day trip, it is forbidden to to make any purchases in North Cyprus. If you do, keep in mind that goods could very well be confiscated by authorities upon your return.

Place names in this chapter are given in their original form, followed in parenthesis by the name used today by Turkish Cypriots. The present place names in the occupied area of the island are a result of a massive renaming campaign carried out in the years after 1974, when even formerly purely Greek Cypriot villages were given Turkish names.

The Turkish names are indicated in this book only in order to assist in the orientation of the traveler. The publisher would like to make it explicitly clear that their indication does not in any way imply an acknowledgment of Turkish renaming policy.

NORTH NICOSIA

The history of North Nicosia (Lefkosha) is the same as that of South Nicosia. The original city, *Ledra*, was situated to the southwest of present-day Nicosia in Ayia Paraskevi. It was absorbed into the kingdom of Salamis sometime before the end of the sixth century. During the early Byzantine Period, the ancient Ledra was called *Lefkon*, in reference to the many poplar trees which lined the banks of the river. **Nicosia ❶** has been the capital of Cyprus since the first Arab invasions in the seventh century. The cener of Nicosia is the old Venetian city, which is surrounded by a sturdy circular wall with eleven bastions.

The walls were hastily built by the Venetians in only three years between 1567 and 1570, incorporating stones of the old Lusignan palaces. Half of the five-kilometer-long walls lie within the Turkish sector. In 1570, they were considered an unconquerable defense against the Turks, who eventually broke through and

took the city. The Kyrenia Gate was one of the three entrances to the walled city built by the Venetians. It was originally known as Porta del Provveditore in honor of the Venetian military governor (*provveditore*) Francesco Barbaro who concieved it.

The main sights of North Nicosia can be seen easily by walking around for a few hours (see the map on pages 146-147). If you need further maps or information, an informal tourist office operates in the Kumarcilar Han, a short distance from the Büyük Han. Tourist Information Offices (tel. 020/228-1057) are also found on Selçuklu Caddesi and in the Kyrenia Gate.

In the **Museum of Barbarism** ㉗, the Turkish Cypriot administration tries its best to convince visitors to the north of their view that the Turkish Cypriots have always been the victims of the cruel Greeks.

Above: The restored façade of the Kumarcilar Han, a 17th-century caravanserai.

The Old Town

Once you have passed the Turkish checkpoint near the **Paphos Gate**, continue walking to the northeast along the outside of the city walls. After entry into the walled city through the Kyrenia Gate, walk on Kyrenia Street (Girne Caddesi). To your left is the **Mevlevi Tekke**, now the **Ethnographic Museum** ㉘. The building more resembles a bath house, with a number of small domes.

The Mevlevi sect was founded in the 13th century by the Turkish philosopher Mevlana Celal ed-Din Rumi, who emigrated from Persia to the central Anatolian town of Konya. A *tekke* is an Islamic monastery, and this one was populated by followers of Mevlana. It was built in the 17th century, with a large dance floor for the followers, known as whirling dervishes because of their swirling dance accompanied by mystical music. The sect was outlawed by Kemal Atatürk in the 1920s, but it continued to exist secretly in many areas even until today. A group from Konya has toured a number of countries demonstrating their traditional ritual.

The museum contains a cheerful eclectic collection of memorabilia from the latter days of the Ottoman Empire. Prayer rugs, dervish costumes with the traditional white robes and tall brown fezzes, and engraved copies of the Koran dominate many of the displays. Some old photos show both King George V and Lord Kitchener, who made the first survey of the island, as well as shots of Kamil Pasha, a notable Anglophile Grand Vizier who died in 1913.

Folkloric objects, such as carved trousseau chests, embroidered linens, copper trays, quaint elevated wooden *hamam* shoes, wedding dresses and calligraphic court records are spread around the rooms. Some traditional musical instruments are on display, including a form of dulcimer known as a *kanoun.*

In the back, in a long domed corridor, are the graves, or *türbe*, of the 16 dervishes who served as heads of the monastery, including Selim Dede, the last Sheikh of the Tekke who was buried in 1954. The Tomb of Feyzi Dede, a sheikh and calligrapher who engraved the inscriptions over the archway of the Kyrenia Gate, is covered with cloths in the traditional holy emerald green and has writing on it.

Kyrenia Avenue leads further to **Atatürk Square** ㉙, formerly known as Konak and then as Sarayonu Square. The Venetians placed a gray **granite column** from Salamis in the center of the square to celebrate their control of the island. It was topped by a Lion of St. Mark, the emblem of Venice, which was lost after the Turks removed the column in 1570. It was re-erected in 1915, and much later the lion was replaced by a copper globe. Coats of arms of Venetian nobles are displayed on the column's base. An **Ottoman fountain** stands on the north side of the square.

To the right off the square are government offices, law courts and the post office. **Rustem's Bookshop**, which has a large selection of English books, is at 22-24 Kyrenia Avenue (Girne Caddesi) just south of the square.

When continuing south on Girne and turning right onto Mufti Ziya Effendi Street, you will come upon one of the finest monuments in town on the corner of Shehit Salahi Shevket Street, the **Arabahmet Mosque** ㉚, built on the site of a church at the beginning of the 17th century and restored in 1845. The mosque has one large hemispherical dome and an elegant fountain, plus a porch with three smaller domes. The **Tomb of Kamil Pasha** can be found in the courtyard of the mosque.

The **Dervish Pasha Mansion** ㉛ is in Beligh Pasha Street in the vicinity, which has managed to retain its historical Ottoman character. It was built in the 19th century for Dervish Pasha, founder of the first Turkish Cypriot newspaper.

The **Armenian Church** ㉜, or *Sourp Asdouadzadzin*, is on the southern end of Shehit Salahi Shevket Street, and quite close to the Green Line. This was originally a Benedictine convent, and was later used by the large Armenian community of Nicosia, which numbered some 2,400 in 1960.

The **Büyük Hamam** ㉝, or "Great Turkish Bath," is on Mousa Orfanbey Caddesi, now two meters below street level due to the sinking of the older building. This was originally the Church of St. George of the Latins, built in the 14th century.

The **Kumarcilar Han** ㉞, or "Inn of the Gamblers," is a handsomely restored late 17th-century caravanserai (an inn for caravan traders) on Asmaalti Square, just 50 meters north of the Büyük Han. The entrance is built out of fragments gathered from other medieval buildings. The two-story structure has a total of 52 rooms. The lower level was originally

North Cyprus

used for storage rooms, while the first floor was the actual guest house, with elegant barrel-vaulted rooms with open fireplaces. Today the building serves as an inofficial tourist bureau.

The **Büyük Han** ㉟, or "Great Inn," was built in 1572, supposedly under Muzaffar Pasha, the first Ottoman Governor. It has 67 rooms, octagonal chimneys, and a small octagonal mosque (in Turkish: *mescit*) supported by marble columns in its center. It, too, was originally a caravanserai, but later served as the principal prison of the city during the early British Period.

The Büyük Han has recently been converted into an intriguing **museum**, displaying folk crafts, antiques and well-preserved national costumes, including some elegant embroidered caftans and wedding outfits. Some of the most interesting displays are those of common

Above: The Bedesten, a church ruin and later a market hall. Behind it is the Selimeye Mosque. Right: Everyday life in Nicosia.

household objects, such as bronze utensils, looms, an old-fashioned iron with a slot to insert coals, ceramics and gas lamps. Farm equipment includes ploughs, copper bells and shepherds' skin bags. The men's sitting room has low-slung divans, water pipes and wooden tables inlaid with mother-of-pearl. The spacious, tastefully-restored Büyük Han evokes the ambiance of everyday life during Ottoman times.

Follow Arasta Street to the ***Selimiye Mosque** ㊱, which was known as the **Cathedral of St. Sophia** before 1570. The Latin cathedral, built during the 13th-century Lusignan era, was the location of the crowning of many Cypriot kings. Compared to its three gloriously decorated portals, the interior is strangely bare after being gutted by the Turks when it was changed into a mosque 400 years ago; in accordance with the Islamic prohibition of human representation.

The Genoese and Mamelukes also pillaged the building, and it was severely damaged by two earthquakes. Furthermore, the carved molding of the door has been filled in by plaster, except in one small section over the central doorway on the west showing the delicate figurines of saints, royalty and commoners. Despite all the alterations to the interior, it is one of the most impressive monuments in Nicosia. Its twin minarets rising above the unfinished western towers of the cathedral provide a distinct landmark of the walled city.

Inside the church, two rows of massive whitewashed columns separate the nave and the aisles with six bays. The Byzantine capitals are painted emerald green with red and yellow stripes above them. Five chapels were once here. Through the northern one is the entrance to what is now the women's gallery of the mosque. The second chapel from the west end was once dedicated to St. Thomas Aquinas. In it are remnants of crusaders' tombstones, once laying on the floor of the cathedral.

The four columns in the apse are probably from Salamis.

On the south side of Selimiye Mosque is the ★**Bedesten** ㊲, or covered market, referring to its years as a textile market place during Turkish rule. It is actually the remains of a church from the Venetian Period which had been built over the ruins of a Byzantine church from the 12th century. The east doorway on the north façade is a stone copy of the marble portal of the cathedral. Above the lintel are carved six Venetian coats of arms. In the center is the figure of a saint that many people assume to be St. Nicholas of the English.

Behind the Bedesten is a little outdoor café, a perfect place to stop for a drink or meal. Next to the Bedesten to the right is a covered produce market. The streets in this area are good for wandering around to get the flavor of everyday life in the Turkish section of the city.

To the west of the Bedesten is the **Library of Sultan Mahmud II** ㊳, a small domed structure which has some gilt woodwork and rare volumes of Turkish, Arabic and Persian books. On the walls of the central room is a poem, written in gilt Arabic, by Turkish Cypriot Müftü Hilmi. Admission is only allowed with a valid permit (available in the Kumarcilar Han on Asmaalti Square).

The **Lapidary Museum** ㊴ is 50 meters east of the Sultan's Library. The building is a picturesque 15th-century Venetian house which now contains stone carvings from churches, cemeteries and palaces, all from medieval times. Especially notable is the exquisite arched Gothic window from the old Lusignan Palace, now destroyed.

For admission, you once again must apply to the Kumarcilar Han, or else find the caretaker near the premises and see if he will let you in.

Up Kirizade Street, close to the home where Lord Kitchener lived from 1880 to 1883 at 1 Haidar Pasha Street, is the former **St. Catherine's Church**, now **Haidar Pasha Mosque** ㊵. The somewhat derelict structure was built in the

14th century in the Flamboyant Gothic style and now has the addition of a minaret and pierced windows. Perhaps the most interesting features are the carvings of roses supported by two dragons and those of human heads on the corbels north of the apse.

MORPHOU, SOLI AND VOUNI

Morphou

The safest and most convenient (but not cheapest) way to take side trips from Nicosia is by hiring a private taxi for the day. Private taxis often wait beside the Turkish checkpoint. Negotiate a price before starting out. Cars can be rented for the day in Nicosia, Famagusta and Kyrenia. Shared service taxis line up at Atatürk Square in Nicosia.

The quickest route to Soli and Vouni is via the town of Morphou (Güzelyurt), about 50 kilometers from Nicosia over a well-paved road. **Morphou ❷** is in the center of the citrus growing area of North Cyprus and is surrounded by lemon and orange groves, which are very aromatic when in bloom. It was probably originally settled by Greeks as a center for *akrides* or "coast-watchers" during Byzantine times.

In the center of town is the **Archeological and Natural Science Museum**. The natural science displays on the first floor of the building include mounted specimens of local birds, such as Eleonara's Falcon and the barn owl, as well as insects and reptiles. On the second floor is the archeological section, which includes finds such as a stone grinder from the Ceramic Neolithic Period and a number of objects including a pithos from Toumba tou Skoura, a Late Bronze Age to Geometric Age site about five kilometers north of Morphou.

This site was excavated from 1971 to 1974 by a team of archeologists from Harvard University and the Museum of

Fine Arts in Boston. They found a wide-ranging cache of objects, including Minoan pottery, African ostrich eggs, Syrian cylinder seals, and a strange artificial mound of bricks. Tomb V had 16th-century B.C. imitations of Tell el-Yahudiya pottery from Egypt, indicating that contact had already been established with this part of the world.

From the Late Bronze Age site of Ayios Iakovos (north of Famagusta) comes a terra cotta fertility goddess with the familiar double earrings. A statue of the Artemis of Ephesus, recovered from the sea near Salamis, dates from the Roman Period.

The main attraction in Morphou is the ornate **Church of Ayios Mamas**, the shrine of one of the most popular Cypriot saints. It was originally a Byzantine church, but in the Middle Ages a Gothic structure was built. This was again reconstructed in 1725, but a number of the original Gothic details remain, including the north and south doorways, the two marble columns in the west window, and the shrine of the saint himself. All of these are in the Flamboyant style popular in the late 15th century.

The iconostasis is outstanding and combines Gothic and Venetian elements. Its four marble columns with Gothic capitals probably date from about 1500. The marble panels are superb examples of Venetian artistry, with figs, grapes and acorns carved in high relief, with Venetian heraldic shields at the corners. The woodwork, painted dark blue and gold, is an excellent example of late 16th-century carving. The altar is supported by five marble columns with Byzantine capitals. The only original icon is a painting of the Virgin Mary dated 1745.

Ayios Mamas' white marble sarcophagus is set in an arched recess on the north side of the church. In the icon here, the saint is shown riding on a lion while holding a lamb in his arms. This is a scene from a popular folk legend of the ascetic

hermit, who lived in a cave near Morphou. When a Byzantine duke issued a decree that every islander must pay taxes, Ayios Mamas protested, saying that he lived in a cave and pointing out that he did not use any public facilities. In response, the duke sent two soldiers to arrest him.

While they were escorting him to Nicosia, a lion jumped in front of them, in hot pursuit of a lamb. Ayios Mamas held up his hand and the lion became tame. He then gathered up the little lamb, climbed onto the lion's back, and rode in this fashion all the way to the duke's residence. The duke was so astonished that he absolved Mamas from ever having to pay taxes again, in itself a miracle many modern citizens would love to be able to perform themselves.

When the Turks bore holes in the saint's tomb, an oily perfumed liquid flowed out, said to heal any wound. Ayios Mamas has acquired a reputation for being the patron saint of animals. This is evidenced by the number of donkeys among

the *tama*, wax forms representing a diseased person, animal or organ, left at the shrine. Worshipers believe that coming here to pray for health and leaving the *tama* will bring about a cure.

The west door is covered with graffiti, including an inscription recording the visit and curing of a man from Moscow in the year 1753. The nearby monastic buildings, dating back to 1779, incorporate columns and capitals of the former church.

Soli

*Soli ❸ was one of the ancient kingdoms of Cyprus and played an important part in Cypriot history. It lies about 17 kilometers southwest of Morphou (Güzelyurt), immediately west of Karavostasi.

The original city of *Sillu* was founded here circa 700 B.C. When the Athenian Solon visited a century later, he gave suggestions on defending the community which were successfully put into effect in 498 B.C., when it held out for four

months against the Persians. According to local legend, the city was thus named *Soli* in honor of Solon. Soli was a thriving center for copper export during Roman times, and is also said to have established the first public library on the island during this period.

In 1932, excavators discovered the ruins of the **Temples of Isis**, **Aphrodite and Serapis**. Each of these had a roofed *cella* (main room) leading to one or more courtyards, which were sometimes surrounded by porticoes (roofed rows of columns).

The famous statue of *Aphrodite of Soli* from this site is now in the Cyprus Museum in Nicosia. Also in the museum is a miniature bronze head of Zeus-Ammon with inlaid silver eyes, dated at between the third and first centuries B.C. The Greek god Zeus is combined with the Egyptian god Ammon, also represented on some coins.

Above: The tranquil harbor of Kyrenia with the Pentadaktylos (Bes Parmak) Range.

The sea view is inspiring from the semicircular Roman Period **Theater**, probably built in the second century A.D., with an auditorium cut into the rock. Apart from some beautiful marble columns and parts of the façade, it has been completely restored and is occasionally used for performances today.

To the northeast of the theater are the ruins of a **basilica** built in the fifth century A.D., containing some interesting mosaics, including a memorable greenish goose. An Orthodox Bishop of Nicosia resided in Soli during the Lusignan Period, but the town had already been abandoned during the beginning of Arab raids in the seventh century. To the west of the basilica is the site of the **Agora** (marketplace).

Vouni

The once wealthy **Vouni Palace** ❹ is about three kilometers northwest on the coastal road. The palace and its accessory buildings were once surrounded by ramparts which can be traced right to the edges of the plateau. The area within the walls is divided into three terraces. The highest of these, to the south, is the site of the Temple of Athena, the second and largest has the palace and its surrounding sanctuaries and chapels, and the lowest one is a residential center that leads down to the seaside.

Most likely the palace was a residence of one of the Cypriot kings in the mid fifth century B.C. It was huge, with almost 140 rooms. As at Soli, it is very difficult to distinguish different phases of the construction. The magnificent view from the **Temple of Athena** over the Bay of Morphou and the tiny isle of **Petra tou Limnitou**, site of a small Neolithic settlement, is rewarding. The open-air sanctuary does not resemble Greek temples. Instead, it is a typical Cypriot sanctuary showing strong Oriental influence in its two open courtyards, the innermost leading to the sanctuary buildings.

Bronze objects from Vouni, including a finely-carved relief of a bull being attacked by two lions and a bronze statuette of a cow, can be seen on display in the Cyprus Museum in Nicosia. Both of these fine works show the influence of Athenian artists, who at this time were breaking away from rigid, archaic forms and imbued their works with expression and fluidity. Other impressive finds attest to the luxury of this community. Silver coins from Cypriot cities and two bracelets that rank among the finest examples of Persian gold work in the world were found along with other coins, bracelets, pendants and silver bowls.

The beaches in this area are fairly good, mostly rocky with a few sandy stretches interspersed, but on windy days the waves are very high.

KYRENIA

Kyrenia ❺ (Girne), the capital of the Kyrenia District, has a charming little horseshoe-shaped harbor and is the most touristic town of northern Cyprus, yet is remarkably unspoiled. The **Pentadaktylos Range (Bes Parmak Mountains) forms a verdant backdrop and is well worth visiting for the castles of St. Hilarion and Buffavento, and the famous Bellapais Abbey.

Years ago, the sun-starved British discovered this area and claimed it as a favorite holiday resort. A large ex-patriot community lived here year round, and a small percentage of them remain to this day. In his delightful novel *Bitter Lemons of Cyprus*, Lawrence Durrell reminisces on the island life during the initially peaceful but eventually turbulent years of 1953-1956.

The original settlement was one of the nine city-states, founded as *Kerynia* around the 10th century B.C. It continued to function as an independent city-state with a king until it was absorbed by Salamis in 312 B.C. During Roman times, it was known as *Corineum*, and some tombs and the breakwater survive from this period. It seems the town was once completely fortified, although only two medieval towers remain. Kyrenia was attacked by the Arabs during their raids beginning in the 7th century A.D., and was looted like the other coastal towns. The port was known as *Gerinia* during the Turkish occupation.

New roads were built in 1880 and 1902, improving communications with Nicosia. The population also began to grow around this time. Kyrenia's harbor was improved and extended from 1886 to 1891, and the breakwater was extended in the 1950s.

Kyrenia Castle

To the east of the idyllic harbor rises ***Kyrenia Castle**, built in the Byzantine style of fortification before the 11th century. Although relatively unscathed by direct attack, its history reflects the shifting

North Cyprus

fortunes of a succession of the island's rulers.

In 1191, the castle surrendered to Guy de Lusignan, and two of the prisoners taken were the wife and daughter of Isaac Comnenos. It was rebuilt and strengthened by the Lusignans in 1208. It was remodeled in the 1290s and afterwards used as a prison. The Venetians, at the beginning of the 16th century, chose to rebuild Kyrenia and Famagusta castles while they dismantled the Castle of St. Hilarion and some of the others. They rebuilt the west wall and added massive towers with gun emplacements. In 1570, Kyrenia Castle surrendered without any resistance to the Turks.

During the British administration, the castle became a prison again. In 1950, it was turned over to the Department of Antiquities, but during the EOKA turmoil in the 1950s it reverted to a prison.

Above: The "Five Fingers Range," prominent backdrop of Kyrenia. Right: The wooden hull of the Kyrenia Shipwreck (300 B.C.).

Keep to the right when entering the castle. Past the steps descending to a watergate is the 12th-century **Chapel of Ayios Yeoryios**. Above the gatehouse are two Lusignan coats of arms. In the main courtyard is the **Tomb of Sadik Pasha**, the Turkish admiral to whom the Venetians surrendered the castle.

The rooms along the sea wall, used as prison cells, are well-preserved. The outer entrance to the south ward is guarded by Roman lions. Below the southeast tower are the dungeons.

Two large halls on the east wall now contain the ***Shipwreck Museum**, dedicated to an ancient ship that sank off the coast of Kyrenia around 300 B.C., at the time of Alexander the Great. The ship was first located by a Kyrenia sponge diver in 1965, who showed it to a team of American archeologists in 1967.

An incredible amount of information about the ship and its crew has been pieced together thanks to underwater excavations carried out under the direction of Michael Katzev of the University of

North Cyprus

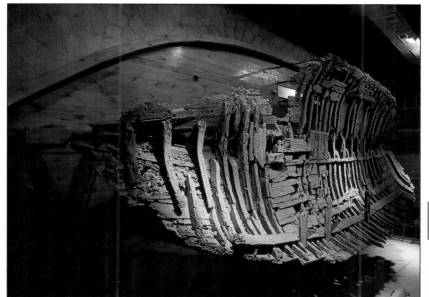

Pennsylvania, which were begun in 1969 and completed in 1974.

The museum is spacious, with clear explanations in English. A replica of the ship, photos of diving and salvaging operations, part of the cargo and other objects are on display. The largest part of its cargo was 400 wine amphoras, mostly from Rhodes. A study of the shapes of the amphoras shows 10 ports of call, the Greek island of Samos being the northernmost. 300 lead weights that have been found support the theory that the sailors fished during their journey.

The Aleppo pine hull of the ship itself has been reassembled and immersed in preservative. It provides evidence that the shell was built first, the opposite of today's methods. Carbon 14 analysis of the 9,000 or so almonds found in the hull and in jars provides evidence that the ship must have been more than 80 years old at the time it sank. Utensils used by the crew, including rigging parts and nails, plus the bronze cauldron from the galley, are on display.

One has a good view of the **Pentadaktylos Range** from the upper level of the castle. These mountains are named because their shape, which looks like the outline of the knuckles of five fingers (in Greek: *pentadaktylos*, in Turkish: *bes parmak*).

A little **Museum of Folk Art** is located on the harbor, open at somewhat irregular hours. It contains a nice collection of household objects, fabrics, a wine press and furniture.

The waterfront restaurants are pleasant places to have a meal or drink.

Castle of St. Hilarion

The ★**Castle of St. Hilarion** ❻ has an exhilarating setting, best viewed on a clear spring day when the pine-covered hillsides are dotted with clusters of wildflowers, including rare white orchids. It can be reached via the new Nicosia-Kyrenia highway, about 17 kilometers from Nicosia and seven kilometers from Kyrenia. The side road leading to the cas-

tle winds through interesting rock formations. You may have to show your passport to enter the castle since this is a military area. It is best to wear sturdy flat shoes: the paths are rocky and can be difficult to walk along.

Travel writer Rose Macaulay portrayed St. Hilarion as "a picture book castle for elf kings," an appropriate description in a nutshell of one of the four defensive fortresses of northern Cyprus. The castle is perched more than 600 meters above sea level between two rocky peaks, which have been nicknamed *Didymoi* or "The Twins." St. Hilarion communicated with the other three castles – Kyrenia, Buffavento and Kantara – by using bonfires and flares.

The castle's name of St. Hilarion did not come from the saint who died near Paphos in A.D. 731, but rather from one of 300 refugees who came here from the

Above: The castle ruins of St Hilarion.
Right:The dramatic ruins of Bellapais Abbey, cradled in the hills near Kyrenia.

Holy Land when it was overrun by Arabs. However, it seems he founded a monastery here and was probably buried on the site. The precise date of its construction cannot be ascertained with certainty, but it was most likely built in the 10th century.

At the end of the 12th century, all four castles were under the command of Isaac Comnenos. After his defeat by Richard the Lionhearted in 1191, the Castle of St. Hilarion was fortified. Emperor Frederick II took control of it for a brief period in 1229. After a struggle with the boy-king Henri I and his patron Jean d'Ibelin, the castle remained in the hands of the Lusignans. Untouched by warfare for the next 140 years, it was used as a summer residence for the Lusignan royal family. It was embellished and used as a refuge during the time of the plague.

In 1373, when the Genoese invaded the island, Jean Prince of Antioch, the regent and uncle of the young King Pierre II, barricaded himself in the castle along with his Bulgarian mercenaries. Persuaded by his sister-in-law Eleanor that the mercenaries were preparing to mutiny, he had them brutally murdered by having every last one of them flung off the peak into the treacherous abyss. The Venetians dismantled this castle and some of the others in the late 1500s in order to cut costs.

The Castle of St. Hilarion is divided into three separate wards: the lower ward, which had the storage cisterns and stables; the middle ward, which is entered through a massive gate house – it has a 10th-century church, restored but without a dome, a vaulted belvedere with a lovely view, and a snack bar in what was once the kitchen; and the upper ward, which is entered through a Frankish arched gate and which is set into the Byzantine wall. The 14th-century Lusignan royal apartments are on this level.

On the west wall is the "Queen's Window," with suitably elegant tracery and

side seats. These windows have stunning views west to Lapithos and Cape Korkomati. The adventurous will want to climb "Prince Jean's Tower," isolated in the center of the castle with sheer precipices on three sides. This is where Prince Jean's Bulgarians met their grisly end.

Bellapais Abbey

Heading southeast out of Kyrenia, one passes **Kazaphani** ❼ village, the name probably a corruption of *Casa Epiphani* or village of Ayios Epiphanios. A medieval church is dedicated to **Panayia Potamitissa** or "The Virgin of the River." Most of the frescoes that covered the walls were badly damaged. At the west end on a south wall is a medieval tomb under a canopied arch with a slab engraved with a man's figure dressed in 14th-century civilian clothes. Local legend says this man was buried here with his three daughters.

Vounos or Vounous, which is situated southeast of Kyrenia between Kazaphani

and Bellapais, was one of the largest Early Bronze Age cemeteries. A lot of finds from there, now in the Cyprus Museum in Nicosia, show evidence of a bull cult, and the graves were provided with ample supplies, including meat, drinking vessels, pottery, daggers and sheaths. Unfortunately, the hillside graves have been looted.

★★Bellapais Abbey ❽ is one of the more memorable sites, set on a natural rock escarpment which drops vertically for over 30 meters in the north. The village of Bellapais, made famous by Lawrence Durrell, has expanded and become more commercial since the time of the English author, yet has managed to retain its charm.

Bellapais Abbey is first mentioned as a house of Augustinian canons, a foundation of the King of Jerusalem, Amaury de Lusignan (1198-1205). In 1205, when the house was known as St. Mary of the Mountain, Kyrenia's first prior received a grant of lands from King Hugo I. In its early period, the abbey was respectfully known as *Episcopia*, suggesting the monastery might have been erected on the site of the residence of the Greek Bishop of Kyrenia. *Episcopia* was later replaced with *Lapais*, which in turn was corrupted from *Abbaie de la Pais* (*Abbaye de la Paix*) to *Bellapais*. In documents of the 15th and 16th centuries, it is also referred to as the "White Abbey," for the white clerical habits of the Norbertine monks. From this name comes *Asprophorousa*, meaning "white-dressed," referring to the highly venerated Virgin of Bellapais.

The abbey swiftly gained in prestige and enjoyed a non-conformist reputation. In 1224 and 1232, the popes had to remind the abbot that he owed allegiance to the Archbishop of Nicosia. A fragment of the True Cross was bequeathed by a knight from Paphos in 1246, attesting to its importance.

Bellapais expanded and became so prosperous under the patronage of Hugo III that he is considered the actual founder of the monastery. During his reign, he brought additional members of the order from Palestine and granted the abbots the privilege of wearing the miter and of carrying a gilded sword and spurs when riding. This caused conflict with the Archbishop of Nicosia at the Bellapais' town residence in Nicosia. Hugo III died in 1284 and was probably buried at the abbey. His successor, Hugo IV, lived in the abbey from 1354 to 1358 and further embellished it with the addition of royal apartments.

This opulence did not escape the attention of the acquisitive Genoese. In 1373, they made off with many treasures, including the fragment of the True Cross. Before the Turkish conquest, the Provveditore Bernardo Sagredo reported on its decline to the Venetian Senate: "The White Abbey of French religion is all in ruins; the services are not maintained; all the brethren have wives and the revenues are assigned to their children so that the brethren live in great penury."

The Turks seized the abbey and its properties, but they permitted the villagers to continue using the church, which they continued to do. As is so often the case with ruined buildings, much of it was quarried for use in nearby village houses. In 1878, further damage was inflicted when the British cemented over the floor of the great hall in preparation for its use as a hospital. In 1912, George Jeffery was given a meager budget to repair the ruins. The ruins of the abbey are highly dramatic, indeed, almost spooky in their melancholy isolation. Three of the most notable areas are the church, the cloister and the refectory.

The **church**, on the south end of the complex, remains in its original form from the 13th century. Minor adjustments were made for the Greek rites with the addition of a modern iconostasis. It is preceded by a simple porch and topped by a substantial belfry. At the north end of the porch is a wall recess which may have been intended as the tomb for King Hugo III. Fragmentary remains of paintings on walls and arches in the southern recesses of the porch are in the Italianate style of the 15th century and earlier. The arches open onto the pillars in the church in an ingenious manner. The pillar capitals are in a 13th-century French style.

The **cloister** to the north has some surviving details that give it a rather distinct character. Corbel carvings vary from foliage to human and animal heads. Among the animals are a fox and a donkey,while the human figures include a head crowned with a diadem and a hero fighting two monsters. Two angle bays in the west wing carry the Lusignan coat of arms. At the northwest corner stands the marble lavabo incorporating a carved marble sarcophagus of the second century A.D.

Right: French Gothic in Famagusta – the Lala Mustapha Pasha Mosque (formerly the Cathedral of St. Nicholas).

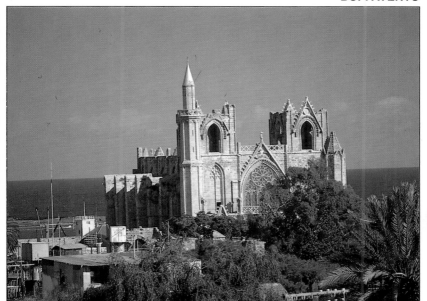

Behind the lavabo is the main entrance to the **refectory**. It is a splendid vaulted chamber of six bays in almost perfect condition, probably the work of Hugo IV. In the north wall near the east end, a staircase leads to the pulpit, where excerpts from the scriptures were read during meals. On the east wall is a beautiful rose window. The windows on the north wall have marvelous sea views, stretching to Turkey on a clear day.

Bellapais itself is still lovely, although the cafés in the vicinity of the abbey, such as **The Tree of Idleness Café** across the street, capitalize on the fame brought to the area by Durrell's account in *Bitter Lemons of Cyprus*. In it he writes, "... I was not prepared for the breathtaking congruence of the little village which surrounded and cradled it (Bellapais) against the side of the mountain.

"Fronting the last rise, the road begins to wind through a landscape dense with lemon and orange trees and noisy with running water. Almond and peach-blossom graze the road, as improbably

precise as the decor to a Japanese play."

A cool drink or snack under the Tree of Idleness will help lull you into the proper state of indolence.

Not far from Bellapais Abbey is the **Castle of Buffavento ❾**. It is best reached from Nicosia via the **Monastery of Ayios Khrysostomos**, several kilometers south of fortress. Two churches, one dedicated to St. Khrysostomos, an Archbishop of Constantinople and the older one said to have been built by St. Helena after her visit to the Holy Land, are distinguished by the huge cypress tree in front.

The Castle of Buffavento, at 954 meters, can be reached in a strenuous but invigorating hour-long hike through a pine forest to its summit high on yellowish rock. Plans have been made to extend the road further up the peak.

Incurable romantics will be rewarded by the setting, with its endless panoramic views to the east, west and south. Buffavento's history, however, is rather grisly: the Lusignan Pierre I (1359-69) imprisoned his friend Sir Visconti there

Above: This ferryboat has just docked at Famagusta Harbor.

and let him starve while political prisoners were tortured to death. Its ramshackle remains with some Byzantine stonework are less impressive than Bellapais or St. Hilarion.

FAMAGUSTA

Famagusta 🔟 (Gazi Magusa) is a remarkable medieval city on a bay 58 kilometers to the east of Nicosia. Gazing at the remants of its formidable fortifications, one realizes Famagusta has seen better days and its history must have been inextricably entangled in its protection from invaders.

Famagusta reached its height as a mercantile settlement during Lusignan times. Its vast wealth was accumulated from Levantine trade, but it went into decline during the Venetian and Turkish Periods. The walled city itself has never regained its former glory. Nevertheless, it is interesting to walk among the wistful ruins which attest to the many different influences that shaped its destiny.

The name is generally considered to be a corruption of *Ammochostos* ("hidden in the sand"), as it is still called by the Greek Cypriots. An alternative possibility is a derivation from *Fami Augusti*, referring to the Roman Emperor Augustus.

Its early history is rather clouded, but Famagusta is believed to have been founded by King Ptolemy Philadelphos of Egypt (285-247 B.C.) and was repopulated in A.D. 648 by Greek refugees from neighboring Salamis. During the early Crusades, it was a rather insignificant village and didn't rise to prosperity until the Lusignan Period.

After the fall of Acre in 1291, King Henri II offered Famagusta as a refuge to Christian refugees from there. It rapidly became one of the richest and most important cities in the Levant, regarded as its principal marketplace. All the business houses of the important trading organizations of Italy and France were here.

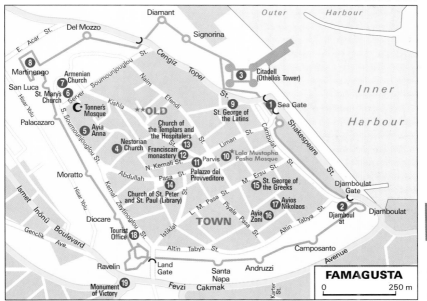

FAMAGUSTA

0 — 250 m

The major religious orders had their convents in Famagusta, and Near East religions, including Greek, Nestorian, Jewish, Jacobite and Carmelite, had their places of worship here as well. It was a city of intrigue and opulence and its nobility was the wealthiest in the world. The buildings were stately, graced by fountains on each corner. As many as 365 churches functioned, many built during this time. More than one visitor commented both on the beauty of the city and its courtesans as well.

The buildings of the Lusignan Period are undoubtedly its greatest legacy. These include the Gothic cathedral, the original fortifications of the city, including the famed walls, and the romantic castles of the Pentadaktylos Range. The design of these buildings is admirable, and the finished structures impressive. However, they are really French or Venetian, not Cypriot.

In 1372, misfortune befell this thriving city in the guise of political conniving, from which it never recovered. Many Lusignan kings of Cyprus were crowned in the Cathedral of St. Nicholas (later the Ayia Sophia Mosque, now the Lala Mustapha Pasha Mosque) in Famagusta. They were crowned both for Cyprus and Jerusalem, although the latter was a symbolic gesture of little significance. During the coronation of the boy-king Pierre II, quarreling broke out among representatives of Venice and Genoa, who both tried to grab the bridle of the twelve-year-old king on the right-hand side, a gesture symbolic of control of the city. In the riot that followed, many Genoese were slaughtered and their loggias sacked. The Genoese avenged this by sending a fleet to Cyprus which ravaged the island. Famagusta became an appendage of Genoa until 1464, when King Jacques II, the illegitimate stepson of Helena Paleologa, drove the Genoese out with the aid of the Venetians.

The Venetians conveniently arranged the marriage of Jacques II to Caterina Cornaro, the daughter of a rich Venetian merchant. Consequently, Cyprus actually

became a colony of "The Mistress of the Adriatic," as Venice was called. Jacques II and his infant son died suddenly, very possibly of poisoning, and Caterina ruled for a few more years. Eventually, her brother Giorgio Cornaro persuaded her to abdicate and return to Venice. She tearfully agreed. In February 1489, the banner of St. Mark's flew at long last over Famagusta, which now replaced Nicosia as the capital. It was an unhappy time for the city, for it was really only a military occupation and its fortunes visibly declined. Trade became sluggish, manufacture ceased, property was abandoned, and a large portion of the population emigrated. Streams overflowed and formed contaminated marshes that facilitated the spread of disease. In little more than a hundred years, Famagusta's former splendor had all but disappeared.

Above: Entrance to the Citadel of Famagusta, with the Venetian symbol of the winged Lion of St. Mark. Above right: Before the fortified walls of Famagusta.

The Venetians busied themselves with fortifying the high, narrow walls, for while fortunes had withered away, its strategic position made her as desirable as ever. They used stone quarried partly from Salamis and Kakozonara on the Karpasia Peninsula. The walls were put to the test in the infamous "Siege of Famagusta" by the Turks, which started in September 1570 and ended in August 1571.

They passed with flying colors. It is estimated that 8,000 Greeks and Venetians and 50,000 Turks died during the Siege. Over 100,000 cannon balls were fired into the city by the Turks, leaving hardly a building standing, but the walls remained mostly intact. The surrender took place with flags still flying when the forces realized no Venetian forces were arriving to support them.

The worst damage was done to the city during the middle of the 19th century. After a tremendous earthquake, much of the building material, including complete churches, was carted off to build the hotels and quays of Port Said. When the British arrived in 1878, they found a number of political prisoners within the walled city, which is described in an 1890 guidebook as having been "a confused mass of ruins and filth." The population at this time was 2,550.

Famagusta's Walls

The walls of Famagusta, surrounding the Old City, are an impressive sight and extremely well-preserved. On average, they are 18 meters in height and at some points reach a thickness of eight meters. They are square and surrounded by a deep dry moat, intercepted in places by bastions and ramparts, with some stables, powder stores and granaries included.

The two original entrances, the **Land Gate** at the east and the **Sea Gate** ❶ at the southwest, remain in addition to three others. The Sea Gate was built in 1496 by Nicolo Prioli, a Venetian captain. The iron-reinforced wooden doors date from the Turkish Period. The Lion of Venice and the coat of arms of Prioli are from Venetian times, as is the iron *portcullis* (moveable grating), once raised and lowered by chains. The colored marble in the background may have come from Salamis. According to local legend, once a year late at night the marble lion standing on a gray marble socle on the inner side of the Sea Gate opens its mouth wide. Whoever sticks his or her hand down its mouth will grab a valuable treasure.

Ten fairly complete bastions are given Venetian names, such as Andruzzi, Palacazaro, Signorina and Othello, though Turkish equivalents are also used. On the southeast end is the **Djamboulat Bastion** ❷, formerly an arsenal, where the legendary Turkish hero Djamboulat Bey died in the siege of 1571. A popular folk legend relates how this brave general saw one man after another of his regiment hacked up by a fiendish Venetian machine made of a wheel equipped with knives. Djamboulat mounted his white horse and rode his steed right into the machine; they were instantly killed. But this brought the spirit back to his men and changed the tide of the conflict. It is said that whenever the Venetians seemed to be gaining, the ghost of Djamboulat Bey would appear, a sword in one hand and his head tucked under his other arm, inspiring his men to go on to victory.

A small **museum** with Bronze Age artifacts, folk costumes, jewelry, Ottoman and Venetian pottery, and other historical objects is in the Djamboulat Bastion, along with **Djamboulat's Tomb**.

Between the Sea Gate and the **Citadel** ❸ to the northwest, portions of the wall are pierced by entrances made soon after the British leased the land in 1878. The Citadel has a colorful history. It was built by the Lusignans in the 14th century to defend the entrance to the natural harbor. During Venetian rule, it was remodeled by Captain Nicolo Foscarini in 1492, and the upper floor was removed. A finely-carved winged Lion of St.Mark is over the main entrance. It has four round towers at its corner and is almost entirely surrounded by a sea moat.

The Citadel, some guides point out today, was the setting for Shakespeare's *Othello*. Christoforo Moro, Lieutenant-Governor of Cyprus from 1506 to 1508, is thought to be the model for the ill-fated Moor because his name and coat of arms (three mulberries) fit in with the legend. The Italian word *moro* means both "mulberry tree" and "Moor." Another candidate is Francesco de Sessa, a dark-complexioned Italian mercenary who fought for the Venetians and had the nickname of *Il Moro*, "The Moor." He was put on trial in 1544 for charges unknown today and banished.

The **Old City

The Old City is entered by way of an old gun chamber near the Land Gate, af-

North Cyprus

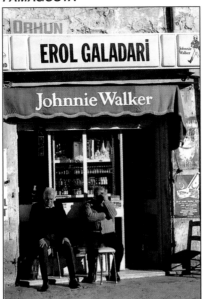

ter which one crosses a 19th-century bridge and continues through a Gothic arch. The following descriptions are arranged for a walk following the West Wall and then proceeding in a circular fashion to the East Wall, ending at Djamboulat Gate. The East Wall overlooks the harbor while the southwest side has gardens.

Following Kemal Zeytinoglou Street, a right turn at the first large junction leads to the **Nestorian Church** ❹, a triple-apsed church dating from 1359 and founded by the wealthy merchant Francis Lakhas.

The Nestorian Church is also known as *Ayios Yeoryios Exorinos* or "St. George the Exiler." This relates to its function of ridding oneself of an enemy by collecting some dust from its floor and leaving it in the enemy's house. The person is then said to either disappear or leave the is-

Above: Dozing in the sun. Right: Famagusta's public library, formerly the Church of St. Peter and St. Paul (later the Sinan Pasha Mosque).

land, a handy way to relieve oneself of animosity without resorting to violence. If you are not motivated to gather dust to make an enemy disappear, the interior is not of great interest since the paintings have been destroyed and the iconostasis is modern.

The **Church of Ayia Anna** ❺ is a little further along on Server Soumounjouglou Street, and is mainly distinguished by its well-preserved building and heavy bell tower. Inside are mural paintings with Latin inscriptions below. Not much is known about the **Tanner's Mosque** opposite the Palacazaro Bastion, once a 16th-century church.

Following the walls to the northwest corner opposite the San Luca Bastion, you come to **St. Mary's Church** ❻. The lovely vaulted 14th-century Carmelite church has exceptional paintings of patriarchs and bishops on the north wall, with coats of arms below.

Opposite it is the **Armenian Church** ❼, dating from the mid 14th century. The Armenian Bishop resided in Nicosia before Lusignan times, and a second prelate was at Famagusta. The interior has earthenware jars embedded in the ceiling to overcome the acoustic drawbacks of vaulted ceilings. The walls have fragments of mural paintings of saints within niches, with Armenian inscriptions below.

The **Martinengo Bastion** ❽, an outstanding example of military architecture built in 1550, is in the northwest corner of the walls. Its walls are six meters thick at some points, and it was considered impregnable. From the top you have a terrific view of the area as far as the Church of St. Barnabas near Salamis. Two enormous caves with ventilation shafts were found here in 1966. Large enough to hold 2,000 people, they might have been used during the siege of 1570-71, when the bastion was attacked by the Turks.

Despite its state of decay, **St. George of the Latins** ❾ is probably one of the most attractive of the Famagusta

churches. It was a fortified church constructed in the French style of the 13th century, perhaps before the walls were built. Not much remains besides the north wall and sacristy. Fragments of a classical temple were probably used in its construction. A capital of one of the wall shafts has a curious cluster of bats.

The splendid Ayia Sophia Mosque or **★Lala Mustapha Pasha Mosque** , the name it has had since 1954, is an incredible French Gothic gem of the early 14th century, far outshining its sister church of Ayia Sophia in Nicosia. Originally dedicated to St. Nicholas, it is huge (55 meters long and 23 meters wide), and its interior has three large doorways on the west with gabled canopies overhead. It resembles the cathedral of Rheims, although it is set among palm trees and a minaret now protrudes from one of its towers. Masses would gather outside in the square in order to catch a glimpse of the Lusignan kings as they were crowned. A balcony over the west door was used for their second coronation as kings of Jerusalem.

It was here that Caterina Cornaro, widow of Jacques II, reluctantly relinquished the throne in 1489, and ceded the kingdom to Agostino Barberigo, Doge of Venice. A couple of tombs remain in the north aisle, but those of Caterina's husband Jacques II and their son Jacques III have disappeared. The building was damaged during the siege in 1571.

The Gothic detail on the apse is indicative of the extensive stonework once decorating the cathedral. Further alterations occurred when it was changed into a mosque: any representation of the human shape was eliminated from the furnishings and altars; the stained-glass windows were removed and the frescoes whitewashed. Although this is regrettable from an artistic point of view, the original architectural details have been enhanced by the simplicity of its surroundings.

The dignity and grandeur of the mosque have not been overwhelmed by Baroque details and garish restorations as has occurred in other cathedrals. The only additions to the original structure are three chapels, two on the south and one on the north side.

The **parvis** (the square in front of a church) is said to one have been the largest in Europe. On it is an aged sycamore tree. Over the central porch of the cathedral is a fantastic six-light rose window, with panels now colored green, pink and yellow; above the side doors are tall double-light windows.

The Venetian **Palazzo del Provveditore** ⑪ consists of three arches supported by four columns from Salamis. In a room above the entrance to the police stables is the cell of the most famous of Ottoman poets, Kemal Bey, or Mehmed Namik Kemal (1840-88), who is often referred to as "The Shakespeare of Turkey." He had been exiled for his defiance of the Sultan, and a bust of him is now in the square.

The **Djafer Pasha Fountain**, with an inscription from an earlier one of 1597 which collapsed, is near the Venetian palace facing the parvis.

Walking along Namik Kemali Street to Kishla Street leads you to the ruins of the **St. Francis Monastery** ⑫. The Franciscans first appeared in Cyprus about 1226 and became large property holders. The south chapel has an altar and had medieval tombstones. Around the apse is a defunct Turkish bath.

Almost opposite St. Francis are the twin 14th-century **Churches of the Templars and the Hospitallers** ⑬. Going north from the cathedral, on Naim Effendi Street, is an **Italian Renaissance House**, one of the few residences in this area.

The **Church of St. Peter and St. Paul** ⑭ (Sinan Pasha Mosque), now a public library, is another remnant of the heydey of Lusignan times. It was built by a wealthy merchant from the proceeds of a single trading venture during the reign of

Right: One of the well-preserved floor mosaics of Salamis.

King Pierre I (1358-69.) Although it was damaged by earthquakes in 1546 and 1548, it is well-preserved.

The church was converted to a mosque in 1571. During the British Period it was used as a storeroom, giving it the name "Wheat Mosque." In 1961, it was restored by the Turks and used as a town hall. Bulky flying buttresses support the vaulting of the naves, and its Gothic north doorway once had coats of arms which have been erased. Close by is the **Tomb of Çelebi**, who was a member of the Janissary corps and served as Ambassador to France.

St. George of the Greeks ⑮ was the Byzantine Greek Orthodox cathedral dedicated to Ayios Epiphanios, Archbishop of Salamis, who was buried here before being removed to Constantinople in 900. On the south side, the apses are all that remain of the original (called Ayios Simeon), destroyed during the bombardment of 1571. Fragments of paintings of New Testament scenes are in the arches and apses, and founders' tombs are on the walls. The larger Gothic building was restored in the 1930s.

This area was the Orthodox quarter. Remains of **Ayia Zoni** ⑯ and **Ayios Nikolaos** ⑰, two other small medieval Orthodox churches are here. Both were once covered with mural paintings, but now only a few scattered fragments survive, most notably one of the Archangel Michael in Ayia Zoni.

The **Tourist Office** ⑱, supplying maps, booklets and schedules, is inside the walls just to the left of the Land Gate. Outside the Old City is the **Monument of Victory** ⑲, at an intersection of three roads. The right road leads north to Salamis, the Karpasia Peninsula and the beaches. The center road goes to the bus station, which has service to Nicosia. A bus to the turnoff for Salamis, less than a kilometer from the ruins, has the name Yenibogaziçi Tuzla or Matluyaka, but ask to make sure that the bus goes close to Sa-

lamis (about one kilometer from the ruins). A taxi stand is also nearby and is preferable, especially if you arrange for the driver to wait while you look at the ruins. Service taxis also go frequently to Nicosia.

A steam engine is located to the southeast of the Land Gate, near the police headquarters off Polatpasha Street, (formerly Anexartisias) at Ilker Karter Street. It once made the run between Famagusta and Nicosia from 1905 to 1951, the last and only railroad in Cyprus, although there is talk of building others.

Just off Polatpasha Street, to the north of police headquarters, are the post office, telecommunications center and a gas station. This street used to lead to Varosha, but it now ends in barbed wire about 500 meters past these buildings.

South of here is **Varosha** ⓫ (Marash), traditionally the Greek Cypriot area, just as the Turkish Cypriots lived in the walled city. The area is now a military zone occupied by the Turkish army and is off-limits to visitors. Varosha, once a posh Mediterranean playground with exclusive restaurants and golden sand beaches lined with hotels, is now a completely deserted ghost town.

Ochre and pink villas languish here, their roofs collapsing and gardens overgrown. Ornate churches, four-star hotels and boutiques whose shop windows feature 1970s fashions, now stand vacant, hastily deserted by their occupants in August of 1974.

Varosha is one of the main negotiating points in talks between the Greek and Turkish Cypriotsts. Its former residents have never lost hope of one day being able to return to it.

SALAMIS AND ENKOMI

**Salamis ⓬ lies nine kilometers north of Famagusta, to the east of the coastal road following Famagusta Bay northwards. The city was one of the most important in ancient times, and its site is vast and impressive. In order to get an idea of the scope of the site it is best to look at an aerial view photo of Salamis, such as the one found in the booklet entitled *Cyprus Museum and Archeological Sites of Cyprus* sold in Cypriot Museums. It gives an idea of the layout of the area and is good to refer to while there, since information at the monuments is minimal and it's easy to get confused. A visit to the Cyprus Museum in Nicosia will also acquaint you with the vast findings from Salamis and Enkomi.

Salamis is believed to have been founded by Teukros, the banished son of King Telamon of the small Greek island of Salamis, when he returned from the Trojan War about 1180 B.C. Artifacts dating to this period have been found, although evidence exists of an even earlier community. Salamis replaced nearby Enkomi as the leading settlement on the east coast in 1050 B.C., when Enkomi was finally abandoned

The 11th century B.C. was one of the most decisive periods in the history of the island of Cyprus. The island entered the Iron Age, and massive migrations from the Aegean region transformed Cyprus into a mostly Greek-speaking world. Whole communities who were fleeing the Dorian destruction formed the capital cities of the ancient Greek kingdoms, including Salamis, Kourion, Paphos, Marion and Soli.

About 560 B.C., Salamis was the first Cypriot city to mint its own coins. In 400 B.C. King Evagoras, an ambitious figure, assured the city's prosperity by strengthening the fortifications, building a fleet, and launching a Hellenic revival by establishing close relations with Athens. His goal was to extend his rule over the whole island, which he achieved by 391 B.C. However, after a siege by the Persians in 381 B.C., he was defeated, but he still maintained his control over Salamis while paying a tribute to Persia. He was murdered about 374 B.C.

During the relatively peaceful Ptolemaic rule, Salamis was replaced by

Paphos as the capital. After being destroyed by two earthquakes in the fourth century, it was rebuilt by Byzantine Emperor Constantine II, renamed Constantia, and once again became the capital. St. Barnabas, who had accompanied St. Paul during his preaching on the island, was a native of Salamis and was killed there by fellow Jews in the first century. It was an early Christian bishopric and a Bishop of Salamis attended the Council of Nicea in A.D. 325. The city was damaged by earthquakes in A.D. 76-77, and again in the fourth century. It suffered the fate of most of the harbor settlements when it was sacked by raiding Arabs in 647-49, and the inhabitants fled to nearby Famagusta.

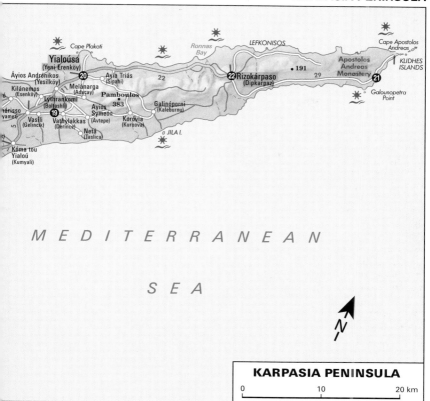

The section of the city walls, seen a short distance after the entrance, can be traced as it rings the central part of the town. It probably marks the city limits as reconstructed by Constantine II after the fourth-century earthquakes.

Starting from the parking lot and tourist pavilion on the north end, the **Gymnasium** is the first of the remains. It was probably destroyed during the fourth-century earthquakes and lay in ruins for some time. Most of the 35 ancient marble Corinthian columns here came from the nearby theater and were re-erected in 1952-55.

The Gymnasium and **Baths**, renovated during Roman times, are set around the **Palaestra**, with its four porticoes where athletes exercised in the nude. Most of the statues found here are in the Cyprus Museum in Nicosia, but a few are left by the rectangular pools, including one of Persephone. The typical areas of public baths can also be identified, including the *sudatorium* (hot air room) and the main building, the *caldarium*, heated by underground furnaces.

A semicircle of over 40 latrines in the southwest corner of the Palaestra is evidence that certain modern prohibitions were not in effect in ancient times. Citizens of Salamis seemed to have had no qualms about sitting here in the open and gossiping.

The white limestone **Theater**, excavated in 1960, is one of the largest in the

201

Eastern Mediterranean, with seating for 15,000 people. It occasionally has performances in the summer. It is a Roman-style semicircle which was built during the time of Emperor Augustus. The orchestra was rebuilt in the third century A.D. to accommodate the staged maritime battles so popular with the Romans. The altar to Dionysus can still be seen here, upon which a sacrifice was made to the god before every event. Most of its columns have been used in the Gymnasium, but a couple of statues of animals remain at either end of the lower seats.

Other remains include a small early Christian **basilica** and a larger one called the **Church of St. Epiphanios**, which has some damaged mosaics. Behind the **Agora**, or marketplace, is the **Temple of Zeus**, with one lone column remaining and bits and pieces lying on the ground.

Above: A dignified Roman Period statue in Salamis. Right: The Mausoleum of Saint Barnabas.

The Royal Tombs

The ***Royal Tombs ⓭** lie to the west of the Famagusta Road. **St. Caterina's Prison** was originally a Roman tomb and the cell of Caterina of Alexandria, an early fourth century Christian martyr imprisoned by her uncle.

Some of the most impressive finds on Cyprus come from the excavations of Salamis. Many of these are from the necropolis, especially the royally furnished Tomb 79, which can be inspected. The huge necropolis, first excavated in 1957, yielded a rich cache of bronze cauldrons containing human remains, wooden royal thrones sheathed in ivory, necklaces, rings and weapons. Many of these are on display at the Cyprus Museum in Nicosia.

The little **museum** behind the custodian's room contains skulls of horses along with the elaborate bronze ornaments they wore, as well as sections of chariots and isometric drawings. These artifacts are proof of the revival of Mycenaean burial rites in Salamis: horses and chariots were buried along with their owners in order to transport them in the next world.

Tombs 47 and 79 contain the skeletons of horses which were ritually sacrificed and buried with their wealthy owners.

The Monastery of Saint Barnabas

Following the road leading to Enkomi, you will reach the **Monastery of St. Barnabas ⓮** to the right. In the monastery church from the 18th century, an icon museum has been established. The right side-chapel of the church was painted by three monks who lived in the monastery until 1974. In four large sections, the paintings illustrate the history of the miraculous discovery of the remains of the saint in the fifth century, which helped lead to the independence of the Church of Cyprus from Antiochia, and thereby to

complete autonomy. In the former monks' cells an attractive archeological museum displays finds from sites in the region, with artifacts from the Neolithic Period to Byzantine times. About a hundred meters east of the idyllic monastery stands a chapel, built in 1953, above the **Tomb of St. Barnabas**, which is set in an underground chamber and which can be accessed from the chapel.

Enkomi

The site of **Enkomi ⑮** is to the southwest of the Monastery of St. Barnabas. The earliest finds of this site, mainly distinguished as the burial grounds of Salamis, are from the Middle Bronze Age (1900-1625 B.C.). Enkomi emerged in the Late Bronze Age (1625-1050 B.C.) as the major harbor town on the east coast when it became a copper-producing center. It was ravaged by seafarers and finally abandoned in 1050 B.C. after its harbor had silted up and the population moved to Salamis.

The excavated areas include a fortress near the North Gate, the Sanctuary of the Horned God, the House of the Pillar and the so-called Great Building.

The site of Enkomi has long been known as the richest cemetery of the Late Bronze Age in Cyprus. Some of the discoveries here include the only written documents in the Cypro-Minoan script on baked clay tablets. Indications of the artistic development of the early inhabitants are evident in many finds, including the hemispherical silver bowl with a wishbone handle found in a 14th-century B.C. tomb. On display in the Cyprus Museum, it has an impressive *niello* inlay of ox heads and flowers.

The fine bronze statue of the Horned God, two feet in height and dating back to the 12th century B.C., is also in the Cyprus Museum in Nicosia. It has been invaluable in providing a link in the development of early art history.

The **Sanctuary of the Horned God** consists of a hall and two inner cult rooms. In the hall was a sacrificial altar surrounded by many skulls of horned animals, mainly oxen. These were probably worn as masks during rituals connected with the worship of the Horned God, a fertility god depicted wearing a kilt and a horned helmet. He has been identified with the worship of Apollo Kerateas in the mountains of Arcadia, Greece, and may have been introduced by the Achaeans. The cult of the Horned God was to survive for at least seven centuries on Cyprus.

To the east is the **Church of Enkomi**, built in 1736, and farther east, the **Cenotaph of Nikokreon**, a platform erected for a funeral pyre, presumably of Nikokreon, the last king of Salamis. A number of gold ornaments and clay statues were excavated in 1965-66, but no human remains were found, leading archeologists to conclude that this was most probably only a symbolic monument.

Further evidence for a leaning towards the Hellenistic world during this period came with the discovery of expressive unfired clay heads of Nikokreon from the cenotaph. They were made by a local artist and reveal a strong influence of Lysippos, a fourth-century Greek sculptor from Attica.

Continuing on this road leads you back to the main road to Famagusta.

KARPASIA PENINSULA

One of the most unspoiled areas on Cyprus is the **Karpasia Peninsula**, the outline of which stretches northeastwards, with its tip pointing directly at the border between Syria and Turkey. The peninsula is not recommended for a day trip from Nicosia because the distances are so great; if you are staying in Salamis, it is best to get an early start.

The peninsula itself has many undeveloped areas and is a refuge for wildlife, including native and migrating birds, the rare wild white donkey, foxes, rabbits and partridges.

Less desirable is the one-meter-long poisonous Coupli snake, with green skin and dark spots, often found around Salamis. The wildflowers here include tulips, cyclamen, the Famagusta lily and wild orchids. The road leading to the Apostolos Andreas Monastery (78 kilometers) at the tip of the Karpasia Peninsula is paved and mostly in good condition. On the way you'll see wheat fields, fruit orchards and vineyards. However, when the grapes here are fermented, they are usually used for *raki* (clear spirits) and brandy, not wine.

The area of the fishing center **Bogazi** ⑯ (Bogaz) on Famagusta Bay has long stretches of almost deserted sand beaches including one called Paradise. Along the coast are several good seafood restaurants with a pleasant view.

A turnoff past **Trikomo** ⑰ (Iskele), a flourishing community 18 kilometers from Famagusta which has the picturesque 15th-century **Church of Ayios Dimitrios**, leads to **Kantara Castle** ⑱, another fantasy fortification which is actually a watch tower, often used as a prison in the past. It was distinguished as the hideout of Isaac Comnenos when he argued with King Richard the Lionhearted. The castle is ruined, although the guards' rooms and so-called Queen's Room can still be identified. Mainly, it is appealing for its panoramic views over the Mesaoria and Famagusta Bay.

Due east of Kantara Castle is **Lythrankomi** ⑲ (Boltashli), a well-developed, predominantly Turkish village. It is famous for the **Kanakaria Church**, which once contained the *Virgin and Child* mosaic, considered to be the most beautiful on the island. But in 1974, after the Turkish invasion, it was crudely pried off the walls and smuggled out of the country, like so many other Greek Orthodox artworks. A landmark court decision

in Chicago in 1990 blocked the sale of the mosaic to Peg Goldberg, an art dealer from Indiana, and ordered that it be returned to its rightful owners: the Greek Orthodox Church of Cyprus.

Of the several churches in **Yialousa ㉠** (Yeni Erenköy), the 13th-century **Archangelos Michael Church** is the most interesting, with some fragments of wall paintings remaining in the newer structure added during the 18th century. The countryside here is ideal for viewing spring flowers, such as crown daisy anemones and giant fennel.

The **Apostolos Andreas Monastery ㉡** is at the very tip of the peninsula, once the site of a temple to Aphrodite Akraia and the Neolithic settlement of Kastros, excavated in 1971-73. The monastery was built in the year 1867, but of greater interest is the quaint little 15th-century vaulted Gothic chapel below on the rocky shore. In it is a small spring, located under two stones in the right corner. This is said to be the source of water that Saint Andrew created to quench the thirst of the sailors when he stopped here while traveling by boat in A.D. 31. In the chapel are numerous *tama*, the ubiquitous wax effigies of Cypriot churches. November 30 is his feast day, widely celebrated in South Cyprus since Andreas is the most popular name for Cypriot Greek Orthodox males. A number of boats hang here also: Saint Andrew is said to protect sailors. Near the silver-gilt icon of Saint Andrew is a glass case with an odd assortment of objects, including eyeglasses, watches, coins and locks of hair, left by pilgrims as offerings.

A good place to stop for a coffee break is **Andreas Kafénion** in the village of **Rizokarpaso ㉢** (Dipkarpaz). The area is known for its tobacco and sizable number of Greek Cypriot inhabitants, some 500 of whom remain by choice. As this minority faces difficulties including lack of education facilities, the remaining Greek Cypriot population is predominantly elderly. In Andreas Kafénion the locals are vigorously involved in card games and *tavli* (backgammon).

MODERN CYPRUS

The economic recovery of Cyprus since the traumatic division of the island in 1974 has been nothing short of miraculous. The Cypriots have worked industriously to repair the damage of the split and get back on their feet economically.

The economists in the Republic of Cyprus have concentrated all their energies on reinforcing their country's position as a prospective member of the European Union after filing for membership in 1990. Cyprus has, for some time, enjoyed a closer customs treaty with the EU and has been slowly structuring its ways of doing business to conform with guidelines laid down in Brussels. Since that time, it has been declared that in keeping with this goal, new legislation will be in

Preceding pages: Shepherd herding along the stark plains of the Mesaoria. Men playing "tavli" (backgammon) in Pano Lefkara. Above: Cypriot woman. Right: Intensively irrigated agriculture on the coast.

harmony with that of the EU. Bankers have urged the government to speed up the process of liberalization, including relaxing currency controls. Some protection was necessary after the 1974 division, but this must be loosened in order for the country to be prepared for the challenges that lie ahead.

Cyprus has also aimed to attract foreign businesses in recent years. It has been very successful because of its liberal tax regime and sunny, hospitable environment. It has rapidly expanded as an offshore center for financial trading and shipping as well. Registered offshore companies now number 6,800, with 800 of these currently operating offices within Cyprus. One of the reasons for this influx of business to Cyprus is the highly qualified workforce. Cyprus has proportionately one of the highest number of university graduates in the world.

In 1992, the country opened its first university in Nicosia, and the existing management academy was expanded. The boom in the economy has meant a level of almost full employment. Per capita income now exceeds US \$10,000, and about 60 percent of the Cypriot women are employed.

Economic growth has been altogether impressive. In 1991, the GNP (gross national product) was about six percent, twice the rate of the developed countries of the EU. The economic prospects for the island are optimistic, although many business people stress the need to diversify the economy to make it less dependent on tourism and agriculture, two sectors that are highly sensitive to unpredictable factors.

Greek and Turkish Cypriots have been cooperating to restore the old part of Nicosia that lies within the 16th-century walls. For some years after the division of the island in 1974, the Old Town within the walls bordering the Green Line deteriorated, especially in the south, and most of its inhabitants moved elsewhere.

Within the last few years, however, impetus has been given to a restoration plan, and several neighborhoods have been rejuvenated, including the addition of smart clubs and galleries. The mayors of the two parts of Nicosia cooperate on a plan for sewage disposal, traffic flow and land use. Visits across the Green Line between party leaders, town planners and journalists have been on the increase.

The Arts and Artists

Cyprus is flourishing artistically as well, with a great revival of creative cultural activity. As is to be expected, much of the poetry and prose after the division of the island in 1974 was centered on the emotional and physical devastation that occurred. Poetry and fiction are especially notable in Cyprus, with an incredible number of working poets and writers in residence, including many women. Notable among the many talents are poets Costas Montis, Panos Ioannides, Niki Marangou and Kyriakos Charalambides.

Christakis Georgiou and Andriana Ierodiaconou are bright lights among the fiction writers.

Art in Cyprus has developed along several distinctive paths over the years, and a number of artists who represent these trends are highly productive. Some of the country's artists who have distinguished themselves include master woodcarver Hambis, Stassinos Paraskos, founder of the Cyprus School of Art in Paphos, Adamantios Diamantis, whose noted oil paintings have earned him the title of the "Father of Modern Cypriot Painting," and Xanthos Hatzisoteriou, who distinguished himself through his expressive folk art.

Yiorkos Skotinos, whose Ayia Napa studio is open to the public, creates earth-toned acrylics and oils that capture the essence of Cypriot myth, making him one of the leading Cypriot painters. He drew on his experience of being forced to leave Famagusta during the division of the island, creating the cycle *Protest Against War And Violence: 1974-75*.

FLORA AND FAUNA

It might surprise visitors to the island of Cyprus to find out that some 90 million years ago it was the bottom of a deep sea now called Tethys. Tectonic movements at about that time resulted in the collision of the African plate with the Eurasian. About 20 million years ago, two small islands rose above the sea, giving birth to Cyprus. The elevation of Troodos and the Pentadaktylos Range to their present height took place about one to two million years ago as the Mesaoria (meaning "between the mountains"), then a shallow sea, emerged as a wide plain to join the two islands.

The flora of Cyprus is unique and diverse, reflecting its complex geology and morphology. There is clear evidence that the island once had many more trees than it does now. Many factors which necessitated cutting down trees took their toll on

Above: A wild tulip in full blossom. Right: The Cedar Valley.

the island's woodlands, including the processing of copper, the ceramics industry of the ancient world, shipbuilding, the day-to-day energy needs of the inhabitants of the island, and the need for arable land. The introduction of the goat on the island had devastating effects in some regions, since these hardy creatures have an astounding ability to completely destroy an area's vegetation within a short period of time.

Today, about 17 percent of the island can be classified as woodland. The main species now present in the island's forests are the brutia pine in the lower reaches of Troodos, the black pine on the higher slopes, three species of juniper, of which two are on the higher reaches of Troodos, while *Juniperus phoenicea* is predominant in what is left of the coastal maquis, mainly in the Akamas region. In such maquis, the lentisc also abounds. Alders, Oriental plane, strawberry trees and the endemic golden oak are common on Troodos. The endemic cedar (*Cedrus brevifolia*) is now restricted to 50,000 trees in the Cedar Valley of the Paphos Forest.

Of about 1,800 species, subspecies, and varieties of plants that grow on the island about 120 are endemic, found only on Cyprus. A wide diversity of habitats exists, far wider than might be expected from an island. Coastal wetlands are of international importance, such as those of Akrotiri Lake and the Larnaca Salt Lake complex. Extensive areas of sand dunes harbor rare and sensitive plant communities. Coastal areas with cliffs are spectacular, such as those at Episkopi and the north coast of Akamas.

The central Mesaoria plain is characterized by low rainfall, often less than 350 mm annually. Little is left of its original vegetation, presumably some type of maquis, which has been used extensively for cereals. Sparse maquis remains on the characteristic flat-topped hills of the Mesaoria along with thyme and the endemic *Onobrychis venosa*, wild orchid (*Ophrys argolica*), and *Pinus brutia*. Here on hillsides and banks of the usually dry riverbeds, the Cyprus endemic bee orchid (*Ophrys kotchyi*) survives.

The foothills that fringe much of Troodos rise to about 750 meters. Although somewhat varied in their geological make-up and characterized by chalks and marls, they generally have very interesting and varied vegetation. Here bee orchids abound, as do many other types. Large areas of untilled land alternate with the remnants of older forests dominated by goat-resistant thorny genista and callicotome bushes. The pink rock rose (*Cistus parviflora*) thrives in many areas, as does the *Pistacia terebinthus*, which has red foliage in the spring and autumn. Cultivated (or wild) carob and olive trees are characteristic of this area.

Where the chalks and marls finish and Troodos starts, with its lava folds and diabase rocks, there is an abrupt change in the vegetation. Here the white rock rose (*Cistus salviaefolius*) abounds in

most areas and on the southeastern slopes of the Troodos Range, as does fragrant wild lavender.

On the higher slopes of Troodos many endemic and rare plants thrive. Helleborines and spectacular red-flowered peonies are characteristic of this region. Cyprus' endemic crocus (*Crocus cyprius*) flowers in early spring while the snows melt on Khionistra, the highest peak of these mountains. On the banks of streams rare orchids, such as the *Dactyloriza iberica* and the *Epipactis veratripholia*, can be found.

Those interested in seeing a large variety of flowers must remember that spring starts early in Cyprus. The first orchids flower in January.

Fauna

Little is known of the early fauna of the island, but much can be assumed from clear fossil evidence. The island was colonized at one stage by hippos and elephants, but most probably as a result of

the absence of predators, these evolved into dwarf species. They disappeared from the island around 8,000-10,000 years ago, apparently when humans first colonized it. Early primitive tools have recently been found on the island in heaps of hippo and elephant bones, suggesting evidence of man's involvement in their demise.

The island's first inhabitants are thought to have brought with them species of deer, wild boar, a type of wild goat and the reclusive wild sheep called moufflon (*Ovis ophion*), the males of which have impressive curled horns. Some of them must have escaped or were released and formed wild populations. With the exception of moufflon and the goat, the others became extinct on the island, probably as a result of hunting and deforestation. The moufflon was at the brink of extinction at the turn of the cen-

Above: A rare shot of some of the almost extinct moufflons. Right: Too often, birds become the prey of weekend trappers.

tury, its population estimated at a few dozen, but it was saved in the nick of time by introduction of strict protection measures. The moufflon is now thriving, with an estimated population of 2,000 living in the Paphos Forest and Troodos. A small number are kept for breeding and conservation purposes at the Stavros tis Psokas Forest Station. Fallow deer, a close relative of the Mesopotamian deer no longer found on the island, were also introduced recently and are kept at this station for breeding purposes.

The indigenous mammalian fauna of the island includes the fox, a hedgehog (*Hemichinus auritus*), the hare, an endemic shrew (*Crocidura cypria*), and several bat species including the Egyptian fruit bat. No native freshwater fish exist on Cyprus, with the exception of eels found in mountain streams without dams, such as the Dhiarizos and Xeros. Freshwater crabs now thrive in many streams on Troodos, rebounding after nearly disappearing from DDT use during the antimalarial campaign. About 20 species

of freshwater fish have been introduced in recent years and are used for stocking dams.

Of the land reptiles, the most noteworthy are the endemic snake *Hierophis cypriensis*, a non-poisonous snake, and the large agama lizard. With the exception of the eastern viper (*Viper lebetina*), none of the other snakes are fanged, although the *Coupli*, about one meter long, and the elusive *Saittaros* are poisonous. Three species of frogs live on the island, one of them the green tree-climbing frog (*Hyla savignie*) which migrates regularly to its main breeding area of Phasouri Marsh in early spring. The striped-necked terrapin, a protected species, also lives on the island in the precious few wetlands that remain on the plains in summer.

Cyprus is a significant stopover point for a fairly large number of species of migrating birds in spring and autumn.

The salt lakes and related wetlands of Akrotiri and Larnaca are also important over-wintering areas for the greater fla-mingo, various species of duck, and other waterfowl. About 10,000 flamingoes pause in Cyprus on their migratory route south, usually in November or December after the rains swell the salt lakes. Coots, ringed plovers, lapwings, sea gulls and sandpipers in large numbers can usually be found by December. Mallards, teals and shell ducks are common. Spring migrants include the glossy ibis and several species of egret, herons and many wading birds. Common resident birds include the chukar, crested lark, wood pigeon, kestrel, and the majestic barn owl, a shrill-voiced bird of prey. Bonelli's eagle is the most common predatory species, and about 20 pairs of griffon vultures breed here. There are several endemic species, such as the Cyprus warbler, Cyprus pied wheatear, coal tit, and the tiny insectivorous Scops owl, a frequent visitor to olive groves and gardens.

The island's tremendously diverse flora attracts a rich variety of butterflies, which are dependent on plants for food for their larvae. About 55 species can be found on Cyprus, an extraordinary number when one considers the same figure applies to all of the British Isles. They fly in several broods, especially noticeable on plains and lower hills. Spring is the season to see the most butterflies. The best time of day for butterfly-watching is an hour or so after sunrise, when these delicate creatures warm themselves in the sun before they lazily take to the air.

Among those common to Cyprus are several endemic varieties, such as the Paphos blue, a species in which the male has electric blue on its upper wings, whereas the female is a drab brown. It is common in the Troodos foothills and Akamas, as is the Cyprus meadow-brown. The yellow swallowtail, distinguished by striking black markings, is found low in the Troodos where its caterpillars nibble mainly on plants of the fennel family. Orange tips, of which only the male has the characteristic orange markings on its forewings, brown argus and speckled wood are common in the Troodos valleys.

A number of rare butterflies can be spotted, such as the eastern festoon on Troodos and in the Akamas gorges, where its caterpillars feed on the exotic Dutchman's Pipe. The rare and spectacular two-tailed pasha, a resplendent marble-patterned butterfly, can be sighted high in the Akamas and at Platres.

The ubiquitous cicada has an amazing life cycle. The larvae spend four years incubating underground, after which they claw their way through the earth into the sunlight. They have a mere six-week life span, at the end of which the female lays her eggs, which will spawn the next generation of cicadas four years later. Both males and females collapse and die before summer is over.

When the weather warms up after the Summer Solstice (June 21), the "song" of

Right: Green turtle hatchlings taking their first "steps" on the way to the sea.

the male cicada can be heard throughout the island. This incredible din is produced by two circular convex membranes called cymbals attached to the cicada's chest and amplified through an elaborate system of resonators.

Marine Life

The productivity of the sea around Cyprus is rather low, about the same as the rest of the Eastern Mediterranean. Nonetheless, it has a diversity of life and clarity that is enviable. The temperature of the sea ranges from about 16°C in winter to about 28°C in summer. The richest marine life lies below a depth of 30 meters. The salinity is about 39 per mill, among the highest in the world. Fisheries in Cyprus depend on a large variety of over 50 species, in comparison to about a dozen or so species in the northeast Atlantic. To the underwater explorer, the bottom fauna in shallow waters is at first somewhat disappointing. Much life is there, but disguised or hidden from sight. Some animals bury themselves in the sand, like several species of sand urchin and starfish, the sauries, and the occasional spectacular flying gurnard. In shallow rocky areas, sea urchins predominate, grazing on algae on the rock surface. The common fish here are peacock and rainbow wrasses, two-banded breams, blennies, and gobbies and the small parrot fish.

A bit deeper, below about 10 meters, the posidonia meadows provide a very characteristic Mediterranean seascape. Posidonia is often thought to be a seaweed, but it is actually a flowering plant that has adapted very successfully to sea life. The meadows, which can be very extensive, are a vital part of the whole Mediterranean ecosystem. This breeding area for many organisms has a rich and varied fish life, including small wrasses, breams, sea perches, groupers, and the odd bullnose ray. Deeper still, usually below 15-20 meters on sandy and muddy

bottoms, caulerpa, a small green algae, takes over from posidonia. It forms extensive beds in which are found the pinna or fan shells, the largest bivalve shells in the Mediterranean. Without a doubt, however, the most fascinating terrain is that of the deep water outcrops, the reefs below 25 meters. The view of submarine hills, cliffs and valleys is breathtaking. The rock itself is invisible, completely covered with animal and plant growth of many hues and forms. The delicate lilac incrustations of lithothamnia contrast sharply with the huge, dark shapes of sponges. Coral knobs house the tubes of elegant peacock fans. In crevices and caves, colonies of fairy-like white and red fan worms of different colors and shapes compete for space with brilliant red slime sponges. Sponges predominate here.

The opening of the Suez Canal in the last century connected the Mediterranean with the Red Sea. For the first time, the Mediterranean's purely Atlantic-origin fauna faced competition from invading Indo-Pacific animals and plants. Many

reached Cyprus and established themselves here. Several well-known species, such as the red soldier fish (*Rossos*) and two siganids (*Prosphygoulles*) are now common in the commercial catches of Cypriot fishermen.

The sea around Cyprus, as is true of most Mediterranean countries, shows signs of overfishing. Fish production is about 2,500 tons per year, valued at about eight million C£. Protective measures, such as establishing closed seasons for fishing or limiting the size of the fleet in closed areas, have been implemented with success. Yet more remains to be done and intensive fishing has inevitably had an impact on the marine balance.

The Mediterranean monk seal, now on the brink of extinction, and dolphins are protected species. Exotic and rare forms of wildlife give Cyprus a special touch. Green and loggerhead turtles breed on the sandy beaches in summer. Both species and their eggs are protected by law, as are some of the most important breeding beaches, such as Lara.

ENVIRONMENTAL PROTECTION

Visitors to Cyprus are often unprepared for the extent of commercial development which has transformed the coastline of southern Cyprus in the years since the division of the island in 1974. Although Cyprus was growth oriented even before that time, a rapid push towards development started in this period, when there was an urgent need for employment of the thousands of refugees, and little legislation was passed strictly protecting the environment on Cyprus.

The over-development in Famagusta was repeated in other places; around Ayia Napa, Larnaca, Limassol and Paphos. "We were striving for confidence and stability," admitted Andreas Demetropoulos, head of the government's Fisheries Department and President of the Cyprus Wildlife Society. "We got it through economic development, but future generations won't see it that way." The boom was largely uncontrolled, though the government belatedly implemented some restrictions in the late 1980s. In 1989, the government also imposed a building moratorium on coastal tourist development and stricter guidelines to regulate other construction.

With a total Greek Cypriot population of just over half a million, Cyprus plays host each year to some two million tourists; the number of hotel beds on the island has climbed to approximately 80,000. As ribbon development already hugs the coastline around major tourist resorts from Ayia Napa in the east to Paphos in the west, environmentalists say the island needs an alternative to mass tourism.

Fortunately, a number of groups and influential individuals are determined to preserve the remaining untampered natural terrain. The hottest issue is the fate of

Right: In the Valley of Windmills, Larnaca, where wind helps to pump water.

the Akamas Peninsula, an area on the west of the island that is Cyprus' last remaining coastal wilderness.

The peninsula contains a large variety of habitats, with a lot of rare endemic plant species, and sightings of Cyprus' dwindling monk seals have been made at its tip. Furthermore, a series of sandy beaches around Lara Bay are one of the few places in the Mediterranean area where the endangered green turtle lays its eggs and where the loggerhead turtle also breeds.

The only link between Lara Bay and nearby Paphos is a 10-kilometer-long pot-holed dirt track off the main road. The hot bumpy ride dissuades most visitors from coming here, and the beaches thankfully remain free of hotels. Three out of five large beaches near Lara Bay are state-owned, as is 90 percent of the peninsula. The Cyprus Wildlife Society was instrumental in stopping construction of a paved road through the peninsula, which would have disturbed the turtle nesting area.

A Greenpeace team attracted media attention several years ago when it demonstrated on the island with the goal of keeping developers' bulldozers away from Akamas and protecting the turtle population. The European Union has already provided funds in the form of grants towards turtle protection under its Medspa program, the first of two that it has approved for Cyprus. The money goes towards funding the Turtle Conservation Project.

Large developers who have bought up key pieces of coastal property, and villagers who feel that the tourist-generated prosperity that has swept over most of the island has left them behind, have put pressure on the government to allow construction in Akamas.

Environmentalists say that if the entire area is to be properly protected, the government of Cyprus will have to declare it a national park, an action it says it plans

Environmental Protection

to take. In the meantime, the debate continues to rage over a number of other key areas as well.

The government has wholeheartedly encouraged small-scale tourism in accommodations owned and run by the villagers themselves in outlying communities on the peninsula. In addition to government plans for assistance to the villagers, environmentalists are also keen to encourage this kind of development and have put together a package called the Laona Project.

The island's environmental protection group Friends of the Earth, assisted by private Cypriot and European Union funds, renovate houses as an example to residents. Grants are provided for them to restore their own homes, and others have been made available for improving the infrastructure and to help with marketing. These small renovated units could serve to accommodate discerning guests in a genuine Cypriot environment, providing a sustainable income for the owners without disturbing the countryside.

With growth rates of 10 to 17 percent over the last three years, tourism revenues accounted for more than 40 percent of all foreign exchange earnings and had been patching up the island's economy, leading to an increasing dependence on the tourist sector to keep it afloat.

Economists, government planners and environmentalists have been expressing concern that the island's tourism is being geared towards the upscale market. Adrian Akers Douglas, a keen environmentalist and moving force of Friends of the Earth, described the decrease of tourism during the years of 1991 and 1992 as the "silver lining" to the Gulf War:

"Everybody realized that the bubble could burst," said Akers Douglas. "When it did, low-level package tours were the first to collapse."

This setback provided quite a jolt, which awakened many Cypriots to the need for diversification of the economy and industry, placing an emphasis on more stable facets with a self-sufficient infrastructure.

TRADITIONAL MUSIC
AND DANCE

The music of the island of Cyprus reflects its geographical position. It has absorbed influences from all the lands of the Eastern Mediterranean littoral – Turkey, Syria, Lebanon, Palestine, Egypt – extending as far east as the Tigris-Euphrates Valley and Persia. Archeological evidence and the culture, language and religion of contemporary Cypriots show, however, that the strongest and most durable influence has been Greek.

The instruments usually used to accompany Cypriot folk dances are the violin and the fretted lute or *laouto*. The *laouto* has a set of four double strings and is played with a stripped eagle's or vulture's quill. Occasionally, a kind of tambourine without metal discs, called a *tambuça*, is used for accompaniment. The *tambuça* skin usually has a design or figures painted on it. The Cypriot shepherd's flute, the *pidhkiavli*, with six finger holes and one thumb hole on the lower side, is rarely used to accompany dances. In the city, a clarinet, in Greek *klarino*, dulcimer or *santouri*, and occasionally an accordion are added to the ensemble.

Generally speaking, Turkish Cypriot and Greek Cypriot folk dances are similar. Turkish folk music, which heavily influenced Turkish Cypriot and Greek Cypriot folk music, is remarkable for its ancient roots. The instruments still used by Anatolian villagers are pictured in Hittite bas-reliefs that date back to 2000 B.C. Stringed instruments, which vary from one district to another, include the *djura* (three strings), *baglama* (six strings), *bozuk* (eight strings) and *azik saz* (nine strings). Of the bowed instruments, the most popular are the *kemence* from the Black Sea area and the *kabak* from the Aegean area.

Right: Colorful folk dancers line up for "karshilamadhes" dances.

Wind instruments play a primary role in Turkish folk music. The *zurna* is the forerunner of the oboe. The *ney*, a flute known as the *mait* by the ancient Egyptians, is one of the primary instruments in the music of the dervishes. The *davul*, a bass drum which usually accompanies the *zurna*, is often heard in folk music.

The *poietarike* is a vocal mode used by the versifiers, or *poietaredhes*, who put events into verse, occasionally at the *poietomakhia* (verse competition). The rhymes themselves are called *çatismata*, from the Turkish verb *çatismak*, meaning "to clash."

These contests are often held at festivals, but can occur at any time where a party atmosphere prevails and at least two versifiers are present. For the most part, these *çatismata*, together with other "songs" whose texts are widely known, are performed at a table where everyone is eating and drinking, as at a wedding. They are also called *Tragoudhia tou Trapeziou* or "Songs of the Table," although the "adversaries" might be dancers who spout rhymes during a break in the music.

The typical folk dances of Cyprus are performed by two people facing each other, the *karshilamadhes*, from the Turkish root *karshi* meaning "opposite" or "counter."

Only in Cyprus are there so many face-to-face dances performed as a suite. The Greek word *antikristoi* meanwhile tends to replace *karshilamadhes*. Traditionally, two people danced, while in recent years there has been a tendency for more people to do so. There must, however, be an even number of dancers. The men are usually heavy-footed while dancing, the women are light. In some of the dances only women dance, in others only men.

The Dance of the Knife, the Dance of the Sickle and the Dance of the Flour Sieve are three distinctive patterns for men which use the same music. The Dance of the Knife is done by two men

standing abreast of each other, linked by a handkerchief. The *schottische* step, three steps and a hop, is used in the beginning. Then the lead dancer draws out his knife, traditionally from his boot, and plunges it into the ground. The pace quickens and excitement begins to mount as the lead dancer dances around the knife, finally does a somersault over it, and picks it up in his teeth while bending over backwards. He then uses the knife to make threatening motions, slashing around the victim's throat and head. He ends the dance by making motions of stabbing the victim, then skins and dresses the carcass.

The Dance of the Sickle is performed by one man only now, but it used to be done by two. The dance was a contest to see who was best at twirling the sickle, much like a baton-twirling contest. Now one dancer twirls the sickle in various proscribed patterns, sometimes utilizing two sickles. Once again the *schottische* step is used, alternating with a hop step.

The Dance of the Flour Sieve (*Khoros tis Taças*) follows the same basic scheme

as the Dance of the Sickle, and is done by one man. He picks up a flour sieve, resembling a tambourine without cymbals, and dances about in a small counterclockwise circle. He places the sieve on the ground and does step-hops while crossing his legs over it. Very agile dancers often put one or two glasses of water on the inside rim of the sieve and twirl it about, being careful not to spill the water or lose a glass, sometimes transferring it from one hand to the other. Now the dancer scarcely does any clearly defined steps, occasionally leaning on one leg.

A number of Cypriot dances are part of a game that lends a humorous tone to them. One is the flirtatious Apple Dance, in which a man tosses an apple at the woman of his desire. She invites him to come closer, sometimes giving him a kiss in the process.

The Arab Dance is probably related to a water-pot-balancing dance originating in Lebanon. In this version, a glass or series of glasses is balanced on a man's head. The dancer may place the glasses

221

on his head himself, or more commonly kneels down so that someone else can place them on his head. The dancer keeps his arms and hands outstretched and will sometimes do tricky variations, such as a back bend after placing a lit candle in the last glass like a vigil light.

One amusing dance is called *O Nicoles*, which seems to be related to the children's game of "Pin the Tail on the Donkey." The first dancer sticks one end of a strip of paper, about a third of a meter long, into the back of his belt. The other dancer has a box of matches, a candle or lighter, and dances around while trying to set fire to the tail, a near impossible task, especially if the dancer has a wicked wiggle to his hips.

The Pepper Dance is a unique and lively Cypriot dance in which the leader holds a leather strap or belt. The dancers unlink and drop to their knees, then rub their right hands on the ground (sometimes their elbows as well), as though they were grinding pepper. Pepper is often considered to be an aphrodisiac, so the dance has erotic connotations. If a participant does not do the dance properly, the leader "beats" him until he does.

Other dances commonly performed include the *Tsiphteteli*, a sensual, somewhat writhing dance referring to double stopping on the strings of a violin. On Cyprus, it is a man's dance, although elsewhere it may be a women's or couple's dance. The man's *Syrtos* is done by two men: the lead holds onto a handkerchief and slowly circles in a counterclockwise direction around the other, who remains still while supporting the lead. *To Zeybekiko*, or the Zeybek, was originally a warrior's dance; in Cyprus it is done by two men facing each other. The rhythm is slow and dramatic, punctuated by slapping the heels or leaping into the air.

A good place to see many of these dances is at a Cypriot wedding. Weddings are held on Sundays, usually between

Above: A solitary folk dancer and musicians. Right: A "tampouras," a musical instrument made out of a gourd.

June 1 and the end of October. Traditionally, they are not held 40 days before Christmas, 50 days before Easter, or on August 15. May is considered a bad month for weddings, as is the whole of leap year.

On the morning of the wedding, the bride and groom are led to the church by their fathers in separate processions, usually to the accompaniment of a lute and violin and with church bells pealing. After the wedding ceremony, the couple go in a procession to their new home, again accompanied by the violin and lute and church bells. Censers with incense are waved near them and they are sprinkled with rose water, representing love and happiness, by people along the way.

The groom's mother greets the newlyweds at the entrance of their home and perfumes them with smoke from incense burning on a plowshare. The groom then slaughters a black chicken with a black-handled knife in order to secure his new home, and they both smash a pomegranate to ensure fertility.

Tables are then set and guests served food and drink. The guests toast the newlyweds and the dancing begins. The Dance of the Wedding Couple (*Khoros tou Andhrogynou*) done by the bride and groom is the only one that a single man and woman dance together. This swaying face-to-face dance in 2/4 time is called the *Mandiloudhin*, or "Handkerchief Dance." The handkerchief is folded once diagonally so that it forms a triangle when the dancers hold the diagonally opposite corners. The offering of a handkerchief by a woman to a man symbolizes her love for him. The silk handkerchief is symbolic of womankind because of the connection with embroidery and silk production, considered feminine crafts.

During this time, the guests give gifts to the bride and groom, i.e., money is pinned onto the couple or a cross and chain. The *koumbaros*, or best man, sprinkles rose water on people while they

sing a song rendering best wishes, praise and advice. *Sandala Mandala*, meaning a collection of useless things, is a comical dance customarily performed on the last night of a Cypriot wedding. In it, a man mimes the actions of a door-to-door salesman who carries the sandals he has for sale on a long pole slung over his shoulder.

The Women's *Syrtos* is the last dance performed at a wedding and is distinguished by the fact that despite its name, it is done by women and men alternating in a chain, not women only, and is the only circle dance done at a wedding. After dancing around several times in a counterclockwise circle, the dancers let go of each other and improvise steps, swaying, turning and even jumping. The vigorous, almost fierce appearance the dancers have while improvising gave rise to the expression "I'll make you dance the Syrtos," meaning "I'll beat you!" The playing of a special tune called *Pologhiastos*, meaning farewell, signals the guests that it is time to leave.

MYTHOLOGY AND LITERATURE

Cyprus is for romantics. Lore and poetry abound, much of it about Aphrodite, whom Sappho called "Queen of Cyprus." The Cypriots have their own epic poet, Stassinos, and Shakespeare's *Othello* is set here. Revered Greek poet Georgios Seferis combined ancient references with local settings in poetry he composed on Cyprus.

The Golden Goddess

The birth of Aphrodite from the sea is lyrically described by an anonymous poet in the second *Homeric Hymn to Aphrodite* (Charles Boer, translator):

... beautiful Aphrodite...
the damp force
of Zephyros breathing
carried her along
on waves of the resounding sea
in soft foam.
In their own fillets of gold
the Horae received her happily,
and happily put
the ambrosial garments
around her.
On her immortal head
they placed a crown
that was carefully made,
beautiful and in gold.
On her silver-white breasts
they arranged necklaces of gold,
which they made themselves.

Decked out in this fashion, the newborn goddess was led to the gods. They reached out their hands to this smiling beauty crowned in violets, and were awed by her and yearned to take her home.

The poet of this hymn does not mention the mutilation and gore of her conception as Hesiod does in his *Theogony*: When father Uranus (Sky) held back the delivery of Mother Gaia's (Earth) off-

Right: Sunset at Petra tou Romiou, the birth-place of Aphrodite.

spring, she cried out for relief and revenge, and son Cronos came to her rescue. He hacked off his father's genitals and hurled them into the sea.

From the semen, blood and sea foam Aphrodite was born, the only deity of her generation not born of Earth. First she drifted near the island of Kythera (Cerigo), then to Cyprus, where she rose out of the sea. Flowers grew wherever the goddess stepped.

Aphrodite's birth was a synthesis of opposites, for out of violence and ugliness the bearer of love and beauty was born. The gods themselves were seduced by the grace and erotic nature of Aphrodite, the goddess who unites humans in love and joy, and fosters social graces and harmony. Through her power, animals mate and all nature reproduces.

On Cyprus, she was identified with the Phoenician fertility goddess Astarte and the divine Ishtar. According to Karl Kerenyi in *Goddesses of Sun and Moon*, she is a symbol of wholeness and union, and a synthesis of opposites.

To Jungians, she represents a synthesizing aspect of the psyche, a combination of male-female attributes, as did Hermaphrodite, the offspring of Hermes and Aphrodite. The so-called Aphroditos is a bearded goddess representing the hermaphroditic form, and others have been found at Aphrodite's shrines such as Amathus.

One can see the very place where Aphrodite was born at Petra tou Romiou, a large rock at the sea edge near Palea Paphos. From here she emerged annually with virginity renewed, according to Robert Graves in *The White Goddess*.

Aphrodite is said to bring harmony and joy but calm as well, for her birth stilled the riled waters. Yet she certainly caused her share of trouble. Her innocence lacks conscience and she can often lie and disregard reason. Artemis, Athena and Hestia disliked her ways, not surprising considering their defense of virginity and

hearth. Aphrodite's unromantic husband Hephaestus had his problems when she bedded down with the war god Aries. Helen said she was powerless against Aphrodite, using this as an excuse for yielding to Paris, which resulted in the ten-year Trojan War.

Despite her naughty reputation, Aphrodite reigned supreme on Cyprus. She was worshiped at many shrines, including Palea Paphos, Idalion, Amathus, Soli, Kourion and one on the highest peak of Mount Olympos. Among her epithets used by outsiders were "Paphian" and "Cyprian," the latter which came to have a lewd connotation. On Cyprus, however, she was often simply referred to as "The Goddess" or "The Lady," and her surname, if used, was *Eleamon*, meaning "The Merciful."

An oiled stone and conical omphalos stones are most likely representations of the goddess. Until recently, new mothers prayed to one of these forms. Other evidence exists to attest to the continuation of the influence of Aphrodite.

At the end of the Mycenaean Era in the late 12th century B.C., temples were built to other gods. Apollo and Zeus came to flourish though they did not displace the goddess of the sea. One is tempted to say that of all the gods Aphrodite came closest to expressing the nature of the inhabitants, being both joyful and sensual.

Tradition has set the location of Aphrodite's temple at Palea Paphos, with different founders mentioned, including Kinyras, King of Cyprus. The priest-king Kinyras, according to the *Iliad*, got into trouble for tricking Agamemnon, commander at Troy. After promising to send 50 ships to Troy, Kinyras, however, sent one real ship and 49 models. Angry Agamemnon captured Kinyras and drove him out. Kinyras eventually met his death as the penalty for losing a musical contest to Apollo.

Other members of the priest's family suffered for their father's ruse. Aphrodite caused his three daughters to sleep with strangers. The fourth, Smyrna (or Myrra) who claimed to be more beautiful than

the goddess, was driven to incest with King Kinyras.

Adonis and Aphrodite

Christian celebrations of springtime rebirth appear to descend from pagan practices. Of the several versions of the story of Adonis and Aphrodite, the following one is traditional: Adonis was born of an incestuous union between King Kinyras and his daughter Myrra, who was turned into a myrtle tree for her sin. When the myrtle trunk was split, baby Adonis was found inside.

Aphrodite loved him from infancy and sent him to Persephone of the underworld to be tended for part of each year. Her warnings against hunting large game were ignored, and the boy was killed by a wild boar. Grieving Aphrodite caused the red anemones of springtime to blossom

Above: Othello's Tower in Famagusta, setting of the ill-failed love affair of Othello and Desdemona. Right: Old man of Cyprus.

from Adonis' blood. Cult rites celebrating the annual rebirth of Adonis included the planting of spring flowers.

In the book *Cyprus, a Portrait and Appreciation* by Harry Luke, the pagan celebration of the return of spring is connected with a celebration at Larnaca reenacting the raising of Lazarus from the dead. Each year on the Sunday preceding Palm Sunday, a boy is draped in funeral garb and laid out on a bed of flowers. He then rises to songs of joy when the priest pronounces, "Lazarus, come forth." Lazarus in another local celebration drifts ashore by boat amid splashing that recalls the playful bathing of Aphrodite's virgins.

Cyprus' Epic Poet

Cyprus had its own Homer in the author of a lost epic entitled *Cypria*. It is a set of stories about events that precede the action of Homer's *Iliad*, but only a paraphrased version of the epic survives. The author, Stassinos, is said to have been a son-in-law of Homer. Covered are events leading up to the Trojan War, including Zeus' plan to wipe out evil, the beauty contest that sets off the conflict when Aphrodite bribes Paris by offering him Helen, the rounding up of reluctant generals, Achilles at Skyros, the deserting of Philoktetes on Lemnos because of his foul smelling wound, and a lot of other myths.

The Roots of Othello

The story of the ill-fated love affair of Othello and Desdemona, a romance set on Cyprus, is the basis of Shakespeare's tragic play *Othello*. Shakespeare's source is Giraldi Cintio's 16th-century Italian novel about a virtuous Venetian beauty named Desdemona who loved a valiant Moorish officer in the service of Venice and married him against her parents' wishes. She went to his new command post in Cyprus, according to legend in Famagusta. The bare plots are much alike. The evil machinations of an ensign (Shakespeare's Iago) play on Othello's naïveté to raise jealous passions and lead to the murder of the innocent Desdemona. Even the lost handkerchief of Shakespeare is in the story.

Motives, Othello's character, and conclusions differ, however. Cintio has Othello and Iago beat Desdemona to death with socks filled with sand and then pull the house down upon her. Othello undergoes drawn-out punishment.

From the bare bones, Shakespeare formed a powerful personal tragedy by making honest Othello too noble to suspect Iago of duplicity. He is so appalled by his crime of suffocating his love, the epitome of goodness, that he can't allow himself to live.

Two possible candidates for the "real" Othello are Christoforo Moro, a Venetian lieutenant-governor of Cyprus, and Francesco de Sessa, an Italian soldier, the latter for his Moorishly dark complexion

and his long imprisonment on unnamed charges.

Georgios Seferis in Cyprus

Georgios Seferis, beloved Greek poet who was a 1963 Nobel Prize winner, lived and wrote on Cyprus in 1953. He dedicated his *Logbook III,* a collection of poems from that period, "To the People of Cyprus, in Memory and Love..."

Most of the poems have local settings and many allude to history and mythology. Seferis often gazed at photographs of local Cypriot scenes for inspiration as he wrote. His poem *Helena* is set in Platres, a lovely wooded village on a slope of the Troodos Mountains. It is based on Euripides' play *Helena*, in which a phantom resembling Helen was sent to Troy while the real Helen stayed in Egypt. The line "The nightingales won't let you sleep in Platres" is especially apt, if listening to their melancholy song leads you to ponder on wars fought for false causes.

227

KOPIASTE : CYPRIOT CUISINE

One of the joys of visiting Cyprus is its eclectic cuisine, a tasty assortment of little tidbits known as *meze*, or *mezedhes* in the plural. *Mezedhes* can be eaten as starters, or a number of plates can be shared by those present to make a whole meal. Cypriot food incorporates influences from both the Mediterranean and Middle East, and the result is a wide range of interesting culinary treats.

Kopiaste means "Come and join us." You will often have this sentiment expressed to you, perhaps out in the country by shepherds eating a simple meal of cheese, olive oil and bread, or by a gathering of city dwellers sharing a sumptuous repast. In either case, the invitation is heartfelt and you will be made welcome if you accept. But be prepared to devote some time to the gastronomic adventure.

Above: The speciality of Cyprus is "meze," an assortment of tidbits. Right: A fisherman softening octopi by beating them on rocks.

Cypriots regard dining out as a sensual, leisurely experience that stretches out for hours. They ascribe to the Mediterranean belief that it is detrimental to drink on an empty stomach, so it is not customary to go out for a drink without nibbling on some snacks along with it. Meals tend to be later than in northern countries: lunch usually starts between 1 and 2 p.m. and dinner between 8 and 9 p.m., or even later in summer.

Cypriot dishes generally call for fresh ingredients and the main fat is olive oil. Garlic, another essential in Cypriot cuisine, has been used in cooking for thousands of years.

Mezedhes that use garlic include *skordhalia*, potent garlic bread sauce used for boiled vegetables and fish filets, especially codfish; *melintzanosalata*, an eggplant dip served cold with bread; and *tahini*, a sesame dip laced with lemon juice and parsley originating in the Middle East.

Houmous, a dip combining sesame paste and chickpeas, is another Middle East favorite. Sesame seeds, grown in Cyprus up to 600 meters above sea level, are used in many dishes and breads. They are high in protein, calcium and lecithin, and contain vitamins C, E and some B complex. Sesame is also used for the rich sweet *halva* blended together with pistachio nuts. In Paphos, a number of different pies with meat or egg inside are made with sesame-sprinkled dough. *Talatouri*, a dip made from yoghurt, garlic and cucumber and accented with dried mint, is a variation of *tzatziki* found on mainland Greece and in Turkey.

Cypriots are especially creative with spicy meat concoctions. One of the best known is *sheftalia*, grilled rolls of pork and beef sausage served as a warm *meze* or main course. *Lountza* is a distinctive Cypriot specialty of smoked filet of pork soaked in red wine and then sprinkled with fresh coriander and hung in the sun to dry for a couple of days.

Hiromeri is another traditional dish of smoked ham marinated in wine. It is served cold, often with melon in the summer, or fried, quite tasty in omelets.

Pastourma is an Armenian speciality, a Middle East *pastrami*. Once made of camel meat, it now consists of spicy beef laden with garlic and hung for several days to dry. *Aphelia* are pork spareribs marinated in red wine.

Gourounopoulo, or tender oven-baked suckling pig, is a favorite festive dish and often the forte of a master chef.

Game dishes include thrush in wine sauce, duck or turkey casseroles, and oven-baked partridges.

Strangely enough, fish is not abundant on Cyprus and much of it served in high season is frozen and imported. For those who crave fresh fish, the Paphos District has the most abundant supply, including *barbouni* (red mullet), *ksiphias* (swordfish) and *maridhes* (whitebait). Also, the fresh trout, *pestropha,* from the Troodos farms is very delicious.

Pastries stuffed with meat or vegetables are an island tradition, and each household has its own special recipe, usually handed down from one generation to the next. *Bourekia*, scalloped fan-shaped pastry stuffed with minced meat or cheese, constitute filling hot *mezedhes.*

A unique Cypriot specialty is *kolokotes*, pastry stuffed with pumpkin, crushed wheat, raisins and sometimes pine nuts, an absolutely delectable dish that is healthy as well.

The most notable soup is *trahanas*, a Cypriot staple made from crushed wheat dried with yoghurt (*trahanas*), cooked in chicken broth and served with *haloumi*, sheep's milk cheese. *Haloumi* is also served alone as a *meze*, usually fried or cooked on charcoal. A by-product of it is *anari*, the delicious bland condensed whey best served warm. One delightful use of *anari* is in *bourekia tis anaris*, a pastry filled with the creamy cheese. Yoghurt, still made locally especially in

Troodos, is a creamy, slightly sweet item resembling cottage cheese.

Vegetables are almost always simmered in casseroles; very flavorful but not crispy. *Imam Bayildi*, a Turkish dish, means "the cleric fainted," presumably because the concoction was so overwhelmingly pleasing. It is an eggplant casserole with tomato sauce, garlic and onions. Tomatoes or zucchini stuffed with rice, spices and cheese are reliable standards. *Kolokassi Mesaritiko* is a typical Cypriot recipe for *kolokassi*, a strange-looking vegetable root similar to a sweet potato that is cooked in a casserole with celery, onions and wine.

The best dessert in summer is probably fruit, plentiful and wonderfully sweet. Besides the usual fare of *karpouzi* (watermelon), *peponi* (melon) and *sika* (figs) are the more unusual *mespila* (loquats), *papoutsosika* (prickly pears) and *rodhia* (pomegranates), also served as a chilled juice).

Gliko are any and every type of fruit (or vegetable) preserved in honey and served

with a glass of water to guests in homes. It is too cloyingly sweet for many palates, but it is an obligatory social gesture to go through the motions of appreciation while eating it (and hope you won't be offered more!). *Shiamali* are semolina cakes subtly accented by rose water, almonds and yoghurt. *Loukmadhes* are a delicacy; little balls of dough fried and dipped in syrup. They are often served at church picnics and fairs, and if properly made and served warm are a delight. *Soutzoukos* is a solidified grape juice sweet made with almonds and formed into sausage-like rolls that are ubiquitous at roadside stands in Cyprus.

Common Menu Items

Soups: *Avgolemeno*: Chicken soup with egg-lemon sauce. *Patcha*: Sheep's brains and innards in broth. *Psarosoupa*:

Above: Men tending Souvla spits. Right: Soutzoukos, a solidified grape juice sweet with almonds, a Cypriot speciality.

Fish soup. *Trahanas*: Boiled wheat and yoghurt in chicken broth.

Mezedhes: *Skordhalia*: Strong garlic bread dip often served with fish. *Taramasalata*: Pink fish roe salad. *Melintzanosalata*: Roasted eggplant dip. *Kolokotes*: Pastry shells stuffed with pumpkin and crushed wheat. *Pastourma*: Smoked, garlicky beef. *Tahini*: Sesame dip laced with lemon and parsley. *Houmous*: A Middle Eastern dip combining sesame and chick peas. *Imam Bayildi*: Baked eggplant casserole. *Talatouri*: Yoghurt, garlic and cucumber dip. *Bourekia*: Pies filled with meat, cheese or vegetables. *Koupepia* or *dolmadhes*: Vine leaves stuffed with rice and meat. *Sheftalia*: Grilled minced pork and beef sausage. *Haloumi*: White sheep's milk cheese. *Lountza*: Smoked pork soaked in red wine. *Hiromeri*: Smoked ham marinated in wine.

Main Dishes: *Aphelia*: Spicy pork goulash. *Keftedhes*: Meatballs. *Klephtiko*: Lamb roasted in a sealed earthenware pot. *Moussaka*: Layered eggplant

and potatoes with minced meat topped by bechamel sauce. *Souvlaki*: Lamb or pork kebab cooked on a spit. *Stiphado*: Veal or beef cooked in a casserole with onions. *Tavas*: Lamb casserole cooked in a sealed earthenware pot. *Yiouvetsi*: Casserole of lamb and pasta.

Fish and Seafood: *Bakalalarios*: Cod. *Barbouni*: Red mullet. *Garidhes*: Shrimp. *Ksiphias*: Swordfish. *Maridhes*: White-bait. *Melanouri:* Local panfish with black spot on tail. *Pestropha*: Trout, raised on fish farms in Troodos.

Salads: *Khoriatiki*: A village salad. *Khorta*: Boiled greens.

Vegetables: *Anginares*: Artichokes. *Bamies*: Okra. *Fasolia*: Green beans. *Kolokassi*: A root vegetable similar to the sweet potato. *Kolokithakia*: Zucchini. *Koukia*: Broad beans. *Louvia*: Black-eyed peas. *Maroulia*: Lettuce. *Pantzaria*: Beets. *Patates*: Potatoes. *Spanaki*: Spinach.

Sweets: *Baklava*: Filo pastry filled with ground walnuts and sometimes pistachios with a fine honey-lemon sauce.

Bourekia tis anaris: Small pastry filled with condensed whey (*anari*). *Gliko*: Preserved fruit in honey. *Halva*: Rich sesame paste. *Loukoumadhes*: Fried bread puffs soaked in honey-lemon sauce. *Shiamali*: Semolina cakes. *Soutzoukos*: Solidified grape juice in a sausage shape.

Fruit: *Karpouzi*: Watermelon. *Kerasia*: Cherries. *Mespila*: Loquats. *Papoutsosika*: Prickly pears. *Peponi*: melon. *Rodhia*: Pomegranate. *Sika*: Figs.

A Few Words about Coffee

If you ask for Greek coffee (the same as Turkish coffee), you will get *kafe*, a potent brew served with the grounds in tiny cups. If you want it without sugar, ask for *sketo*, with a little sugar *metrio* and with a lot of sugar *gliko*. The grounds can be used to tell your fortune, an art which is still practiced by some locals.

Nescafé is found almost everywhere and, occasionally, filtered (sometimes called French) coffee as well. Very refreshing is *frappé*, drunk cold.

CYPRIOT WINE

Cyprus is considered one of the first countries to practice viticulture (growing of grapes) and to produce wine. The earliest known reference to Cypriot wine is from a playful painting circa 900 B.C. on the so-called Hubbard Amphora. The appreciation of wine extends to immortals in this image of a free-spirited goddess on a throne sipping wine through a straw from decorated containers, as her attendant replenishes the supply.

According to the dramatist Euripides, the ancients referred to wine as *Cypriot Nama,* which in the era of Christianity means the "Wine of the Holy Eucharist," showing the reverence in which they held it. Allegedly when Mark Antony presented Cyprus to Cleopatra he gallantly said, "Your sweetness, my love, is equal to that of Cyprus Nama."

During the Classical Age, a society flourished with its prosperity based on the growing of grapes, wine production and trade. Many mosaics, drawings and sculptures from this period indicate the importance of wine in daily life. A chalice dating from the sixth century B.C. found at the ancient city of Marion, close to modern Polis, has an inscription which says "Be happy and drink well."

Many writers, from ancient times until the present, have commented on Cypriot wine. It was praised by Homer, the poet Pindarus and Roman writer Pliny, who considered Cypriot wine superior to all others in the world. When the Jews worshiped in the Temple of King Solomon, the High Priest's offerings included the famous wine of Cyprus *Yen Cafrissin.*

Many of the world-renowned wines are made from vines introduced into Europe from Cyprus after the Crusades. A charming tale traces the origin of Champagne to Cyprus. Early in the 1300s,

Right: A cozy taverna in the vineyards of Omodhos, Troodos.

Count Thibaut IV of Champagne was returning from a crusade and stopped on Cyprus. While there, a young noble of the Queen's court had been sentenced to death for sneaking into the royal apartments to visit his betrothed. Count Thibaut asked that his life be spared under the condition he take him along to Champagne.

Once there, the young noble pined away for his love. Count Thibaut finally urged him to return to Cyprus, marry his sweetheart and return to Champagne. More than a year later, the Count was surprised when a visit was announced from the noble and his new bride. The happy couple presented gifts to Thibaut. The bride offered a rose bush, which became the fragrant rose of Provence. The noble brought cuttings from the best vines of Olympos, which, when planted on the chalky cliffs of the Marne, became Champagne.

During the period following Richard the Lionhearted's conquest of the island in 1191, Cyprus' most famous wine, *Commandaria*, was made for the first time. The production of the legendary dessert wine was carried on in the commanderies of the Knights of St. John, which gave their name to the wine. These three commanderies derived their wealth from the vast number of vineyards planted in the 40 villages of the area. The recipe for *Commandaria* wine was already described by Hesiod in 800 B.C. as "Leave the grapes ten days in the sun and then ten nights and then five days in shade and eight more in the jar."

Immature *Commandaria* wine is yellowish-white in hue, becoming a ruby-red color through aging. The grapes, grown above 900 meters in the villages of Zoopiyi, Kalokhorio and Ayios Konstantinos, are picked late in the season when they are sweetest. Hesiod's recipe is still followed as they are spread out in the sun for 14 days to concentrate the sugar content. The wine is kept in the

Commandaria villages for two years and then kept at least a year in a barrel in Limassol. Fully mature wine, called *Mana*, Greek for mother, remains in oak barrels until added to the immature wine, and is allowed to sit with it for seven years before it is sold. The oak barrels of the Mana never stand empty.

Another wine popular during medieval times was *Malmsey*, the name derived from the port of Monemvasia in the Peloponnese, but it was made on Cyprus as well. The red *Malvoisie* grape is still grown on Troodos slopes.

Wine production was really refined during the Lusignan and Venetian Periods. Martoni, in the 1500s, wrote of Nicosia, "In this city there is an abundance of bread and wine, and the wine is generally sweet and kept in large jars. I intended to remain there for a month or so, on account of the abundance of bread and wine..."

It is said that the fine wines of Cyprus are what led the Turkish Sultan Selim II (better known as Selim the Sot) to over-

run the island in 1571, beginning 300 years of occupation. Although there was a decline in the quality of wine produced on Cyprus during the Turkish Period, it was still the main agricultural export product. It seems the local population also had its share of it. Seigneur de Villamont, from the Duchy of Brittany, wrote about the Turks in 1589: "And although their law forbids them wine, yet they will drink to excess without scruple or shame."

Some of the oldest wine on the island is available privately. A delightful local custom calls for burying a jar of wine near the house when a child is born. When the child marries, the jar is dug out and its contents served to the guests at the wedding party.

Four big wineries produce most of Cyprus' wines. The large cooperative SODAP, founded in 1947, owns two large wineries in Limassol and Paphos. Members and shareholders are all vinegrowers. Seventy-five percent of SODAP's production is destined for ex-

port, mainly to the United Kingdom, other European countries, Canada and the United States.

ETKO is the successor to the C. Hadjipavlou Company formed in 1844. The new winery is in Limassol and exports 75 to 80 percent of its products to the United Kingdom and the rest of Europe, the United States, Japan and even Nigeria.

LOEL is a public company formed by vinegrowers in 1943. Eighty percent of its products are exported, much of them to Eastern Europe and the countries of the former Soviet Union, besides the United Kingdom and Japan.

KEO was formed as a private company in 1926, but it now belongs to the Hellenic Group of Mining Companies. The KEO enterprise has four wineries, two on Troodos, one in Paphos, and the main plant in Limassol. It owns three experimental vineyards, and one of its many

Above: This vintner obviously seems to be proud of his wine products.

achievements is the introduction of new scientific methods in the wine industry. It is rapidly taking the lead in the export market. KEO introduced the first Cypriot sherry in the early 1930s and had a monopoly on exports to the United Kingdom. It now exports to the United States, United Kingdom and the rest of Europe, Japan and Australia. KEO also makes a good lager beer.

Sunshine is essential for the production of top-quality grapes, but not scorching heat, which weakens the acidity of the crop. The southern slopes of the Troodos Mountains and high altitude villages in Limassol and Paphos offer perfect temperatures for grape ripening. The rocks of the Troodos massif and sedimentary rocks of Limassol and Paphos offer sufficient support for the vines.

Commandaria wine is made from the two most popular grape varieties, the largest portion from the *Mavro* red grape with the addition of the *Xynistri* white grape. Together with the *Maratheftiko* and *Ofthalmo*, two potent red grapes, they cover close to 100 square kilometers of the total 110 square kilometers under cultivation.

Over 100 varieties of grapes are grown on Cyprus. About 55 percent of the grapes are grown in the Paphos District, but Limassol is the chief wine-making and exporting center.

Newer white varieties that have been introduced to Cyprus since the 1950s and 1960s include Iberian *Palomino*, imported from Spain in 1958, and Alsatian *Riesling*. The prevalent *Cabernet Sauvignon*, black grapes imported from France in 1954, and black *Chiraz*, imported from Australia in 1950, have made big headway in popularity. The white *Lefkas* was brought over from the Greek island of Lefkada, and *Malaga* white came from Spain in 1936.

While visiting Cyprus, experiment by ordering lesser-known labels. Look for domain-bottled products from regional wineries and monasteries.

Some of the more interesting labels to sample while visiting the country are:

Red Wines

Agravani (Ecological Winery of Ayios Amvrosios): Blend of *Cabernet*, *Carignan* and *Mataro*. **Semeli (ETKO)**: Blend of *Mavro* and imported varieties. **Kilani Village (Ayia Mavri)**: Estate-bottled *Xynistri*. **Peratis (Menagros Winery)**: Dry blend of *Mavro*, *Carignan Noir* and *Grenache*. **Plakota (Vouni-Panayia)**: Blend of *Mavro*, *Chiraz* and *Mavrotheftiko*. Distinguished by a characteristic aroma.

White Wines

Ayios Andronikos, Monte Royia (Khrysorroyiatissa Monastery), Cellar Antoine (KEO): Crisp dry wine of *Xynistri* grapes. **Kilani Village (Ayia Mavri)**: Blend mostly of *Mavro*. **Amathus (LOEL)**: Fragrant *Palomino*

and others. **Ambelida (Ecological Winery of Ayios Amvrosios)**: Dry, light wine produced from *Xynistri*. **Cellar Arsinoe (SODAP)**: Well-balanced *Xynistri*.

Rosé Wines

Rosé wines are made from red grapes but the must is not fermented on the lees, resulting in the lighter color. The blending of white and red grapes to make rosé is forbidden.

Coeur de Lion (KEO), named for King Richard the Lionhearted: Dry, light wine made from *Grenache Noir*. **Mirto (SODAP)**: Fine wine with pleasant aroma produced from *Mavro* grapes. **Pampela (Vouni-Panayia)**: Dry, light wine made from a blend of *Mavro*, *Ofthalmo* and *Lefkas*.

The major wineries all offer tours of their premises. A good time to sample different types of wine is at the Limassol Wine Festival, held since 1961 for 11 days in September in the Municipal Gardens. Wine-tasting, typical local specialties at low prices, music, dance and theater performances are part of the festivities. Enjoy yourself, but remember to pace your drinking and to eat as well. Although Cypriots are fun-loving, they disapprove of drunkenness, particularly in women.

Poke around in local *cavas* (wine shops) to find unusual bottles of vintage standard. Most labels give information on the grape variety and the taste of the wine. Wineries also make brandy, and some of the fruity ones are very tasty. The *brandy sour*, correctly made with fresh lemon juice, is a big favorite in the summer.

Another by-product that separates the faint-hearted from the robust is *zivania*, a clear, deceptively innocent-looking spirit produced from grape mash. This locally-produced firewater is sometimes offered by mountain villagers and, once downed, produces a warm glow.

CYPRIOT ARTS AND CRAFTS

Cyprus has a rich folk-art tradition. Purchasing a sample of it is a pleasant reminder of your trip and makes an unusual present for the people back home. Traditional items favored by visitors to Cyprus are embroidery, lace, pottery and woodwork.

In 1975, the Cyprus Handicraft Service was established by the government to preserve and revive local crafts, maintaining standards of workmanship and marketing at fair prices. Shops of the Cyprus Handicraft Service (CHS) have been established in Nicosia, Limassol, Larnaca and Paphos. Outside Nicosia, a workshop has been set up where one may telephone to make an appointment to see artisans at work. Products of the service are labeled (CHS) to assure the purchaser of high standards and authenticity.

In villages one can find craftspeople creating their wares for local shops, and many will be glad to give you an informal demonstration. Available from the Cyprus Tourist Organization is a booklet entitled *Diary of Events*, listing celebrations and fairs which often have demonstrations of folk crafts and sell the products. For centuries, the lace of the village of Lefkara has been prized abroad. *Lefkaritika*, as the work is called, was made well before the Venetians came to admire and acquire it, at the same time lending new designs to the tradition. Embroidered lace and cutwork are done on off-white linen, or nowadays sometimes on cotton, in tablecloths, curtains, placemats, doilies and dresser sets. If you want authentic *Lefkaritika*, you should examine goods carefully and ask questions to avoid buying a crude imitation of the authentic handicraft.

Paphitika fabric from Paphos features loom embroidery in geometric designs and muted colors. Brightly-striped *Lefkonika* fabric, named for the village where it was originally made, is now woven commercially and is available as place mats, towels and aprons. *Alatjia*, a finely-woven, striped cotton with a silk-like sheen, comes in a range of clear, true colors. Items made of or trimmed with crocheted lace are especially lovely.

In stores and CHS shops one sees white and off-white blouses, curtains and tablecloths made with insets and edging of hand-crocheted lace. Woven and crocheted cotton rag rugs, called *pefji*, many vividly striped, and also goat hair and wool rugs are made in mountain villages. Wool knit and crocheted shawls, scarves and blankets range from soft, light and clinging, to coarse and heavy, in colors both dyed and natural.

Cyprus mined copper even before the Bronze Age was truly underway, and copper pots, saucepans and planters make charming additions to the kitchen. Gold and silver items of jewelry are often eye-catching copies of ancient designs and often a real bargain. One unusual item seen in many jewelry shops is the *kapanisty*, an ornate silver pot used in Cypriot churches to burn olive leaves for a blessing. It makes a lovely incense burner for the home as well.

Pottery making has been practiced since Neolithic times. Popular souvenir items are terra cotta ware with white decoration, copied from museum pieces. A lively sense of humor and striking creative expression characterize the pottery of Ara Nigogossian and Nancy Hocking, a couple who have made replicas of the earthenware pieces of the Bronze and Iron Ages (Treskelian Pottery Shop, Neokhorio).

Another country tradition is the decorating of gourds, called *koloki*, which are painted or etched by burning and put to such uses as planters, vases, carafes and scoops. In Giorgios Seferis' poem *Details on Cyprus*, the poet watches a monk paint

Right: This modern Cypriot girl is selling delicate handmade lace at Paphos Market.

a gourd with pictures of sinners of various types, including cheaters, slanderers, haters and, next to them all, a lowly worm. This art form is still practiced in Platres.

Native reed and cane are turned into such items as baskets, trays and chair seats, and such non-portable items as fences and ceilings. Many villages in Paphos, such as Mesoyi, produce their own basket weaving, often woven with bright ribbons and colored with distinctive designs, such as the *tsestos*, perfect for a wall hanging.

A specialty of the Kouklia region is *anathrika*, a small, light, square stool made of fennel stalk. Originally designed for children, it proved strong enough for adult use and makes a good footstool. One can easily tuck one into a flexible bag to take back home.

Woodcarvers still work in traditional designs. Pine dowry chests, called *sandoukia*, are often decorated with rosettes, flowers, birds, trees and religious images, all rich in symbolic implications.

New ones can be made to order at CHS shops, and you can have them shipped to your home. They also make pieces small and light enough for a traveler to carry, such as small boxes and shelves.

Also for sale are long wooden boards, called *sanidha*, or the pine troughs known as *vourna*, a speciality of the Troodos mountain village of Moutoullas, used to raise dough in country kitchens. These add a folksy touch to your own kitchen and can be used for bread making, or else they can be painted and used for a decoration in the living room or patio.

Cyprus Handicraft Service (CHS) Shops

Nicosia: 186 Athalassa Avenue, tel. 302751; Laiki Yitonia, tel. 303065.
Larnaca: 6 Kosma Lyssioti Street, tel. 30327.
Limassol: 25 Thermidos Street, tel. 30118.
Paphos: 123 Archbishop Makarios III Avenue, tel. 40243.

METRIC CONVERSION

Metric Unit	US Equivalent
Meter (m)	39.37 in.
Kilometer (km)	0.6241 mi.
Square Meter (sq m)	10.76 sq. ft.
Hectare (ha)	2.471 acres
Square Kilometer (sq km)	0.386 sq. mi.
Kilogram (kg)	2.2 lbs.
Liter (l)	1.05 qt.

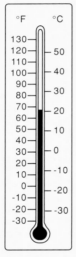

PREPARATIONS

Climate / Travel Season

Cyprus has a Mediterranean climate, with long, dry summers from mid-May to mid-October and mild winters from December until February. In the spring, temperatures average between 12° and 20°C; in summer between 25° and 30°C. The warmest time of the year is July and August, when midday temperatures reach 40°C. The coolest period is January and February, when temperatures average between 10° and 11°C; they only rarely get as low as freezing and usually only in the mountainous areas.

Rainfall reaches about 300-400 mm per year and is heaviest in January and February, when snow often coats the Troodos peaks.

The sun shines year round, with an average of six or seven hours of sunshine in January and February, and 12 or more in mid-summer. It is possible to swim almost any time of the year with the exception of the coldest periods.

Hiking and walks in the countryside are most rewarding in spring, when splendid wildflowers, many of them indigenous or rare species, bloom.

Clothing and Equipment

Experienced travelers generally like to travel light, bringing clothes they can wash out and dry in hotel rooms. Lightweight clothing is suitable, along with cardigan sweaters and windbreaker jackets. Bring comfortable, sturdy boots for hiking, and tennis shoes and sandals for strolling in towns. You may want to buy sandals in Cyprus, as well as cool shirts, blouses, cotton skirts and beach towels. If you go in fall or winter, bring warm clothes and a light coat, as well as a travel umbrella.

Unless you are traveling on business you will not need a suit or formal attire. You can dress for the evening in resort wear and sandals, although it is best to bring proper clothes for better restaurants or clubs. To enter churches you will need modest clothing.

You will need good sunglasses and a hat for protection from the exceedingly bright light, glare and heat. Suntan lotion with a protective filter is highly recommended. A small line for drying hand laundry is convenient, as is a wide, flat sink stopper.

Entry Requirements / Visas

For a stay of up to 90 days you will need a valid passport, but no visa is required for citizens of the U.S., Canada, Australia, New Zealand or west European countries. Children and teens under 16 years of age must have a passport or be entered in the passport of an accompanying parent.

Visitors may enter or exit the Republic of Cyprus only via the international airports of Larnaca and Paphos, or the sea ports of Larnaca, Limassol and Paphos. Day trips from Nicosia across the Green Line are usually permitted by the Cyprus Government. Vaccinations are not required, but having a tetanus shot before travel is recommended.

Currency / Foreign Exchange

The Cyprus Pound (C£) is divided into 100 cents. Notes are in 5, 10 and 20 pound denominations; coins in 1, 2, 5, 10, 20 and 50 cent denominations. One C£ = US $1.87 / UK £1.15.

Eurochecks, traveler's checks and credit cards are accepted, though not all banks serve all of them. There are exchange services at airports and ports. There is no limit to the amount of currency you may bring in. Amounts in excess of the equivalent of US $1,000 must be declared on arrival, if you plan to take more than that amount back out of the country when you leave.

Customs and Import Regulations

Visitors may import articles for personal use, as well as the following articles without payment of duty: 200 cigarettes or 50 cigars or 250 grams of tobacco; 1 liter of spirits; 0.75 liter of wine; 0.30 liter of perfume; other articles (except jewelry) up to a total value of C£50.

There is not much point in bringing along a pet: animals must be quarantined for six months upon arrival.

Warning: The export of antiquities without permission and a licence from the Department of Antiquities is forbidden and could result in arrest.

Motor vehicles, trailers and boats can be imported toll-free for a period of up to three months. For information, rules and advice regarding bringing a motor vehicle to Cyprus, contact the Cyprus Automobile Association, 12 Chr. Mylonas St., P.O. Box 2279., Nicosia 141, tel. (02) 313233.

An international or national driver's license and certificate of registration are required. Green card insurance is not accepted in Cyprus. Visitors must take out a short-term insurance policy with a company on the island.

GETTING THERE

By Plane

More than 30 airlines connect Cyprus with major European and Middle Eastern cities. Cyprus Airways flies from and to Athens, London, Gatwick, Birmingham, Manchester, Paris, Berlin, Munich, Frankfurt, Zurich, Geneva, Tel Aviv, Jeddah, Dubai, Riyadh, Bahrain, Kuwait, Dhahran, Cairo and Damascus, among other cities.

Cyprus Airways: Nicosia, 21 Alkeus St., P.O. Box 1903, tel. (02) 443054, fax. (02) 465428. Ticketing Office: 50 Arch. Makarios III Ave., tel. (02) 441996. Branches in Limassol, Larnaca, Paphos and Athens.

From the Paphos airport there is an hourly bus service into town. From Larnaca's airport there is no bus service, though taxis are available round the clock. Both airports offer the following services: tourist information, foreign exchange, coin-operated telephones, car rental, hotel reservation assistance, facilities for the physically handicapped, duty-free shops, health inspector's office, cafeterias.

By Ship

Passenger ships and car ferries connect Cyprus with Greece (Piraeus; Athens' harbor) and many other Mediterranean countries (e.g., Israel, Lebanon, Egypt). An information sheet on boat transportation can be obtained from the Cyprus Tourism Organization offices in Cyprus and abroad.

Guidelines

Ferries to and from Piraeus

Poseidon Lines: Piraeus, 32 Alkyondon Ave., tel. (01) 965-8300; Limassol, 124 Roosevelt Ave., tel. (05) 745666, fax. (05) 745577.

Salamis Lines: Piraeus, 9 Filellinon St., tel. (01) 429-4325, fax. (01) 429-4557; Limassol, C. Hadjipavlos St., Salamis House, tel. (05) 355555, fax. (05) 364410.

Louis Cruise Lines: Athens, 3 Karageorgi Servias St., tel. (01) 322-7852, fax. (01) 322-3054; Limassol, 63B Gladstone St., tel. (05) 363161, fax. (05) 363174.

Salamis and Louis also offer two to three day excursions to Egypt and Israel.

TRAVELING IN CYPRUS

You can travel within Cyprus by bus, taxi, service taxi or rented car. There are no trains. Tours and sightseeing cruises are organized all year round by various tour operators.

By Bus and Taxi

Bus: Various bus companies operate between towns and resorts. Urban buses run frequently during the day, but operate only until 7 p.m. in summer in tourist areas. Village buses make one run to the city each weekday, leaving the village early in the morning and returning in the afternoon. All major bus stations and connections are given in the *INFO* section of each travel chapter.

Service Taxis: This is a convenient and reasonable form of transportation between main towns. Usually seven to ten persons share one large taxi. Passengers arrange in advance to be picked up and let off at the stop of their choice along the route. Make sure to make a return reservation at a specific hour and location, especially on weekends when most taxis are full. Your hotel or the local tourist office can help you with schedules and reservations. Service taxis are frequent, reliable

and cheaper than private taxis. Most service taxis make their last run at 7 p.m., so bear this in mind when you plan your arrival or while on excursions within Cyprus. One service taxi company in each town operates on Sundays.

Private Taxis: Your hotel reception desk can call and have you picked up promptly. If you want a chauffeured excursion, agree to a price ahead of time. The charge is often based on time.

By Car

You drive on the left side of the road in Cyprus. Main highways and city streets are in good condition. Some country roads are only partially paved and lack shoulders, occasionally narrowing to a single lane. Some mountain roads are narrow dirt lanes. Drive slowly and watch for vehicles, animals and pedestrians.

Distances and speed limits are posted in kilometers, and road signs are in English as well as Greek. The speed limit on main highways is 100 kmh and on other roads 80 kmh unless otherwise posted. In most settled areas the speed limit is 50 kmh. Use of seat belts by front seat passengers is compulsory. Children over five may occupy the front passenger's seat if it is equipped with a child's safety belt.

Avoid driving west in the glare of the setting sun. Getting your rental car back to town before sundown is a good idea.

You are legally drunk if your blood alcohol level is 0.9 per mill or higher.

By Rental Car

There are numerous rental agencies in towns; the Cyprus Tourism Organization publishes a list of them. A valid international driver's license or license of one's country is required. The driver sits on the right, British style, with the gearshift to the left.

The car is generally delivered to the driver with a full tank of gas, but the gas must be paid for at the time of pickup. However, if there is still gas in the tank when you return the car, you are not compensated for it. By prior arrangement, a car may be picked up at one place and delivered to another.

Before setting out on a longer excursion, take the car on a test drive with someone from the agency to make sure it is working properly. Don't underestimate the difficulty of switching to the British system if you are unfamiliar with it.

Hitchhiking

Hitchhiking is not forbidden in Cyprus but one must use good sense when doing so, as is true anywhere else. Generally, it is best for female hitchhikers to pair up with someone else, preferably a male, and to restrict the activity to the daytime. Cypriots are generally hospitable and will often pick up hitchhikers. It can be a lovely way to meet the locals while out in the mountains or countryside, and will spare you from waiting for hours for one of the local buses.

By Ship

Cruises: One-day sightseeing cruises are organized from May to October. Details are available from local sightseeing tour operators. Itineraries: From Limassol Harbor to Lady's Mile Beach and back; from Paphos Harbor to Coral Bay, Peyia area; from Ayia Napa to Paralimni, Protaras and back; from Larnaca along the coast to Ayia Napa and back; from Polis along the Akamas coast.

Yachting: *Larnaca Marina*, tel. (04) 653110, fax. (04) 624110. Weatherprotected berthing for 400 yachts. Amenities (reasonable charges): Water, electricity (240v / 50hz), telephone and fax, fuel (N. Pier), repair facilities, laundry, showers, lockers, duty-free shop, post boxes. Ten minute walk to city center. Larnaca Marina has stringent 24-hour security. Customs and immigration formalities can be cleared here.

Limassol Sheraton Pleasure Harbor, P.O. Box 1064, tel. (05) 321100 ext.

3312, fax. (05) 324394. Protected by breakwater, ideal for sail and motor boats. 227 berths. Water, electricity, telephone, television hookup. Shuttle bus and water taxi, 24-hour security, market and yacht repair. Yachts arriving and leaving can clear customs in office.

Organized Tours

Over 250 travel agencies operate on the island, many of which are IATA members (*International Air Transport Association*). Cyprus also has its own travel association, ACTA (*Association of Cyprus Travel Agents*), and issues a directory each year. ACTA, P.O. Box 2369, Nicosia, tel. (02) 366435, fax. (02) 467593.

Many travel agencies operate full or half-day tours within Cyprus to major sights, and a few offer evening outings to clubs featuring music and folk dances.

Some reliable agencies are:
LIMASSOL: **A.L. Mantovani & Sons Ltd.** (American Express Agent), 1 Archbishop Kyprianous St., Loukiades Building, tel. (05) 362045, fax. (05) 377842. *NICOSIA:* **Amathus Travel Ltd.**, 17 Homer Ave., tel. (02) 462101, fax. (02) 451329. *POLIS:* **Century 21 Travel Agency**, Aphrodite St., tel. (06) 321658, fax. (06) 321693. *PAPHOS:* **Exalt Tours**, 24 Agias Kyriakis St., tel. (06) 243803, fax. (06) 246167. *LARNACA:* **Iason Tours,** Stratigos Timagia Ave., tel. (03) 636499, fax. (03) 821988.

PRACTICAL TIPS FROM A TO Z

Accommodation

Hotels in Cyprus are modern, and few are without air conditioning or private bathrooms. The *Cyprus Hotels Guide* printed by the Cyprus Tourism Organization lists almost all hotels, guest houses, B & B's and campsites, classifying them by the star system and giving price ranges and telephone numbers. It is strongly recommended to reserve accommodation

Guidelines

before you arrive in Cyprus during summer in beach communities, and all year round in Nicosia, for it hosts many conventions. Most hotels offer discounts during the low season (November 16 to March 15), and Cyprus' mild climate makes it suitable for winter vacations.

Upon arrival at your hotel, clarify upon what terms you are staying (bed and breakfast, half-board, etc.). A charge of 50 percent is added to a bill if guests vacate the room after noon but before 6 p.m. Complaints about accommodation can be reported to the nearest office of the CTO.

An alternative to hotels is the apartment hotel, some with two bedrooms, many of them located at the seaside. They are an ideal choice for families, allowing more room for children to play, and kitchen facilities that can cut down on dining expenses.

Camping

Camping is legally restricted to authorized campsites licensed by the CTO. Facilities include showers, toilets, minimarkets, small restaurants, and washing facilities. Electricity is extra.

LIMASSOL: **Governor's Beach Campsite**, tel. (05) 632300. Twenty kilometers east of Limassol. Capacity for 111 caravans, 247 tents. Open year round.

PAPHOS: **Yeroskipou Zenon Gardens Camping**, P.O. Box 99, tel. (06) 242277. Three kilometers from Paphos. Capacity for 95 tents/caravans. Open April to October; **Feggari Camping**, Coral Bay, 11 kilometers north of Paphos, tel. (06) 621534. Open year round.

POLIS: **Polis Camping**, tel. (06) 321526. 500 meters from Polis in a grove on the beach. Capacity for 200 tents/caravans. Open March to October.

AYIA NAPA: **Ayia Napa Camping Site**, tel. (03) 721946. Near beach. Capacity for 150 tents/caravans. Open March to October.

TROODOS MOUNTAINS: **Troodos Camping Site**, tel. (05) 421624. Two ki-

lometers from Troodos Hill Resort, off main Troodos-Kakopetria road. Open May to October.

Electricity

Electricity is 240 volts. Three-pronged adaptor plugs may be necessary and are available at hotels and shops.

Environmental Action Groups

Cyprus Wildlife Society and Turtle Conservation Project, c/o Andreas Demetropoulos, P.O. Box 4281, tel. (02) 303279, fax. (02) 365955; *Friends of the Earth and Laona Project*, tel. (04) 332139; *Cyprus Ornithological Society*, 4 Kanaris Street, Strovolos, 145, Nicosia, tel. (02) 420703.

Festivals and Holidays

Holidays and special events are celebrated throughout the year. Visitors are welcome; accommodation is quickly booked out at some local celebrations. For information visitors can consult these publications of the CTO: *Monthly Events*, available at hotels and local CTO offices. The *Diary of Events* (for the entire year), which can be obtained at CTO offices locally and abroad, lists drama festivals, sports events, concerts, fairs, exhibitions, saints day festivals, and so on. On national holidays major sites and museums stay open, except at Easter. Banks, shops and businesses close except for a few shops in resort areas.

January 1: *New Year's Day,* presents are exchanged among family and friends.

January 6: *Epiphany Day,* blessing of the waters.

Variable: *Shrove Monday*, 50 days before Easter.

March 25: *Greek National Day* (Independence Day).

April 1: *EOKA Day.*

Variable: *Good Friday, Easter Sunday and Monday* (according to the Greek-Orthodox calendar).

May 1: *Labor Day.*

August 15: *Assumption Day.*
October 1: *Independence Day.*
October 28: *Greek National Day (Oxi Day,* commemorating the Greek Army's resistance to the Italians in 1940).
December 25: *Christmas Day.*
December 26: *Boxing Day.*

Besides these national holidays, there are local festivals and religious celebrations. One is *Kataklysmos,* celebrated mainly at Larnaca (with a large street fair) and other seaside towns, starting 50 days after Easter. Everyone joins in the fun and splashes their friends with sea water. The ritual is said to commemorate Noah's flood and the coming ashore of the resurrected Lazarus, with pagan elements reminiscent of Aphrodite's purification.

St. Paul's Feast is celebrated at Paphos on June 28 and 29. *Limassol Carnival* occurs in March (generally); the *Limassol Wine Festival* in September. In summer, plays are performed at the ancient sites of Kourion and Paphos.

Holidays in North Cyprus:
January 1: *New Year's Day.*
April 23: *Children's Day.*
May 1: *Labor Day.*
May 19: *Sports and Youth Bayram Day.*
Variable: *Seker Bayram,* two days at the end of Ramadan; *Kurban Bayram,* four-day Feast of Sacrifice.
July 20: *Day of the "Peace Operation."*
August 1: *TMT Day.*
August 30: *Victory of the Turks over the Greeks in 1922.*
October 20: *Turkish Independence Day.*
November 15: *Anniversary of the Proclamation of the "Turkish Republic of North Cyprus."*

Opening Hours

Banks: Monday to Friday 8:30 a.m. (in July and August 8:15) to 12:30 p.m., Mondays also 3:15 to 4:45 p.m. Some central banks provide afternoon tourist service Monday through Friday from 3:30 to 5:30 p.m. (October to April) and from 4 to 6:30 p.m. (May to September).

Shops: Monday through Saturday 9:30 a.m. to 6 p.m. (November to March), otherwise until 7 or 7:30 p.m. Some shops close from 1 to 4 p.m.

Postal Services

Post offices are open Monday through Saturday from 7:30 a.m. to 1 p.m., Thursdays also from 3 to 6 p.m. Afternoon service in **Nicosia**: Eleftheria Square. **Limassol**: 1 Gladstone Street. **Larnaca**: King Paul Square. **Paphos**: Thermidos and St. Paul streets. To claim poste restante mail you must show your passport.

Press

The English-language daily newspaper is *The Cyprus Mail.* A lively and informative weekly newspaper is *The Cyprus Weekly. Time Out* is an entertainment and information guide. *Sunjet* is Cyprus Airways' interesting in-flight magazine.

Radio and Television

News and weather forecasts are given in English each evening on the radio by the *Cyprus Broadcasting Corporation* (CyBC) on 498 or 603 on the AM band.

Socializing

Cypriots are gregarious people and love to socialize. They also adore children, so you'll find bringing the kids along to most restaurants is no problem.

If you are invited to a Cypriot's home for dinner, a party or a wedding, make sure to accept! You can really get an insight into the culture this way and are sure to be treated to an abundance of good food and wine. Almost all Cypriots understand some English, so you will easily find a number of people with whom you can converse. Social customs call for bringing a gift of some sort when visiting a Cypriot household. Flowers, a bottle of wine, or sweets, such as boxed *baklava,* will be most welcome.

Cypriots celebrate Name Days or the Saint's Day after whom they have been

Guidelines

named, rather than birthdays. On the days of the most popular saints, such as Maria on August 15 or Andreas (the most popular man's name on Cyprus) on November 30, family and close friends come calling with flowers and sweets. The honored person offers food and wine in a continual open house. If you are invited to stop by a Cypriot house on a Name Day but cannot do so, you should at least call to extend your greetings. Cypriot hospitality is legendary, so give up any notions of going "Dutch Treat." Your host will usually insist on picking up the tab when dining out, so accept graciously with a smile.

Sports

Bowling: Nicosia: *Kykko Bowling,* near Ledra Hotel, five kilometers from the town center. Limassol: *Limassol Bowling:* In hotel area, east of city center.

Bicycling: Cycling is popular throughout the year. Bikes can be rented in towns and resorts. Races in spring and fall organized by The Cyprus Cycling Federation, P.O. Box 8126, Nicosia, tel. (02) 450875.

Diving: Spear fishing is prohibited in areas marked with red buoys. For spear fishing with scuba gear a special license is required. It is forbidden to take sponges and antiquities from the sea bed!

Fishing: No license is required for salt-water fishing. Thirteen reservoirs are stocked with fresh-water fish: trout, perch, bream, catfish and other species. Anglers older than 12 must apply for a license at the District Fisheries Department. Some reservoirs observe a fishing season. Fisheries Offices for fishing and spear fishing licenses and regulations: *Nicosia*: 13 Taymatarkhou Pouliou and Capota St. tel. (02) 303527. *Limassol*: Near the entrance of the Old Port. tel. (05) 330470. *Larnaca*: Piale Pasha Ave., at the fishing shelter, tel. (04) 630294. *Paphos*: Paphos Harbor, tel. (06) 240268.

Hiking: Hiking excursions can be arranged by tour organizers. *Troodos Area:* Numerous marked nature trails. *Akamas*

Area: Two posted nature trails. *Cape Greco:* One Forestry Department trail. *Stavros-tis-Psokas Area:* Two marked trails in Paphos Forest.

Nature walks, hikes to out-of-the-way places: *Exalt Tours, Iris Travel,* 10 Gladstone St., Ktima, Paphos, tel. (06) 237585, fax. (06) 233960. *Cyprus Ornithological Society,* 4 Kanaris St., Strovolos, 145, Nicosia, tel. (02) 420703.

Hikers are advised to take walks only with companions, never alone, carry water and rations, have sturdy hiking boots, a compass and a whistle. Inform someone at your hotel or lodging where you are going and when you expect to return.

Horseback Riding: *Lapatsa Sporting Center,* Dheftera, 11 kilometers southwest of Nicosia. tel. (02) 621201. *Elias Beach Hotel and Country Club,* Limassol-Nicosia Road, five minutes drive from hotel area, Pareklissia Junction, tel. (05) 325000. Both centers are open year round. Phone for hours.

Sea Sports: Swimming is popular from May until November. Some truly hardy persons swim year round. CTO public beaches offer changing cabins, parasols, chairs and lifeguards.

Paphos Public Beach, Yeroskipos, three kilometers east of Paphos Harbor, tel. (06) 234525; *Dassoudi Public Beach,* five kilometers east of Limassol city center, tel. (05) 322881; *Larnaca Public Beach,* 10 kilometers east of Larnaca center, tel. (04) 621311. Sea-sport sites are strung along beaches. One can rent speed boats, water scooters, sailboats, windsurfing boards, canoes and pedal boats.

Skiing: On Mount Olympos (Khionistra) from January to March. The *Cyprus Ski Club*, P.O. Box 2185, Nicosia, tel. (02) 365340, fax. (02) 369681, operates four runs, two on the north face and two in Sun Valley, which has a cafeteria and three restaurants. Equipment and toboggans for rent, instruction offered.

Tennis: *NICOSIA: Field Club,* Egypt Ave., in the city center, tel. (02) 452041;

Eleon Tennis Club, 3 Ploutarchou St., Engomi, tel. (02) 449923; *Lapatsa Sporting Center,* Dheftera, 11 kilometers from town. *LIMASSOL: Limassol Sporting Club,* 4 J. Zachariadou, west of town, tel. (05) 359034; *Famagusta Tennis Club,* 3 Mesaorias St. (in center), tel. (05) 335952. *LARNACA: Larnaca Tennis Club,* 10 Kilkis St. (in center), tel. (04) 656999. *PAPHOS: Yeroskipos Tourist Beach,* three kilometers east of Paphos Harbor, tel. (06) 234525.

Telecommunications

Using the telephone is uncomplicated. Operators speak English and directories are printed in Roman letters. Pay phones may be used for local and international calls. Instructions are posted on the phone. Expect hotels to add a surcharge to the basic rate. Card and coin-operated phone booths are installed in convenient locations in towns and villages. Telephone cards are sold at kiosks, souvenir shops and post offices. Almost all hotels have fax service available at an extra charge, and the main post office has the same service for the public.

The country code for Cyprus is +357. For directory assistance in Cyprus dial 192 for national numbers and 194 for international numbers.

Tipping

A 10 percent service charge is added to the bill in restaurants, but not all of this goes to the waiter. It is polite to leave up to five percent more. Service taxi drivers who handle luggage, and porters and hotel maids should be given a reasonable tip at the end of the stay.

Tourist Information

The Cyprus Tourism Organization (CTO) has offices in several countries and in towns in Cyprus. Their literature is available free and is helpful in planning your itinerary. The CTO has maps and booklets for special needs and interests.

The *Cyprus Traveler's Handbook* is a useful general-purpose guide for phone numbers of public services and recreational facilities.

For details on planning a conference or incentive travel program, contact the head office in Nicosia. Most 4- and 5-star hotels offer conference facilities. Nicosia has a new Conference Center capable of hosting up to 1,200 delegates.

Information: CTO Head Office, P.O. Box 4535, CY-1390 Nicosia, tel. (02) 337715 fax. (02) 331644, e-mail: cytour@dto.org.cy.

CTO offices for different regions are listed in the INFO section of the relevant chapters. CTO offices abroad: *U.K.:* 213 Regent Street, London W1, tel. (071) 734-9822, fax. (071) 2876534. *U.S.:* 13 East 40th St., New York, N.Y. 10016, tel. (212) 683-2800, fax. (212) 683-5282.

Cyprus in the Internet: The homepage for Cyprus' tourist board is www.cyprustoursim.org.

Chamber of Commerce and Industry, 38 Grivas Dighenis Ave., P.O. Box 1455, Nicosia, tel. (02) 449500, fax. (02) 449048. Branch offices are in Limassol, Larnaca and Paphos.

Tour Guides

Private tour guides can be hired for half or full days and are especially useful for people whose time is limited and whose needs are specialized. Contact the Cyprus Tourist Guides Association, P.O. Box 4942, CY-1355 Nicosia, tel. (02) 765755, fax. (02) 766872.

LANGUAGE GUIDE

Greek

Greek and Turkish are the official languages in the Republic of Cyprus, although news broadcasts are also given in English in the evening. Almost all Cypriots speak some English, but they are delighted if you know at least a few basic Greek words and expressions. The dialect of Cyprus is called Kypriaka. It contains ancient Greek words, as well as Turkish.

Greek and Turkish are very different languages, but Greek and Turkish Cypriots have body language in common. Mobile hands and expressive gestures are the way of life in the Mediterranean. For example, *yes* is indicated by a slow downward nod, *no* by a sharp jerk of the head backwards, usually accompanied by a "tsssk" made by the tongue. A more subtle form of *no* is expressed by a mere raising of the eyebrows. Never expose your open palm with fingers extended to a Greek Cypriot. This *munza* literally means "Go to the Devil" and is considered extremely insulting.

Some Remarks on Pronunciation

kh is pronounced as hard ch, as in Bach; ch pronounced ch as a throaty hiss.

Common Words and Phrases

good morning	*kaliméra*
good afternoon	*chérete*
good evening	*kalispéra*
good night	*kaliníchta*
hello (plural or polite)	*ya sas*
hello (singular, familiar)	*ya su*
goodbye	*addío*
please	*parakaló*
thank you	*ephcharistó*
yes / no	*ne / ochi*
excuse me	*signómi*
none	*kanéna*
no problem	*kanéna provlima*
okay	*endáxi*

How are you?

plural or polite:	*ti kánete?*
singular, familiar:	*ti kánis?*
Fine, thanks.	*kalá, ephcharistó*
My name is....	*onomásome...*
Do you speak...?	*ezis miláte...?*
English	*angliká*
I don't understand	*then katalavéno*
I'd like....	*thélo...*
I'm happy	*chérome*
I'm hungry	*pináo*
I'm thirsty	*thipsó*
I'm lost	*chátika*
it's urgent	*íne épigon*
Where is...?	*pu íne...?*
I'm sick	*íme árrostos (fem. árrosti)*
Help!.	*voidia!*
How much?.	*póso?*
How many?.	*pósa?*
How?.	*pos?*
Where?	*pu?*
When?.	*póte?*
What time?.	*tí óra?*
What?	*tí?*
Who?	*piós?*
Why?	*yatí?*
Is there?	*ipárchi?*
there is....	*ipárchi...*
there isn't.	*then ipárchi*
Where is?	*pu íne?*
expensive.	*akrivó*
cheap.	*phtinó*
beautiful.	*ómorpho*
ugly.	*áschimo*
near.	*kondá*
far	*makriá*
left	*aristerá*
right	*theksiá*
today.	*símera*
tomorrow	*ávrio*
yesterday.	*chtés*
hour	*óra*
day.	*méra*
week	*evdomáda*
month.	*mínas*
cold / hot	*kríos zestós*
open / closed	*aniktós / klistós*
one half	*misó*
one	*éna*
two	*thío*
three.	*tría*
four	*téssera*
five	*pénde*
six	*éxi*
seven	*ephtá*
eight.	*okhtó*
nine	*enniá*
ten.	*théka*
hundred	*ekató*
thousand.	*chília*
million	*éna ekatomírio*

Monday	*dephtéra*
Tuesday	*trítí*
Wednesday	*tetárti*
Thursday	*pémpti*
Friday	*paraskeví*
Saturday	*sávvato*
Sunday	*kiriakí*

Turkish

The Turks used the Arabic alphabet from about the year 670 A.D. until 1928, when Kemal Atatürk ordered the change-over to the Roman alphabet.

Turkish is fairly easy to pronounce. It has no diphthongs as in other languages, and each consonant is pronounced separately. Words consist of a root and one or more suffixes added to it. For example, *ev* means "house," *evim* "my house," *evimder* "in my house" and *evimdedir* "he is in my house."

Some Remarks on Pronunciation

I i	(dotted i) ee as in fee
I i	(undotted) uh as in were
C c	j as in jolly
Ç ç	ch as in champion
G g	hard g as in get
g .	after a,u,o lengthens preceding vowel
after e,i,ü,ö :	y as in yellow
J j	j as in journal (French pron.)
S s	sh as in shore
Ü ü	ew as in new
Ö ö	ur as in purr

Common Words and Phrases

good morning	*günaydin*
good afternoon	*tünaydin*
good evening	*iyi aksamlar*
hello	*merhaba*
goodbye	*Allaha ismarladik* (said by person leaving)
	güle güle (response)
please	*lütfen*
thank you	*tesekkür ederim / mersi*
you're welcome	*bir sey degil*
yes / no	*evet / hayir*
excuse me	*affedersiniz*
none	*yok*
That's right!	*tamam*

come in	*girin*
Help yourself!	*buyurun*
How are you?	*nasilsiniz*
very well	*çok iyiyim,*
thanks	*tesekkür ederim*
so-so	*söyle-böyle*
My name is...	*adim...-dir*
Do you speak...?	*...biliyor musunuz?*
English	*Ingilizce*
I don't understand	*anlamiyorum*
I'd like	*istiyorum*
Help!	*yardim edin*
How?	*nasil?*
Where?	*nerede?*
When?	*ne zaman?*
Where is?	*nerede?*
	nerede... dir?
What time?	*saat kaç?*
What?	*ne?*
Who?	*kim?*
Why?	*niçi?*
Is there?	*var mi?*
there is...	*var...*
Where is the toilet?	*tuvalet nerede?*
I'm sick	*hastayim*
fever	*ates*
sunburn	*günes yanigi*
cold tablets	*grip haplari*
Call a doctor!	*bir doktor çagirin*
there isn't...	*yok...*
How much?	*ne kadar?*
How many?	*kaç tane?*
expensive / cheap	*pahali / ucuz*
left / right	*sol / sag*
today	*bugün*
tomorrow	*yarin*
yesterday	*dün*
hour	*saat*
day / week	*gün / hafta*
month	*ay*
cold / hot	*soguk / sicak*
open / closed	*açik / kapali*
one half	*yarim*
one	*bir*
two	*iki*
three	*üç*
four	*dört*
five	*bes*
six	*alti*

Guidelines

seven	*yedi*
eight	*sekiz*
nine	*dokuz*
ten	*on*
Monday	*pazartesi*
Tuesday	*sali*
Wednesday	*çarsamba*
Thursday	*persembe*
Friday	*cuma*
Saturday	*cumartesi*
Sunday	*pazar*

CYPRUS AT A GLANCE

Information given here refers to the Republic of Cyprus, the internationally recognized government of the island.

Name: Republic of Cyprus.

Capital: Nicosia.

Founded: August 16, 1960.

Flag: Map of the island in gold above two crossed olive branches on a white field.

Description: The third largest Mediterranean island, Cyprus has an area of 9,251 square kilometers, its greatest length is from the tip of Akamas to the tip of the Karpasia Peninsula, and its greatest width is 95 kilometers. Its coastline stretches for 778 kilometers. It is located in the Eastern Mediterranean 65 kilometers from Turkey, 95 kilometers from Syria, 380 kilometers from Egypt, and 386 kilometers from Rhodes. The highest peak is Khionistra (Mount Olympos) at 1,951 meters. The two main mountain ranges are the Pentadaktylos Range (Kyrenia Mountains) in the north and the Troodos Mountains in the south.

Government: A democratic presidential republic with a 56-member parliament elected for four years.

Population: The entire island has a population of about 760,000; 604,000 in the south and 156,000 in the north. In 1960 the population was made up of 77.1 percent Greek Cypriots, 18.1 percent Turkish Cypriots. 4.8 percent Maronites, Armenians, Latins and others. Nearly two thirds of Cypriots work in the service industry; five percent work in agriculture.

Education: Since September 1992, the University of Cyprus has been in existence in Nicosia. The largest university in North Cyprus is the Mediterranean University in Famagusta.

Commerce and Industry: Agriculture, wine, copper and gypsum mining, manufacture of textiles, shoes, cement. Tourism is an important source of income.

Membership: Commonwealth, Council of Europe, EU Association, OECD.

AUTHORS

B. Samantha Stenzel, project editor of this book, was born in Chicago. "Sam" is an Athens-based foreign correspondent, travel writer and editor who has covered the Eastern Mediterranean for over a decade. She wrote the chapters "The Little Paris of Cyprus" and "North of the Green Line." Together with Corine Vallois she wrote "Aphrodite's Home." She also contributed to the history chapter, "Aphrodite's Island," and wrote the features "Modern Cyprus," "Kopiaste: Cypriot Food," "Cypriot Wine" and "Traditional Music and Dance."

Nita Clothier, Professor Emeritus in Liberal Studies at Western Washington University in Bellingham, has taught humanities courses there for over 20 years. She has divided her time between the academic life on campus and conducting study tours for students in Athens and the Eastern Mediterranean. Her research for a documentary on the birthplaces of the gods first took her to Aphrodite's Island. She wrote "Mythology and Literature" and "Cypriot Arts and Crafts."

Andreas Demetropoulos, a Cypriot marine biologist and oceanographer, is a founding member of the Cyprus Wildlife Society and has been its president since 1984. In 1988, he received the "Global 500 Award" from the United Nations Environment Program for his tireless campaigning for the protection of turtle nesting beaches and for the creation of the National Park on the Akamas peninsula. He penned the chapters on "Nature Walks" in the travel section, as well as the feature "Flora and Fauna."

Lana der Parthogh, headed radio programs on the Cyprus Broadcasting Corporation from 1964 to 1985. She has written several childen's books, and her television and book reviews have enlivened the pages of the *Cyprus Weekly* since 1979. For this guide she wrote the chapter "Divided Capital."

Mary Frances Finch, a Cypriot-American travel writer and journalist, has spent all of her summers on Cyprus. She specializes in sociology and contemporary issues, including ecology. "The Gateway to Cyprus" and "Karpasia Peninsula" were written by her.

Kerin Hope, an erstwhile archeologist, is a British foreign correspondent who lived for a year in Cyprus. She now covers Greece and Cyprus for the *Financial Times* of London. She co-authored the chapter "Aphrodite's Island."

Ken MacKenzie, Scottish foreign correspondent for *The Observer* and *The Economist* of London, has lived in Cyprus for many years. He contributed to the chapter "Aphrodite's Island."

The late **Ted Petrides** was a Greek-American, a leading folklorist and dance instructor who devoted his life to the study and perpetuation of regional folk dances. He studied Cypriot folk dances for many years and in his travels there documented a great deal of information in the posthumously-published *Dances of Cyprus*. He co-authored the feature "Traditional Music and Dance."

Corine Vallois, a Parisian resident of Cyprus, is a foreign correspondent for various publications and radio stations, including the BBC. She has a special fondness for the Paphos District, in which she lived for a long time. Along with Samantha Stenzel she wrote "Aphrodite's Home."

Special thanks to the Cyprus Tourism Organization, Public Information Offices of the Republic of Cyprus and North Nicosia, and Stuart Swiny, Director of the Cyprus American Archeological Research Institute in Nicosia.

PHOTOGRAPHERS

Acquadro, Aldo / Look   44, 62, 72/73, 78, 84, 126, 166, 227
Ali Acar, Mehmet   187
Archiv für Kunst und Geschichte, Berlin   25L, 26, 28L, 28R, 29, 32, 33, 40, 41
Bärmann, Fritz   188, 199
Brey, Hans-Jörg   cover, 35, 149, 167, 181, 211, 213, 230
Cyprus Museum   223
Cyprus Tourism Org.   221, 222
Couteau, Pierre   52, 60, 65, 74, 93, 94, 110, 125R, 129, 153, 157, 229, 233
Demetropoulos, Andreas   214, 217
Hackenberg, Rainer   46, 86, 141, 180, 186, 189, 191, 192, 194L, 196, 202, 205
Henninges, Heiner / Free Lance Press   80, 107, 114, 215, 219
Janicke, Volkmar   178
Lintzmeyer, A.   210
Malecos, Andreas 16, 18, 19, 20, 21, 23, 24R, 30, 34, 64, 68, 102, 132, 148, 206/207, 212, 225
Mauzy, Marie   36, 37
Sierpeklis, Zenon   174L, 174R
Skupy-Pesek, Jitka   8/9, 100, 118, 184, 203
Thiele, Klaus 43, 61, 67, 69, 88, 95, 106, 109, 122, 136/137, 143, 151, 152, 156, 158, 162, 165, 176, 208/209, 228
Thomas, Martin / Look   10/11, 12/13, 14, 24L, 25R, 38, 48/49, 50/51, 56, 76, 85, 89, 91, 92, 98/99, 111, 113, 115, 120, 121, 125L, 127, 130, 131, 138, 144, 159, 161, 163, 170/171, 177, 194R, 197, 226, 231, 234, 237
Tzschaschel, Sabine   172.

Guidelines

Explore the World

NELLES GUIDES

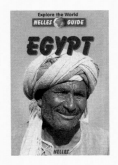

AVAILABLE TITLES

Australia
Bali / Lombok
Berlin and Potsdam
Brazil
Brittany
Burma → *Myanmar*
California
   Las Vegas, Reno,
   Baja California
Cambodia / Laos
Canada
   Ontario, Québec,
   Atlantic Provinces
Canada
   Pacific Coast, the Rockies,
   Prairie Provinces, and
   the Territories
Canary Islands
Caribbean
   The Greater Antilles,
   Bermuda, Bahamas
Caribbean
   The Lesser Antilles
China – Hong Kong
Corsica
Costa Rica
Crete
Croatia – *Adriatic Coast*
Cyprus
Egypt
Florida

Greece – *The Mainland*
Greek Islands
Hawai'i
Hungary
India
   Northern, Northeastern
   and Central India
India – *Southern India*
Indonesia
   Sumatra, Java, Bali,
   Lombok, Sulawesi
Ireland
Israel - *with Excursions*
   to Jordan
Kenya
London, England and
   Wales
Malaysia - Singapore
   - Brunei
Maldives
Mexico
Morocco
Moscow / St. Petersburg
Munich
   Excursions to Castles,
   Lakes & Mountains
Myanmar (Burma)
Nepal
New York – *City and State*
New Zealand
Norway

Paris
Philippines
Portugal
Prague / Czech Republic
Provence
Rome
Scotland
South Africa
South Pacific Islands
Spain – *Pyrenees, Atlantic*
   Coast, Central Spain
Spain
   Mediterranean Coast,
   Southern Spain,
   Balearic Islands
Sri Lanka
Syria – Lebanon
Tanzania
Thailand
Turkey
Tuscany
U.S.A.
   The East, Midwest and South
U.S.A.
   The West, Rockies and Texas
Vietnam

FORTHCOMING

Poland
Sweden

Nelles Guides – authoritative, informed and informative.
Always up-to-date, extensively illustrated, and with first-rate relief maps.
256 pages, approx. 150 color photos, approx. 25 maps.

Explore the World

NELLES MAPS

AVAILABLE TITLES

Afghanistan 1 : 1 500 000
Australia 1 : 4 000 000
Bangkok - *and Greater Bangkok*
  1 : 75 000 / 1 : 15 000
Burma → Myanmar
Caribbean - **Bermuda, Bahamas,
  Greater Antilles** 1 : 2 500 000
Caribbean - **Lesser Antilles**
  1 : 2 500 000
Central America 1 : 1 750 000
Central Asia 1 : 1 750 000
China - *Northeastern*
  1 : 1 500 000
China - *Northern* 1 : 1 500 000
China - *Central* 1 : 1 500 000
China - *Southern* 1 : 1 500 000
Colombia - **Ecuador** 1 : 2 500 000
Crete - Kreta 1 : 200 000
Dominican Republic - Haiti
  1 : 600 000
Egypt 1 : 2 500 000 / 1 : 750 000
Hawaiian Islands
  1 : 330 000 / 1 : 125 000
Hawaiian Islands – **Kaua'i**
  1 : 150 000 / 1 : 35 000
Hawaiian Islands – **Honolulu**
  - O'ahu 1 : 35 000 / 1 : 150 000

Hawaiian Islands – **Maui - Moloka'i
  - Lāna'i** 1 : 150 000 / 1 : 35 000
Hawaiian Islands – **Hawai'i, The Big
  Island** 1 : 330 000 / 1 : 125 000
Himalaya 1 : 1 500 000
Hong Kong 1 : 22 500
Indian Subcontinent 1 : 4 000 000
India - *Northern* 1 : 1 500 000
India - *Western* 1 : 1 500 000
India - *Eastern* 1 : 1 500 000
India - *Southern* 1 : 1 500 000
India - *Northeastern* - *Bangladesh*
  1 : 1 500 000
Indonesia 1 : 4 000 000
Indonesia **Sumatra** 1 : 1 500 000
Indonesia **Java - Nusa Tenggara**
  1 : 1 500 000
Indonesia **Bali - Lombok**
  1 : 180 000
Indonesia **Kalimantan**
  1 : 1 500 000
Indonesia **Java - Bali** 1 : 650 000
Indonesia **Sulawesi** 1 : 1 500 000
Indonesia **Irian Jaya - Maluku**
  1 : 1 500 000
Jakarta 1 : 22 500
Japan 1 : 1 500 000

Kenya 1 : 1 100 000
Korea 1 : 1 500 000
Malaysia 1 : 1 500 000
West Malaysia 1 : 650 000
Manila 1 : 17 500
Mexico 1 : 2 500 000
Myanmar (Burma) 1 : 1 500 000
Nepal 1 : 500 000 / 1 : 1 500 000
Trekking Map **Khumbu Himal -
  Solu Khumbu** 1 : 75 000
New Zealand 1 : 1 250 000
Pakistan 1 : 1 500 000
Peru - **Ecuador** 1 : 2 500 000
Philippines 1 : 1 500 000
Singapore 1 : 22 500
Southeast Asia 1 : 4 000 000
South Pacific Islands 1 : 13 000 000
Sri Lanka 1 : 450 000
Taiwan 1 : 400 000
Tanzania - Rwanda, Burundi
  1 : 1 500 000
Thailand 1 : 1 500 000
Uganda 1 : 700 000
Venezuela - Guyana, Suriname,
  French Guiana 1 : 2 500 000
Vietnam, Laos, Cambodia
  1 : 1 500 000

*Nelles Maps are top quality cartography!
Relief mapping, kilometer charts and tourist attractions.
Always up-to-date!*